SHATTERED

The Seth Alfaro Miracle

The times when our lives feel the most shattered are precisely the times when God is making us whole.

Christine Alfaro

Cover Photo: Seth Alfaro
Cover Art by Caleb Alfaro
Formatting by Andrea Alfaro

Copyright 2024 by
Christine Alfaro

ISBN: 9798336200959
Imprint: Independently published

Dedicated with deep gratitude to

My husband and children for their undying, sacrificial love.

Our extended family and friends,
St. Thomas the Apostle Parish community,
and the thousands of prayer warriors around the world,
whose prayers helped bring Seth back to us.

God, who has shown me repeatedly that
His will is perfect and beautiful even when I don't
understand it and even when it hurts.

*"Trust in the Lord with all your heart, and do not lean on
your own understanding. In all your ways acknowledge
him, and he will make straight your paths."*
(Proverbs 3:5-6)

"My God is Good"

February 13, 2017, is a date that will be etched in my memory forever. In one unexpected moment our lives were changed. Joy turned into fear as our family was thrust into a nightmare. Without warning, one of my greatest fears became my reality. A reality that I had hoped I would never have to face. A reality that shattered life as we knew it…

My routine day had become a busy and exciting evening. My husband, Chris and I were busy getting our things packed and making final arrangements before leaving on our vacation the next day. We were about to leave the cold winter of Michigan and fly to California for a week of sunny, warm weather where we would be visiting my husband's family.

I couldn't believe that we were actually going to be able to get away without the kids. We had five children still living at home, ranging in age from nine to twenty-one. We were definitely ready for a break. This was also going to be the first time in years that all of my husband's siblings and their spouses would be together with his parents. We were excited! However, our kids were not as excited about us leaving, especially the two youngest ones who had been home sick from school that day.

That evening, sick and anxious children were sprawled out on the couches in our family room, suitcases were partially packed, toys were strewn across the floor, dirty dishes were piled in the sink, schedules and meal plans were waiting to be finalized and laundry needed to be folded. It was sure to be a very busy evening. As I worked on one task, I was constantly making mental notes of other last-minute preparations that needed to be done. I was excited but was quickly feeling tired and a little overwhelmed as the evening went on. Around 7pm, I had made my way to the dining room, where I was cleaning up after having fed 10 daycare children there earlier that day.

Busy and focused on my "to do" list, I was suddenly startled by an unusually loud, quick, and frantic pounding, at the front door. The unusually loud and urgent banging gave me an immediate feeling of panic as I ran to the door wondering who it could possibly be. My heart plummeted in fear with what I saw. There in the darkness, stood a police officer with a look on her face that said it all, but before I could utter a single word, she said, "Seth Alfaro had a bad accident! Come with me." With my voice shaking, I screamed for my husband, who was in our family room in the back of the house. He came running with the kids trailing behind him, knowing from my scream that something was terribly wrong. Without explanation, he and I rushed out of the house leaving our four youngest children watching in disbelief and shock. Following a police escort to the hospital, we drove... legs shaking, hearts pounding, minds racing, not knowing if we would find our son dead or alive...

CHAPTER ONE
- ALL BOY -
God is Good... in All Life

Let me tell you a little bit about our son, Seth. At this point in time, at the age of twenty-one, Seth was at the top of his game, or so he thought, with his whole life of dreams in front of him. He was immersed in the rap scene and was determined that he was going to be a famous R&B, hip-hop artist one day soon. He was deep into the rap culture. It was harsh, crude and dark. Working on his music often meant Seth was in an environment surrounded by drugs and immorality. But it was his dream, and he was willing to do what it took to get it. He had a strong work ethic and worked hard on his music, often into the early hours of the morning even though he had to work the next day.

Seth was always on the go. He didn't like to sit around. If he wasn't working, he was playing or on some sort of adventure. He was an incredible athlete, super fit, and always active. He was a certified personal trainer, but struggling to get clients, Seth began working for his cousin's husband in construction shortly after his twenty-first birthday. He worked construction long hours during the day and then would hang out with friends. After that, he often worked on his music late into the night, getting very little sleep. He, like many college aged kids, didn't seem to need much sleep. He drank his coffee and energy drinks and kept on going. Even watching a movie felt like a waste of time to Seth. He always wanted to be on the go, living the dream. He saw life as an adventure and wanted his life to be full of experiences. He was strong and good looking, got the beautiful girls, was the life of the party and the envy of many. In many ways, Seth thought he had it all...

Let me go back a little first. Seth was born Franklin breech, which meant that he came out butt first. We often joked that we should have known right then and there what we were in for. Seth was full of life and all boy right from the start. He was either hot or cold, without much in between, but he filled our home with energy and laughter like none other.

Seth was third in our family of seven children. He was raised Catholic and went to Catholic schools his whole life. He was a very honest child and a strong rule follower. He was a super funny kid and often the class clown in school. His humor was something we, his family, all loved and took great delight in. Seth had a way of making us laugh even when we were mad. He was goofy and fun. Watching a comedy with him was the best. He would laugh so hard that it made all of us laugh too. When he was in high school, he would search for funny YouTube videos, and laugh so hard that he could be heard all throughout our house. His laugh was contagious and lit up our family and home. It was definitely one of the things we all treasured most about Seth.

Seth was the most athletic in our family. His speed was evident from a very young age. When it came to playing sports, he was just naturally gifted. He had amazing control over his body and its movements. I'll never forget his siblings telling me to watch as Seth came running into our living room and did a full front flip with no hands. He could pretty much watch any movement and then just do it. He would watch sports and then go out and play them, being one of the best without ever having played them before. When he was in middle school, his football coach would have to pull him out of the game out of mercy for the other team. His coach would tell us that Seth could pretty much score at will. He was fun to watch.

Seth and his dad really bonded over sports. Chris helped coach him in football, basketball, tennis, track and pole vaulting. Chris traveled wherever was needed to support Seth and proudly watched him compete. Every sport Seth played, he looked to his dad for approval. One of his first football games, Seth scored four touchdowns, and each time, the first place he looked was over at his dad with a big smile.

In high school, because of his size, Seth switched from football to tennis and made the varsity team his first year playing. Then as a senior, after he had finally grown, Seth decided to play rugby for the first time and was awarded the most valuable back, scoring three tries in the semifinal game, leading his team to the state championship.

Seth was a lot like his dad. He was fun, but also fiery. He either made people laugh or cry. As a small child he had a bad temper and tested us quite a bit. His dad understood him and had a way of calming him down. Chris always had an extra soft spot in his heart for Seth. Seth had a way of getting away with things that the other kids couldn't. Because they were so similar, his dad could understand and relate to Seth in many ways. When Seth was a little boy, I often didn't know how to handle his temper. The more upset I got, the more upset Seth got, and I did not know how to calm him down. In our family, I was usually the patient one, but with Seth, Chris was the one that could remain calm. It was like he understood what was going on inside Seth. Chris used to tell me that I needed to stay calm and appeal to the Seth inside, because Seth didn't really want to act the way he was. Chris would stay so calm, telling Seth "I know you don't want to act this way. You are so much better than this. You need to fight that temptation to be mad and selfish and be the strong and kind boy that I know you are and want to be." It was amazing how he could calm Seth down and bring the best out of him. It was obvious that Chris understood what he was going through when he was acting out or throwing a fit.

Seth stayed true to his convictions through high school, often standing up for what was right, even if others didn't. As he got older, however, his faith became just a bunch of dos and don'ts, rules that he felt held him back from having a good time. I used to tell him that he was missing out on the best part of his faith; that being, the love relationship with God, but Seth never seemed to really understand that. So, after high school he embarked on a new adventure, one that left most of his rules and morals behind. He became the life of the party, the hottest guy with the hottest girl, the one that many of his peers envied and sought to be. Seth was drinking and smoking pot and living a life opposite of how he had been raised, and outwardly he didn't seem to care. However, he always felt in his heart that he would eventually come back to his faith. He just wanted God to look the other way for a while so he could have some fun.

Seth still lived at home during this time, so homelife became rough. He became more and more distant from the family because he knew he was not living for God, and darkness cannot stand the light. Our whole family felt it. It seemed like most conversations of any importance with Seth became arguments, as Seth defended his lifestyle and tried to pretend everything was okay.

Seth's two older siblings, Michael and Andrea, lived on their own, so Seth was the oldest at home during this time. The next sibling was Ethan who was three years younger than Seth. Their personalities were about as different as they could be. Consequently, they fought quite a bit growing up, and even more the older they got. Seth's three youngest siblings, he really didn't know and didn't seem to care. One day he told me, "I don't really know Caleb, Mary, and Peter." I said to him, "Yeah, you really should spend more time with them and make an effort to get to know them better." To which Seth replied, "Nah, I'm good." And that pretty much summed up his mentality toward his family as a nineteen/twenty-year-old.

It got to the point where his dad, during a confrontation one night, told him outright, "Seth, I don't even know what you stand for anymore!" That was shocking to Seth, and he fought it. But he had truly become someone that we could hardly recognize. To the world, Seth was fun and happy and everything they wanted to be. It seemed like he had a great life. But to us, he was short tempered and no longer the fun kid that we all knew and loved. He was self-absorbed, rarely ever looking beyond his own needs and desires. On the outside, things didn't look too bad. In fact, he really wasn't much different from most people his age, but that was the problem.

The words Chris had spoken to him, "I don't even know what you stand for anymore" seemed to be a bit of a wake-up call for Seth. In fact, before his twenty-first birthday, Seth was really trying to come around and straighten out his life. His faith started to resurface and show in his words and actions again. He even got the words, "Viva Cristo Rey," meaning "long live Christ the King," tattooed on his arm. He admired his dad so much that he had it written in Chris' handwriting too. When he was explaining to his girlfriend why it was important to him that it be in his dad's writing, he said, "If I could be even half the man my dad is, I'd be happy."

Seth eventually broke up with his girlfriend. He knew the relationship wasn't good for him. He knew that he was not living the way he should, and he felt the emptiness. He knew he was living a lie and didn't love her for the right reasons.

Deep down Seth had always planned to come back to his faith someday, and he was trying. However, coming back wasn't that easy. He was deeply entrenched in the ways of the world. His confidence was wrapped up in social media, his status, and the approval of others. The rap culture, too, was dark, and since Seth still loved making that music, he was still in that environment surrounded by drugs and immorality. Seth worked hard to keep his songs clean by not using the typical crude and degrading language. He tried to be a witness, but it was a struggle because he loved the party life and the popularity and status that came with it. He also still loved being with his ex-girlfriend, and even though they were broken up, he had still been seeing her some. He was not a perfect person by any means, nor will he or any of us ever be, but Chris and I could tell that his faith was important to him and he was at least striving again. This gave us comfort.

As Seth's desire to straighten out his life grew, things at home started getting better. He spent more time talking to us and was grateful for our help and direction once again. He sought out support and counsel from his older siblings, Michael and Andrea too, and he was trying to find more Christian support and friendships. He was an active and passionate young guy, working full time during the days, and then often out at night till all hours in the morning either working on music or adventuring. He was full of life and energy.

Seth's adventurous spirit always scared me though, because he had no fear and would act without thinking. He would leave late at night with a backpack and tell us he was going adventuring. I didn't know exactly what that meant, and I didn't really want to. He had, at times, alluded to the fact that he had been on top of buildings and billboards in downtown Grand Rapids, MI where we lived, as well as on and off moving trains. We had no idea what all he was doing, but we knew Seth. It was no secret that Seth did a lot of crazy, dangerous, and stupid things. In fact, I used to tell him that I didn't want to get a phone call from the police someday saying he was dead or in jail...

CHAPTER TWO
- LIFE ALTERING MOMENTS-
God is Good... in Heartache

On February 12, 2017, Seth (21) and his brother, Ethan (18) got into a big fight. They argued a lot, but occasionally it got worse and they would grab each other and throw a couple punches before one of them would come to their senses and stop. They knew exactly what to say and do to hurt each other, and they said some pretty terrible things to each other that day. It was undoubtedly a life altering moment that neither of them realized would cause great heartache in the days that followed.

Later that evening, Seth was in the living room waiting to go out with some new friends. I felt compelled to go talk to him, even though I didn't want to. I was very upset with Seth for how he had treated Ethan, but I knew in my heart that I needed to talk to him and find out what was going on. He had totally overreacted and lashed out at Ethan. The boys argued, like brothers do, but when it escalated into a bigger fight, it was usually because there was something else going on in one of their hearts, something that had nothing to do with their brother. There was usually an underlying factor that led them to take it out on each other.

Fighting my own emotions, I went out to the living room to talk to Seth. I am so glad that I did. Little did I know at the time that it would end up being a pivotal conversation, for which I would be forever grateful. As I talked with Seth, I discovered that he was very angry at his ex-girlfriend. I didn't even realize at the time that he had been hanging out with her again. His being with her again, wasn't a good thing, and it had him uptight. We discussed that for a minute or two, but the conversation quickly turned from that to where it usually did, Seth's typical question, "Where is my life going?" Seth was always worried about where his life was headed and what the future held for him. He wanted to be a famous singer/rapper more than anything.

Seth always had very lofty goals and dreams, the type that many people never attain. However, Seth was serious about reaching his dreams, and he worked extremely hard and constantly at his singing, determined to become famous. Most of the time he stayed positive and confident about it, but at times the uncertainty of his future frustrated him, and this was one of those nights. My message to him that night was that no matter how many dreams and goals he reached or what he accomplished in this life, he would never truly be happy or fulfilled unless he was in God's will. I told him that if he sought God first, everything else would fall into place as it was meant to be.

My husband, Chris, eventually joined our conversation. He asked Seth what success meant to him. Seth's version of success was fame and fortune. Chris shared with Seth that success is faithfulness, and that he had learned to measure his own success not in what he did or how much money he made, but rather in his faithfulness to God and helping his wife and children get to Heaven. He challenged Seth with the scripture, Mark 8:36 "What does it profit a man to gain the whole world but lose his soul in the process?" As Seth was leaving that night to hang out with new friends, Chris also challenged him to praise God more, to turn his mind and heart from himself, and put it on God, thanking Him for all the good.

Seth spent that night at his friend, Nate's house. Seth had just met Nate the week before. They bonded right away because of the fact that they were both Christians and because of their mutual love for music and making videos. Early the next morning, February 13, 2017, Seth rushed home from Nate's house with just enough time to change and leave again for work. He told us quickly before he left that it had been a good night, that he and Nate had even done some praise and worship together. He was definitely in a much better mood than when he had left the night before.

In Michigan, winters are long, typically lasting from November to April. But if there's one thing people know about Michigan weather, it's that you never really know what you are going to get. You can have temperatures in the forties one day and eighties the next.

With temperatures in the sixties, February 13th of 2017 was one of those days.

Being an unusually warm and sunny day for February in Michigan, Seth got permission from his boss, Michael, who was also his cousin-in-law, to get off work early in order to go downtown with Nate and some other friends. They were going to scout out good locations for shooting Seth's next music video. He and Nate had been making plans to make a music video together for Seth's newest song.

Seth seemed so happy that afternoon as he was going to meet up with Nate. Chris and I were both home and remember vividly the joy he exuded as he left the house that day. His energy was contagious, and we were excited for this opportunity for him as well. We both said goodbye to him and told him to have a great time. He smiled and walked out the door so vibrant, lively and happy. It was shaping up to be a great day!

The sunshine and sixty-degree weather in mid-February seemed to raise all of our spirits. However, Chris and I had even more reason to be happy. We were preparing to leave for California the next day. I actually couldn't believe we were going to get to go. Chris and I didn't get to take trips like this very often. We had been planning it for a while and were super excited to see Chris' parents and all of his siblings. Even his sister, Monica and her husband, Dallas and their children, were going to be there from Hawaii. However, as excited as I was for the trip, for some reason this time, I was really afraid that we weren't going to be able to go.

I didn't usually think like that, but Mary and Peter, our two youngest, had been home from school with the stomach flu. I told myself that they were old enough to leave even if they were still sick. After all, it wasn't like they would be alone. Our oldest son, Michael (27) and his wife, Meg (24) and their two little boys, Christopher (3) and David (8 months), were going to stay with them for the week at our house.

Unfortunately, worry was sort of second nature for me. So I started worrying about Chris or I getting sick. Still, I figured the only way we wouldn't get on that plane was if one of us was actively throwing up at the time. I kept my worried feelings to myself and just prayed that we would not get sick. I had recently just finished writing a whole book about surrender. It was very fresh in my mind, so I knew I had to trust God and place the whole trip in His hands. I remember that in my head, I kept repeating, "Your will, Your way, Your time, Lord."

This brings me to that unexpected, life shattering knock on our door at 7pm that evening, February 13, 2017. It was not a typical knock. It was a loud, rushed, and very frantic knock. As soon as I heard it, I quickly and automatically went over in my mind where each of our kids were. They were all home except for Seth. But I knew Seth had his house key, because he had taken his car. I thought maybe he forgot something and, leaving his car running, was hurrying to get into the house to grab it. When I opened the door, I never expected to see a police officer standing there. It was a moment I never could have imagined. It was the sort of moment I had always feared…

As the officer said, "Seth Alfaro had a bad accident," my immediate thought was a car accident, but she went on to say that Seth had been skateboarding and fell off a roof. She guessed that maybe he had been doing parkour but admitted she really didn't know what had happened. I couldn't imagine Seth skateboarding off a roof. He did a lot of risky things, but he didn't do parkour. I didn't understand. It made no sense to me.

The police officer had gone to school with Seth's older siblings and recognized our last name. Knowing where we lived, she headed straight to our house to inform us while her partner stayed with Seth. I asked her if Seth was okay, but she couldn't say. All she knew was that the paramedics had resuscitated him and were rushing him to the ER.

From the back of the house, Chris heard a blood curdling scream as I yelled for him. Our youngest three children were in our back family room with Chris and heard my scream too. Sadly, their first thoughts were that Seth and Ethan may be fighting again. They knew by my voice that something was very wrong. Chris immediately came running out, with Caleb, Mary, and Peter following close behind him. The officer waited for us, so she could escort us to the hospital in order to get us there as quickly as possible. We were running around frantically trying to find shoes, coats, keys, etc. In the panic, Chris couldn't find his wallet. Not really thinking straight, we decided that I needed to drive since he didn't have his license and there was a police officer standing right there. In hindsight, given the situation, I don't think she would have cared about the license.

Having me drive was not a good idea, since I normally drive slow. And on top of that, I tend to panic and freeze in emergency situations. As we were leaving, I realized we hadn't even told Ethan, our eighteen-year-old, anything. Mary had run up to his room to tell him, and he was running down the stairs as we were running out the door. I saw him on the landing of the stairs and all I managed to say was, "We gotta go," as I rushed out the front door of our home. We left them with no explanation, and the four of them, Ethan(18), Caleb(14), Mary(13), and Peter(9) stood there in shock, scared and not knowing what to think or do.

Following police escort, it was a stressful drive to the hospital. I struggled to keep up with the officer as she rushed through intersections with yellow lights that were about to turn red. I couldn't even think straight. Chris had to keep telling me to hurry up and stay with the police car. As we drove, my leg, which was in a brace because of a torn MCL, was shaking uncontrollably.

I was so afraid they were going to tell us Seth was dead. All I could say was, "oh my gosh, oh my gosh, oh my gosh," over and over. The same words, "oh gosh, oh gosh" ran through Chris' head repeatedly, but unlike me, he didn't say them out loud. Instead, in his head he kept telling himself, "Don't panic. Don't go there." He was working very hard to keep his mind from wandering to his deepest fears.

Chris is very good at not thinking ahead about things that could happen. He stayed calm and was reassuring to me. He said, "Let's not panic. We don't even know what we are dealing with yet. Let's just stay in the moment." He is very good at staying in the moment, while I tend to jump to the worst possible scenario, which is definitely where my mind was at that moment.

On the way, Chris immediately began calling family members. He called our oldest son, Michael, first. Michael(27) has always been a rock in our family, someone the other kids all look up to. Being the oldest and always the protector, he dropped everything without hesitation, got in his car and drove straight to Spectrum Health ER. Michael's wife, Meg, didn't know any details, but she knew that Michael had to go.

Shortly after Michael left, Ethan called Meg. Meg's mom and two sisters were at their house visiting from Delaware at the time. Leaving her mom, sisters, and three-year-old son, Christopher behind, Meg grabbed their eight-month-old son, David, and headed straight to our house to be with Ethan, Caleb, Mary, and Peter. She, being a mother herself, was a great comfort to them. They gathered together and began praying a rosary for Seth.

The next call was to our daughter, Andrea(23). She was in a night class. On her break, she noticed she had several missed calls and a text from her dad that said, "Call me. Seth's been in a bad accident." When she talked to Chris, he told her that she could stay in class because we didn't know anything yet, but there was no way she could have stayed. Her mind was only on Seth. She was the closest in age to Seth and they had always been quite close. Being so close in age, they shared a lot. She packed up her things immediately and drove straight to our home to be with the rest of the family.

Chris then called our sister-in-law, Sarah. She and my brother, Dave, are Seth's godparents and lived just around the corner from us. Sarah ended the call with Chris and immediately called Dave, who was in a meeting about forty-five minutes away in Lansing, Michigan. Right in the middle of a dinner meeting, Dave got up and left immediately, and headed straight home to Grand Rapids. Sarah began calling the rest of my family and our close friends in order to get everyone praying for Seth.

The final call before reaching the hospital was to Chris' dad, asking him to please contact the rest of his family for prayers, as well as inform them that we most likely would not be coming to California the next day. Chris' mom and dad and three of his sisters and their families all lived in California. His fourth sister and her family lived in Hawaii but had just flown to California for the week. They all began praying right away. Chris didn't have any details for anyone. We had no idea what we were dealing with yet, but as we followed the speeding police car, we knew it was serious. The best thing anyone could do at that point was pray.

I was so afraid the hospital staff was going to tell us that Seth was dead. We parked the car and rushed into the emergency room. We were immediately ushered into a private room and told that the social worker was going to come talk to us. "The social worker?" I thought. "That must mean Seth is dead." Michael got to the ER shortly after us. The three of us sat silently in that little room, waiting...

The social worker never came in. Instead, the trauma doctor, who had been working on Seth, walked into the room and sat down grimly facing us. My heart was pounding. What was he going to say to us? Dr. Gibson began by telling us straight out that Seth had fallen about twenty-five feet and had a severe brain injury. They had already done a CT scan, which showed Seth had bleeding in his brain. Dr. Gibson went on to explain to us that there was nothing he could do about the damage that was already done to Seth's brain from the fall, but that their job now was to keep the swelling in his brain down in order to keep him alive and limit any further damage to his brain.

He told us that they had intubated Seth and put him on a respirator which was breathing for him. They were also putting Seth into a medically induced coma. I couldn't really process everything he was saying. As bad as it was, in some ways it felt like good news, because prior to that I had been pretty convinced they were going to tell us Seth was dead.

Dr. Gibson finished his explanation and asked us if we had any questions. I could only think of one. "Could Seth die from this?" He answered, "Yes. He could." He told us that the next twenty-four hours would be critical, and that it would be up to Seth. He told us that this was going to be a marathon, not a sprint. We had no idea how long that actually meant. But it didn't matter. At that point we couldn't think of anything else to ask. We were in shock and just wanted to see Seth.

After getting the report from Dr. Gibson, Chris called home and talked to Andrea. Having just gotten the news that Seth had a serious brain injury and was in an induced coma and in critical condition, she and Ethan went upstairs to talk. Caleb, who was only fourteen at the time, went upstairs and saw Andrea and Ethan talking and crying. Andrea told Caleb to go back downstairs because they didn't want to scare the younger kids. Mary, age thirteen, also wanted to go upstairs to find out what was going on. Meg told her to wait and stay downstairs. Our adult children were very mindful in trying to protect the younger ones and not scare them. As much as Meg wanted to go upstairs and talk with Andrea and Ethan, she knew she needed to stay downstairs with the younger kids. So consequently, she learned of Seth's condition in bits and pieces. After getting the initial report on Seth, they (Meg, Andrea, Ethan, Caleb, Mary, and Peter) all prayed another Rosary together for Seth.

As we waited to see Seth and Chris talked to Andrea, I pulled out my phone to make arrangements for my job the next day. I was a childcare provider and ran a daycare out of our home. Even though we were supposed to be flying to California the next day, I was still scheduled to watch kids in the morning. I took out my phone to try to formulate a text message to the parents, but I just sat there staring at my phone as it shook in my hands. I couldn't think straight. Michael looked at me and said, "Mom, what are you doing?" I told him I had to let the parents know I wouldn't be able to babysit in the morning but couldn't figure out how to do it. He was sweet and told me to put my phone away. He called Meg, and she took care of it for me. That was a huge blessing because I could hardly function at that point.

Before long, Dr. Gibson took Chris and me and Michael back into the ER to see Seth. He was scraped up, in a neck brace, and had many tubes and wires hooked to him already. He laid there unconscious, with his chest rising and falling to the rhythm of the ventilator. It was so hard for us to believe that it was Seth lying there so beat up and lifeless. Nothing could have prepared us to see him that way.

It was so surreal. Just a few hours earlier, he had walked out of the house so happy, so full of life. It just didn't seem possible that he was laying there lifeless, so weak, so broken, and teetering on the edge of life and death. I just kept picturing the big smile on his face as he walked out of the house just a few hours earlier. Never could I have imagined things would end like this. I wondered if we would ever see Seth smile again. Could that have been his last goodbye?

Doctors told us Seth had purposeful movement. He was reaching for the breathing tube, which meant that he recognized something was there that didn't belong there and it was irritating him. They said that was a really good sign. Doctors and nurses vigorously rubbed Seth's sternum trying to make him uncomfortable in order to arouse him, while also talking loudly and forcefully to him trying to get him to respond to simple commands, such as squeeze my hand, give me a thumbs up, open your eyes, etc. They said if he could respond to a command, that would be a great sign. Despite all their attempts, Seth did not respond at all.

I stepped away to call my Dad who spends winters in Alabama. While I was away on the phone, the nurses were having trouble getting an IV in. Seth was pulling his arm away, which was a good purposeful movement, but it was making it virtually impossible for them to get the IV started. So Chris helped hold Seth's arm down while the nurses put it in.

This took Chris back seventeen years as he remembered when Seth was four years old and having surgery. At age four, Seth had to have a type of hernia surgery. He could only have one parent with him while he was put to sleep. He wanted his daddy with him. Chris held Seth as the anesthesiologist was putting him to sleep. He told Seth not to fight it and that it was ok to just go to sleep. Seth trusted his daddy would protect him, and he peacefully closed his eyes and did not fight the anesthesiologist. That was so difficult for Chris, because we all know there can be complications with general anesthetic. Now, seventeen years later, Chris was back in that position once again, imploring Seth to trust him and not fight the IV's. Chris reassured Seth, but this time it was terrifying and heartbreaking for him because in all honesty, he really had no idea whether Seth would be okay or not.

Michael stood at Seth's side in the ER with a steady stream of tears running down his cheeks. "How could this be?" he thought. Earlier in the day, Michael had just been at church thanking God for all his blessings, as he thought about how good everything was in his life right then. This couldn't possibly be happening.

Being the oldest in the family, Michael had already faced a lot of tragedy in his life, as a two-year-old, a three-year-old, an eight-year-old, and an eleven-year-old brother. He has his own story of pain, heartache, grief, and fear. At age two he lost his brother, a brother that would have been close to him in age and potentially would have been the best friend he's always wanted but never really had. At age three, he lost his first sister. He was angry with her for leaving him. At age eight, his little brother died in his arms. He still remembers it vividly. He also remembers the fears it left in him later. And then again at age eleven, he lost another brother, one who looked a lot like him. By the time Michael got a living sibling, he was so much older that he was always looked at as the older one, the big boy, the helper, and the mentor. And he lived up to all those things. He had let go of four siblings already, and standing there in the ER with Seth, he was not willing to let go again.

Michael and Seth were six years apart, and very different. Michael and Andrea were very quiet and well behaved. When Seth was born, he brought a new energy to our house. He was full of energy and aggression. He was either happy or mad with very little in between. Michael could play for hours using his imagination, while Seth was very physical, always running, jumping, flipping, or kicking, hitting, or throwing any kind of ball. Seth loved all sports, gymnastics, or anything physical. While Michael was thoughtful and careful about what he did, Seth would try just about anything without even thinking of the consequences.

Though they were very different, they had a mutual respect for each other. Michael admired Seth's athleticism and physical abilities, while Seth always looked up to Michael and counted on him, knowing he would always be there with sound advice when Seth wanted it. As they grew, Michael definitely questioned Seth's judgment and willingness to try anything without thinking. Being older, it concerned and frustrated Michael.

Now he stood at Seth's side bawling and thinking, "You better pull through this Seth!" But he also couldn't help thinking, "but when you do, I'm gonna kill you." None of us knew yet what Seth had been doing that night or how he fell, but we all knew Seth did a lot of super risky things. The tears were uncontrollable as Michael stood there thinking, "Oh Seth, what have you done?"

The friends who were with Seth when he fell showed up at the ER shortly after us. Michael stayed with Seth while Chris and I went to talk with them. They were the only ones who actually knew what had happened to Seth. We knew of Nate but had not met him yet. Apparently, Seth and Nate met up with a couple of other of Nate's friends, Jake and Hunter, and one girl, Brooke, whom they were just getting to know. Nate, Jake, and Hunter came to the hospital to talk to us and see how Seth was. They were obviously very shaken up and in shock as they tried to relay the events of the evening to Chris and me.

They told us that they had been skateboarding around downtown Grand Rapids, when Seth wanted to climb up on a roof to get a good view of the sunset over the city. So he and Hunter climbed up, while the others waited below. While Seth doing parkour didn't make any sense to us, this did. Seth loved a good view!

Coming down after watching the sunset, Seth and Hunter had to make an approximate eight-foot jump from one roof down to an attached roof below. Hunter was going to jump first, but then at the last minute, Seth decided to go first. When Seth jumped, the roof below collapsed upon impact, sending him straight through it. Seth must have tried to grab on as he went through, which would explain why his thumb was all ripped up. Hunter explained that the roof collapsed so fast that it didn't even slow down Seth's fall. He went straight through it, falling about twenty-five feet onto concrete. Hunter said Seth hit a radiator on the way down, slid off it, and landed face down on the concrete floor of a car repair shop.

Completely stunned, Hunter yelled down to the other guys. None of them realized how badly hurt Seth was. They kind of thought he would just get up and walk out of the building. They waited a few seconds with no sign of Seth. Instead, they heard a moaning or sort of snoring sound coming from the building. They broke a window of the building to get in and found Seth in what they described as probably the only place he could have landed without being impaled. They knew that was a miracle in itself. God is good.

Afraid they may get into trouble for being in the building, the boys rolled Seth over onto his back and dragged him out of the building. Brooke called 911. The 911 operator told them that the snoring noise meant he was not breathing and that they needed to start doing compressions on him. When the ambulance arrived, the paramedics resuscitated Seth and rushed him to Spectrum Health hospital emergency, which was thankfully very close by.

We were thankful that the guys came to the ER, so we could talk to them and find out what had actually happened to Seth. While Seth didn't belong on that roof, we were grateful to know that he was only making an eight-foot jump that he could have handled if the roof had been sound. It would have been even more difficult for me to handle and reconcile the situation in my mind and heart if Seth had been doing something completely reckless.

Because of the nature of the accident, Police detectives were assigned to Seth's case right away. They had to make sure everything happened the way Seth's friends described it, and that there was no foul play involved since the guys had broken into a building.

The detectives questioned us about what little we knew. It was kind of scary. I wondered if there could be legal trouble for being on that roof and for the damage that was caused. We didn't even know where or what building it was. The detectives took Seth's phone as well as the phones of all the other guys who were present when it happened to make sure all their stories lined up and that they didn't have any pictures or anything that would prove differently. From my perspective, it was all too much to handle. All I wanted to do was be with Seth.

The three guys' stories all lined up, and in the end the detectives determined that it was all innocent, just boys being boys. The detective said something to the effect of, "Man, which one of us hasn't ever done something like that!?" I could tell he felt extremely bad for us and for Seth being so seriously injured. He very kindly offered his prayers and best wishes for Seth to pull through.

I was relieved and thankful when that got resolved. But the fact remained that reckless or not, Seth jumping off that roof was a life altering moment that caused incredible heartache. As quickly as that roof collapsed, his life and ours had been shattered. We would all have to learn and trust that God is good even in this heartache.

CHAPTER THREE
- THE SICU -
God is Good... in Tragedy

Around 8pm they moved Seth out of the ER and into the Surgical Intensive Care Unit (SICU) on the fourth floor. We were able to go right up in the elevator with Seth. Andrea and Ethan met us there once Seth was in the SICU. They both stood silently at Seth's side with steady streams of tears running down their cheeks, just like Michael had. Michael held it in once they got there. He was always the older brother and protector, so he switched off the tears and assumed that role as soon as Andrea and Ethan got to the hospital.

As parents, it was so hard to see Michael, Andrea, and Ethan's pain too. Seeing the suffering and anguish on the faces of our oldest children as Seth laid there on the verge of death was incredibly painful on so many levels. But neither Chris or I could cry. They all thought we were so strong, because we didn't cry. Truthfully, for me it didn't feel like strength. Rather, I was in shock, and I literally felt sick, like I was going to throw up. It was all so surreal. Neither Chris nor I could believe it was happening.

We held each other at Seth's bedside in utter disbelief, thinking, "How many, Lord? How many is it going to take?" Our minds couldn't help but go back to all those years ago in the neonatal intensive care units with our dying newborn babies. We had begged God for the lives of our babies, yet four times we left the hospital empty handed. We had buried four children in nine years. Never did we ever imagine that sixteen years later we would be back in this position again with our twenty-one-year-old son. God wouldn't possibly ask us to surrender yet another one of our children, would He?

My brother, Dave, and his wife, Sarah, also met us in the SICU shortly after 8pm, and stayed for several hours with us. Meanwhile their daughter, Regina (17), went to our home to be with our other children. She didn't want to be alone. Another niece of ours, Hannah (24), my brother, Mike's daughter also went to our house. We have a very close family, with many of the cousins having grown up together. It was amazing how the family began to gather together in prayer and support, no matter where they were.

Those first few hours in the SICU were busy and chaotic. Chris and I were being flooded with questions trying to get Seth's medical history. There was a steady flow of doctors and nurses in and out of Seth's room, hooking him to more and more machines and monitors. They were also constantly trying to get him to respond. "Seth, open your eyes, wiggle your thumb…" they would command. Chris and I, Michael, Andrea, and Ethan all chimed in as well, "Come on Seth," we pleaded. "Give us a thumbs up. Wiggle your toes." Doctors were looking for him to be able to follow any kind of simple command. If Seth could do that, they said it would be a great sign. But every time there was nothing, absolutely nothing.

Doctors told us that if Seth didn't respond by midnight they would have to drill into his skull and put a wire into his brain to measure the pressure from the swelling. They needed to make sure there was enough room for the brain as it continued to swell. This was crucial to keep Seth alive and protect his brain from further damage.

It was imperative that Seth respond on command. For the next four hours, doctors and nurses would poke and prod Seth about every fifteen minutes trying to get any kind of response from him. We all tried too. I dreaded it every time they came in to check. I was so scared each time. I wanted so badly for Seth to respond. I was desperate to see any kind of life in my son. My heart was breaking. But each time they tried and there was still no response, my heart would sink even further into the pit of my stomach.

I felt so sick that I seriously thought I was going to throw up. I didn't know if it was my nerves or if I was getting the same flu that Mary and Peter had been home sick with. At one point I finally sat down in the corner of the room and put my head down. I prayed, "Lord, I can't do this. I can't feel sick now. This can't be about me. I've got to be present for Seth. I need your strength.

Please give me your strength." At that very moment, I experienced a little miracle as God's strength and grace came upon me immediately. He was so good to me. He heard and answered my prayer, and I was able to stand at Seth's side and try to face this unimaginable situation.

Chris watched as they hooked more and more wires to Seth. He knew from our experience with the babies that the more they hooked to him, the harder it would be to get close to Seth. Desperate to hold his son one more time, Chris seized a brief opportunity when none of the medical staff were around Seth. He leaned over Seth's bed and wrapped his arms around him, loving and comforting him. He was holding his little boy again, only this time he was a grown man. Seth laid there so big and muscular, yet so broken. He was our strongest and Chris had come to count on him, especially for his physical strength. Chris couldn't wrap his mind around it. Seth still looked so strong, yet there was no strength there at all. He wasn't even breathing on his own. He was teetering between life and death. It was so hard for Chris to see Seth this way. He couldn't believe this was happening. He held his helpless, broken, grown son and whispered in his ear, "Oh Sethy, what have you done?"

Our parish priest, Fr. Jim had been notified late that night of Seth's accident. He had been our priest for the past twenty years, since Seth was one year old, and had been very instrumental in the spiritual growth of our family, even with Seth, particularly in the past year of his young adulthood. When Fr. Jim received the call about Seth, he was heading out to see another parishioner who had asked him to come pray with them and their elderly, dying father. Having just received the call about Seth, he was very distressed when he got to the other family. So together they all stopped and prayed for Seth, right in the midst of their own suffering with their dad who was close to death. Their love and support for us in those critical moments was so beautiful and selfless. We were blown away by their love and care for us right in the middle of their own suffering.

When Fr. Jim arrived at the hospital, it was close to midnight. He immediately gave Seth the Sacrament of the Sick and Absolution from his sins. Then he prayed with Chris and me, Michael, Andrea, Ethan, Dave and Sarah as we all surrounded Seth's bed. We prayed together for Seth's life, his healing, and the grace needed for all of us to get through this. This sort of marked the beginning of our marathon vigil at Seth's side, begging God to spare his life.

When Fr. Jim left the hospital, Seth was still unresponsive. He would occasionally move a little if the doctors or nurses pinched him or messed with him causing pain, but he would not wake up or respond to any verbal commands at all. The doctors told us they would have to drill into Seth's skull so they could insert a small wire, called a bolt, into his brain. It would measure the pressure, called intracranial pressure (ICP) in his brain as it swelled. We had to leave the room while they put the bolt in. While we were out of the room, they also put a central line into his chest and an arterial line into the artery in his left arm, which would give them a constant blood pressure reading.

We all waited in the waiting room during these procedures. While in the waiting room, my sister Kathy's daughter, Karianna, who was a nurse at the adjoining children's hospital, came over. Karianna was the same age as Andrea and was one of Andrea's best friends and closest cousins. Karianna and Andrea and Seth had done some silly things together, especially YouTube videos. She was scared for Seth and her heart ached for Andrea's. Karianna worked nights and took a break to come over to the SICU as soon as she could. The minute she stepped off the elevator, Andrea caught sight of her. When their eyes met, Andrea ran into Karianna's arms and broke down and sobbed.

Seth's best friend, Tyler, also joined us at the hospital. Thankfully, Ethan had thought to call him since he was away at college across the state. Ethan knew how close Seth and Tyler were. Seth had helped bring Tyler back into his Catholic faith after a difficult time. Then as Tyler grew in a closer relationship with Christ, he ended up being a faithful friend and support for Seth when he was struggling with his faith. They were very good for each other.

After receiving the news from Ethan, Tyler didn't know what to do. In shock, Tyler called his mom, CJ, who was like a second mom to Seth since he spent a lot of time at Tyler's house. She picked up the phone to hear complete silence. Finally Tyler quietly said, "Mom." CJ waited for him to continue. "Seth's in a coma," Tyler said, barely able to get the words out. He talked to his mom, wanting to leave school and come home but was unsure because he had an important exam the next day. Neither of them could think straight. They were stunned and didn't know what to think or do. Shortly after ending the call, CJ called Tyler back to tell him just to come home. Tyler was already in the car on his way. He knew there was no way he could stay, knowing that Seth was fighting for his life. Tyler arrived at the hospital close to 1am and never left that night.

It was very surreal sitting in that waiting room as family members of other ICU patients were sleeping there. We all, Chris and I, Michael, Andrea, Ethan, Dave, and Sarah, sat there trying to take in all that was happening and somehow make sense of the nightmare we had been thrown into. Little did we realize then that this was just the beginning of the marathon the doctor spoke of, and that we, too, like the other families, would make our home there...

Although we had been in the ICU many times before, this time our main support was different. All those times we had lost our babies, our children were all young, and we were surrounded by my family. In fact, throughout many of our parenting years, we and my parents and siblings and their families all lived within ten minutes of each other. All of our kids were raised together and were such close friends. We were each other's constant support through everything.

During recent years, however, my family had been gradually separated. My Mom had passed away eight years earlier, and now my Dad and his new wife, Erma, lived in Alabama for half the year during the winters. My brother, Mike, and his wife, Mary, and their youngest two kids moved to Portland, Oregon for work. And my sister, Kathy, and her husband, Keith, and their two youngest kids moved to Appleton, Wisconsin also for work. So with many of my family members gone and Chris' whole family in California and Hawaii, Dave and Sarah were our only siblings in town.

Along with Dave and Sarah, this time it was our adult children, Michael, Andrea, and Ethan who became our main support. They were at the hospital around the clock, day and night with Chris and me. Between all of us, we made sure not to ever leave Seth alone. Though it was extremely difficult for our children, there was nowhere else they wanted to be. They were a great comfort and tremendous support to us. There was something so beautiful and special about having them there with us and going through it together.

We still had three other younger children at home though, who we felt were too young to be at the hospital at this point. We wanted to protect them from it. We didn't tell them the gravity of the situation and didn't want them to see Seth this way. It was very scary to see him so lifeless, and we didn't want the kids to be afraid and have nightmares or anything, especially since we couldn't be with them to help them process it.

Our beautiful, strong, faithful daughter-in-law, Meg, without ever being asked, just moved into our home with her two sons and took over the care of Caleb, Mary, and Peter. She was completely selfless. She loved Seth so much too and wanted to be at the hospital, but she put her own feelings aside and stayed with the kids, so that the rest of us could be with Seth and not have to worry about anything else. Meg's mom, who had been visiting from Delaware, extended her trip and stayed a couple more weeks to help. It gave me peace to know that Meg was there for my younger three kids, and that Meg's mom was there for her.

While it was different from our past experiences and hard not to have our parents and siblings with us, it was such a blessing to be surrounded by the love and support of our own children. Each one of our children, even the younger ones, did their part, and provided the perfect support we needed. God is good even in the midst of tragedy.

CHAPTER FOUR
- LONG, LONELY HOURS -
God is Good... in Darkness, Silence, and Freezing Cold

Walking back into the SICU after the bolt was put in, Seth's room was marked as a "no stim" room, which meant that there could be no noise, no light, no stimulation of any kind for Seth's brain. The doctors no longer tried to get Seth to respond to them, and we were asked not to talk to him either. Just like that, Seth's room had gone from chaotic activity to complete darkness and silence. The only sounds were the beeping of monitors when something was wrong. That's a sound we would never get used to.

Seth was naked in the bed with only a small cloth over his private area. His body was burning up, but when we touched his hands, they were ice cold. He had a dangerously high temperature which they were trying to control by putting a cooling blanket with ice water running through it on him and ice packs under his arms, as well as keeping the temperature in his hospital room freezing cold. While Seth was naked with ice packs, we were sitting there with winter coats, hats and gloves on, and were still freezing.

It was a terrible feeling to be told not to talk to Seth. He lay there so still, so lifeless, with only his chest moving up and down to the rhythm of the ventilator. There was so much I wanted to say to him and ask him. I wanted to tell him how much I loved him. I wanted to tell him to fight to come back to us, that we needed him. There was so much I wanted to say but couldn't. Luckily the doctor did tell us that we could whisper to him once in a while very calmly and softly just letting him know that we were there and loved him, but that's about it. They didn't want anything to agitate him or stimulate his brain. Whenever we whispered anything, we would stare at the monitor watching his ICP number to make sure we weren't causing any pressure in his brain. It was extremely stressful, yet at the same time, it was unbearable not to be able to talk to Seth.

Because there could be no noise or stimulation, they also only wanted two or three people in the room at a time. Chris and I were in there all night and the others took turns being in Seth's room or in the waiting room. When Tyler came in, he would just sit in the corner silently praying. No one got much sleep that night. The kids may have gotten a little sleep in the waiting room chairs when they were out there. Chris and I didn't sleep at all. I was in shock and completely numb. I was there, and Seth was there, but I just couldn't believe it. It didn't seem real. It just couldn't really be happening.

We sat there hour after hour as one day blended into another. We sat in darkness, silence, and freezing cold. Friends had brought us bags with food and supplies

41

to pass the time, but the lights had to remain off, so it was often too dark in the room to see what was in them and even the crumpling of a bag felt like too much noise. We couldn't even talk to one another. So while we were all there together, we each felt very much alone in our thoughts and prayers. We each sat in darkness, silence, and freezing cold while wrestling with our own thoughts, memories, regrets, and fears…

My husband, Chris, did what he always does. He prayed the rosary. He paced back and forth at the foot of Seth's bed with his rosary beads in his hands. The rosary calms him, centers him, and gives him peace. He prayed nonstop! He said he just felt compelled to completely cover Seth in prayer.

Praying the rosary also kept Chris' mind occupied. An idle mind can be the devil's playground, and he did not want to allow that. Chris fought constantly to not let his mind wander to his worst fears. He knew, from having gone through it when our newborn daughter, Nicole was in the ICU, that if he let himself think ahead he would become overwhelmed and tempted to despair. So he fought constantly to stay in the moment. There were horrifying moments of fear and doubt that would seep through the cracks tempting to break the dam. He knew that if he let the dam break, he would not have the strength to get through it. Literally every single minute was a very conscious and constant battle for him to not allow his mind to go to that dark place and sink into the terrifying abyss of "what ifs."

I wish I could say the same for myself, but I am not that strong and disciplined with my thoughts. I kept trying to pray Hail Marys but honestly couldn't focus on actually praying the rosary. I just kept thinking about the conversation I had with Seth the night before. I was grateful beyond words that I had gone against my own will and had followed the inspiration of the Holy Spirit to talk to Seth that night. It ended up being a blessed conversation and opportunity for me to connect with Seth. I wondered if that was the last real conversation I would ever have with him. My heart ached, but the light and beauty I saw in him through that conversation gave me comfort as I sat in the ICU with him hanging on the edge between life and death. I knew his heart was good and striving for God.

As I sat there though, I couldn't stop thinking about one specific thing I had said to Seth during our conversation, "You will never truly be happy or fulfilled unless you are in God's will." Those words played over and over in my mind like a broken record. I thought, "Lord, this is definitely not what I was talking about when I said that. How could this be your will for Seth?" Deep in my heart, I did believe that if this was God's will for Seth, then somehow it was best. At this moment though, I just didn't know how I could possibly ever accept it and live it.

I had just finished writing my first book, "The Delight of My Heart," about my experiences with grief when our babies died and all that God had taught me about trusting Him completely and surrendering my will to His. I knew I truly believed what I had written in that book, but I didn't know how I could possibly surrender Seth and trust God in this. I kept telling God, "No! Not this!" I was very weak and afraid.

Seth was lifeless… My son, who as a little boy, was so full of energy that even when he smiled it looked like he was going to burst. As I sat there, I thought about my little Sethy, as we used to call him. From a very young age, even as a baby, Seth seemed to have so much pent up aggression and energy. He often looked like he couldn't contain it, and many times he didn't! He had a strong will and a temper to match it. He was always very physical and not very verbal. As a young child, he didn't really know how to express what he was feeling verbally.

Seth was the roughest and toughest acting of our older kids, but he was also the most sensitive. I remember when he was little always thinking that if any of them were going to be ill or suffer much, that it couldn't be Seth. I just didn't know how he would handle it. Yet, it was Seth laying in a coma, fighting for his life…

He may have been small while growing up, but he was mighty and had a big personality! And when it came to sports and speed, he had what we referred to as "the X factor." In junior high, Seth was ranked in the state for pole vaulting. He had a huge collection of medals he had won at track meets. I used to love hearing people's reactions at track meets, when this little tiny kid would pour on the speed and pull way ahead of all the other kids coming around the track. Sitting in the ICU, I could get caught up in these memories, but then they almost made the reality of his situation even worse. It was so painful and completely unimaginable to think that he may never wake up again.

As a toddler, when Seth was sleeping, he looked so peaceful, but when he would wake up he was, as Chris called it, "like a little demon child!" He would wake up in the worst mood, all out of sorts, and would just tear through the house crying, yelling and throwing a fit. We never wanted to wake him up!! Now we found ourselves sitting at his bedside, and all we wanted to do was wake him up. Instead, we weren't even supposed to talk to him. We had to sit there silently, patiently waiting, hoping and praying that his brain would stop swelling and that the pressure inside his head from the swelling would not damage his brain any further or worse yet, claim his life.

I wanted to talk to Seth so badly. I kept thinking about when he fell. I wondered what went through his mind as he was falling. I felt so bad thinking about how terrifying that must have been for him. I hurt for him, for his pain physically and emotionally. I hurt for all he had been through and all that may lie ahead for him. It hurt to think I wasn't there for him, that I couldn't protect him from that pain and fear.

I wanted to ask him all about it. I missed him. I just really wanted him to wake up and talk to us. I wanted to know how he was. As I stood at his side, I prayed that God would bless him and take care of him. I prayed that God would show himself to Seth, let him know that He loved him, and be present to him while he was in his coma. Sometimes that prayer brought me peace, thinking of the possibility of Seth growing closer to Christ through this. And then in the very next moment, I could be overcome by fear that this could damage Seth's relationship with Christ. I mean, Seth was a guy that didn't want to waste a second of his life. How would he feel when he woke up and realized that he had missed whole days? It scared me thinking that this could possibly make Seth really mad at God. My emotions were all over the place, changing from minute to minute.

Physically, I was a mess too. I couldn't eat anything at all. Friends and family brought food to the hospital for us. I remember having to force myself to eat, even just a bite or two in order to try to get at least a little nourishment. It was all like a bad dream. It was unfathomable that Seth was laying there, not even breathing for himself. My mind just couldn't even process it. I thought about Seth leaving the house that day, so vibrant, so happy. Seth was so full of life, full of dreams, athletic, and strong. I wondered if we would ever get Seth back the way we knew him.

We all knew that brain injuries often changed people's personalities if they survived. We were terrified of that. It's funny the things you think of when you're faced with losing someone. Even the annoying things become endearing. I thought about how Seth would always plop down on the couch next to me late at night and lean over onto my lap asking for a back rub. I would be so tired, practically falling asleep and would not want to do it. I often did, but a bit begrudgingly. Suddenly I was sitting there in the ICU wishing for even just one of those moments back again. As I stood at Seth's side, I was dying to just rub his arm. He used to love that. But I wasn't even allowed to do that, since Seth couldn't have any stimulation at all. I leaned over and whispered in his ear, telling him how much I loved him and wanted him to fight to come back to us, and that I had a lot more massages to give him!

Chris and I had experienced a lot of loss together. Chris was my faithful rock through it all. This was a new experience for us though as we not only supported each other but were also watching the heartbreak and pain in our older children, Michael, Andrea, and Ethan as they spent countless hours at Seth's side, holding his hand, thinking and praying.

Ethan stood there as fear, sadness and regret gripped his mind and heart. Bawling, he couldn't stop the tears. It was terrifying for Ethan not knowing what was going to happen to Seth, especially since they had just fought the day before. Ethan didn't know if he should feel sad because Seth might die or upset because he may never get to make things right between them. He didn't know what to think or do. So many emotions were running through his head. In some ways he felt every emotion and in other ways he felt completely void of emotion.

It's hard for him to describe it, but overall, he just felt empty, and no matter what he did, he couldn't stop the tears. They were automatic and uncontrollable. He hurt so bad and felt so cold and alone even though he was surrounded by family. Things looked and felt so bleak.

I don't think any of us could fully understand the depth of what Ethan was going through. Seth and Ethan's last words to each other were not kind, and definitely not the way Ethan wanted his relationship with Seth to end. Ethan was living a nightmare deeper than many of us can imagine. Filled with sorrow and remorse, Ethan stood beside Seth in the ICU with a steady stream of tears running down his cheeks. He cried to his dad saying, "Dad, the last thing I said to Seth is that I hated him. Things just can't end like this. I need to tell him I'm sorry and that I didn't mean what I said. It can't end this way..." Ethan desperately wanted to apologize to Seth, but he didn't know if he would ever get that chance. In that moment, nothing else in the world mattered to him, but Seth. None of their differences or past struggles mattered anymore. He instantly forgave Seth, letting go of all their differences, past struggles and hurts. He knew he loved his brother and would do anything to get him back.

Although Seth and Ethan were very different, Ethan always admired Seth for his hard work ethic and determination. When Seth made up his mind to do something, there was no stopping him. He would do whatever it took to make it happen. He was a very motivated person, and Ethan really looked up to Seth for that. Seth was, in Ethan's mind, one of the strongest people he knew, both physically and mentally.

As Ethan stood vigil beside Seth's lifeless body, he thought of all these things, and he hoped and prayed he would get his strong and determined brother back. Also one of the things Ethan wanted back the most was Seth's humor. He thought about all the times and ways Seth could make him and all of us laugh. He thought of Seth's contagious laugh and just hoped and prayed that he would get his goofy brother, Seth, back. But no matter how Seth came out of this, Ethan knew that he would always be there for him.

Andrea too thought a lot about Seth's humor. Just thinking about it brought smiles to our faces in that dark time. Seth was a goofy kid, and he and Andrea together were pretty goofy. In fact, as Andrea sat in the hospital going through pictures of her and Seth together on her phone, she could hardly find a serious picture of them together!

Seth was kind of shy when he was little, while Andrea was not. Being so close in age, Seth really relied on Andrea when they were young. I remember when Andrea started kindergarten, Seth missed her so much. He used to sit at the living room window and cry for her almost every day after we dropped her off at school.

Now Andrea was the one crying for Seth. She dropped everything as soon as she got the call about Seth's accident. Her mind and heart were with Seth. I think her every thought and whole life became about Seth from that moment on. She couldn't imagine life without him. Hour after hour, she sat with us at Seth's side, praying and holding his hand. I remember one night in particular when she laid across three hard straight-backed chairs, and that was how she slept. She didn't ever want to leave the hospital. Here is the letter Andrea wrote to Seth while sitting in the ICU:

"Hi Seth,
Right now I am sitting in your room with you, and even though I've been spending so much time with you since the accident, this is still all so surreal. I know that it is you lying in the bed, but I still can't fully process it. I still can't fully accept the fact that I can't just call you or talk to you or take ridiculous selfies with the weirdest faces that no one is ever allowed to see.

We've been through a lot together, but I never anticipated that this was going to be something we'd have to go through. Being only a year and a half apart, we have a pretty close bond, and it breaks my heart to see you like this. I love you so much, Seth. I miss you. I've been listening to your music more than I have ever done before. Even though it's painful, it helps to hear your voice. I've even downloaded the soundcloud app just for the sole purpose of listening to you. (When you wake up I'm sure this will make you very happy. Also- I just heard your new song, Tourist, and I very much like it!)

I've also been going through all the dumb photos we have together. Trust me- there are a lot (most of them cannot be shown to the outside world because we both have a knack for making the weirdest and ugliest faces that no one else ever needs to witness.) My life is full of amazing memories with you, and I know that when you wake up we will share many, many more.

We've both had our moments where we've struggled with our faith, but we both have been fortunate to turn back and strive for goodness. When you started wanting to make a change and turn back to your faith, you expressed it (as you express all things) through a song. In the song you say 'fighting for my life right now. So much bigger than the night tonight right now.' I know when you wrote those words, you didn't know about this situation you'd be in now, but those words are so encouraging to me. You are a fighter. You always have been. I know you are fighting for your life right now, and I know you can pull through this. I can't wait till you wake up, Seth. But until then, I'll be here by your side praying.

Much love,
Andrea"

Michael, too, did not want to leave Seth's side. However, being a manager in a grocery store, he could only miss so much work. It was a particularly tough time at his job because his department was understaffed. His assistant had just gotten promoted and moved to another store and one of his other associates quit around that same time too. Having no one to pick up the slack for him, Michael would often leave the hospital late at night and go straight to the store. He would work through the night trying to catch up and prepare ahead for the next day, so that he could get back to the hospital to be with Seth as quickly as possible. He had very little time with his wife and kids during that period, next to no sleep, and no time by himself to process all he was feeling. Michael tried to be strong and hold it all in. Alone in his car was about the only place he could let it out. He remembers getting bad news one day while he was driving. He yelled, "No! No! No!" at the top of his lungs as he drove, punching the ceiling of his car over and over again. Everything in him did not want to believe or accept that this was happening to his brother.

Sitting at Seth's side, Chris came across the remake of an old song called "I Will Be Here" by Steven Curtis Chapman. As he listened to it, he was brought to tears. He played it over and over and just wept inside. As the song said, "Tomorrow morning if you wake up and the sun does not appear, I will be here...Tomorrow morning if you wake up and the future is unclear, I will be here…" Chris knew that no matter what was to come, he would always be right there at Seth's side. As he leaned over Seth, he would whisper, "We're here for you, Seth. Mom and Dad are here, and we will always be here for you all the way through."

During those long, lonely hours, we all had some happy moments thinking of the many times and ways Seth had brought our family so much joy. I would at times sit there and watch old videos of Seth that made me laugh. It felt good to get lost in the memories. However, it was both joyful and sorrowful at the same time because in a split second, I'd be brought back to the reality that I may lose him and never see his smile or hear his laugh again.

With such a severe brain injury, we knew that if Seth survived, he could end up with a different personality. I remember having conversations with both Michael and Andrea about that. We were all so afraid of losing Seth… Seth, as we knew him, the Seth they grew up with, the Seth that either made us laugh or cry. He didn't have much in between. He was so passionate about life, lived it to the fullest, rarely ever stopping to sit still. He had a humor that made us laugh even when we were angry and didn't want to laugh! Oh how we wanted our goofy Seth back. He brought so much joy and laughter to our family. Whether we were talking about it or not, we knew that the fear of Seth's personality being different was in the forefront of each of our thoughts.

This fear plagued our minds in those dark and silent days of waiting.

As we sat there hoping and praying to get Seth back as we knew him, it became increasingly important to Chris that the doctors and nurses knew who Seth was. Like the rest of us, he thought much about Seth's humor and contagious laugh, and he wanted everyone to know the incredible, full of life, fun-loving guy that Seth was. He wanted them to know the person they were caring for under all those wires, tubes, and machines. He wanted them to see him for who he was, not just another lifeless body.

Chris told the nurses all about Seth and what he was like. He showed them pictures and videos that Seth had made. He also asked our kids at home to print pictures of Seth. Chris hung the pictures all over Seth's hospital room. He even put one right on Seth's pillow so doctors and nurses would see who they were taking care of. He wanted desperately for them to not just see another patient hooked to machines, but to see Seth, his son. One of Seth's ICU nurses was so young and cute. We kept thinking, "Man, it's too bad Seth is missing out on this! He would have enjoyed being awake to see her!" We all joked that Chris was still trying to set Seth up, even while in a coma. Sharing stories about Seth and joking around gave us little moments of joy, which kept Seth alive and well in some small way in our hearts. God is good even in darkness, silence, and freezing cold.

CHAPTER FIVE
- THE BODY OF CHRIST -
God is Good... in the Prayers and Support of Others

While we sat quietly in Seth's ICU room feeling quite isolated and alone, we were, in actuality, being supported in many, many ways by family, friends, acquaintances and even strangers. The support that was shown for us was truly overwhelming. Hopefully as you read, you will see the many various ways that we were supported throughout this time. We can't express enough our gratitude to the many, quite possibly even thousands, who became involved.

As soon as Chris' sister, Amanda, who lived in California, heard about Seth's accident, she made a post on facebook about Seth, asking for prayers. Chris and I have always been pretty private people, and we wanted to protect Seth's privacy too. So we weren't comfortable with this. Chris called Amanda and asked her to please take it down. We didn't really think about how many more prayers we could get for Seth through it. Honestly, we didn't know what to think or how to handle any of it. Respectfully, Amanda took it off facebook right away for us, and people continued spreading word of Seth's accident and asking for prayers by word of mouth.

Actually, the word was also being spread by the Holy Spirit! God was calling together prayer warriors, and there were little miracles and signs of God's providence and care for us all along the way. For example, I received this text message from a friend: "Thinking of you and wrapping Seth and your family in prayer. My circle of prayer warriors is on it, too! A friend of mine said that God put it on her heart to pray for someone named Seth on Monday. Amazing..." Monday being the day of Seth's accident, God was constantly showing us that He was in control, and He had Seth in His hands. We just had to completely rely on Him and trust...

The first morning after Seth's accident, my very close friend, Carol, brought Communion to the hospital for Chris and I. We sat in the SICU waiting room and prayed together. As Carol gave me the Eucharist, for the first time since that fateful knock on the door, peace came over me, and I knew right then exactly how I was going to be able to get through this. I knew it would only be with Christ that I, or any of us, would get through it, and in Him is where we would find peace. God had shown me years ago after we lost our newborn son, Jacob, that He can bring joy and peace right in the middle of our suffering. For a split second that morning when I received the Eucharist, I felt that peace again. Small tears filled my eyes, but I still could not cry.

Emotionally I was still very numb and unable to wrap my mind around the looming reality that Seth may die.

We were so blessed though to have friends like Carol to support us and cover us in prayer. Word of Seth's accident traveled fast, and by noon on that first full day many people had gathered in Adoration before the Blessed Sacrament at our church to pray for Seth. The response of friends and the people of St. Thomas the Apostle, our home parish, was overwhelming. Immediately everyone was praying.

Back in Seth's ICU room, it was a constant waiting game, and we really had no idea how long it would go on. After a sleepless night, it became clear that as much as we didn't want to leave the hospital, we were going to have to in order to get some sleep. Chris and I took turns going home to nap. Chris went home first, and then I went later in the day after he got back to the hospital.

When I got home and walked into our bedroom, I saw Chris' beard trimmer laying there. It was like an arrow pierced my heart. You see, Seth used to always come up to our room and use Chris' beard trimmer to shave. It used to drive us crazy because he often didn't clean out our bathroom sink when he was done. After seeing the razor, I turned the corner into the bathroom to find Seth's hair trimmings from shaving all over our bathroom sink. I collapsed onto my bed and sobbed out loud.

It's interesting how even the little things that were once irritating, can trigger so much emotion. Seeing that little piece of Seth in my room was what finally opened the floodgates for me and got me to cry for the first time since his accident. Oh how I hoped Seth would someday be back home to use that razor and make a mess in our bathroom again! Suddenly, the mess was the least of my concerns. Actually, for several days to follow, whenever I used the sink, I was very careful not to let any of those hair trimmings wash away. I found out later that Chris had been doing the same thing when he was home. We both desperately wanted to hold onto any sign of Seth, alive and as we knew him.

Because Chris and I were supposed to be leaving for a week in California, we both already had the week off work and everything such as paying bills, grocery shopping, and laundry had already been taken care of at home. This ended up being an incredible blessing for us. It allowed us to just stay with Seth without really having to think about anything else, and it also made running home a bit of a respite for us rather than a stress. It's amazing the little blessings you can find even in the midst of suffering. God is good. He always knows what we need even when we don't.

Once we got through the first twenty-four hours, it quickly became apparent that the critical period was not necessarily just twenty-four hours as Dr. Gibson had originally indicated. As long as the brain was continuing to swell, Seth's life was in danger. Doctors told us the peak swelling may not actually come for three to four days, possibly even five to seven days...

The ICU nurses worked tirelessly to make sure that every little detail was attended to. It was eye opening to see how each level affected another. They were all so attentive to even the tiniest of details, and we were so grateful for that because Seth's life was literally in their hands. They were amazing, and so very caring and respectful too. Even though Seth was completely unresponsive in a coma, every time they had to do anything to him, they would talk to him and let him know exactly what they were doing, apologizing for any pain they may cause and warning him of their cold hands before they touched him.

Seth had so many monitors and so many wires and tubes coming from his body, that nurses who would come in from other rooms to help reposition him, would comment saying he took the prize for having the most things hooked to him. He had at least ten leads on his head monitoring any possible seizure activity in the brain, a feeding tube in his nose, the breathing tube in his mouth, at least five IV bags running into him, an arterial line measuring constant blood pressure, the bolt going into his brain measuring his intracranial pressure, a central line in his chest, etc. They were monitoring so many things that it took three monitor screens and still all the readings didn't fit. The nurses had to unhook some things in order to get the readings of others when needed.

As the hours continued to pass with no sign of improvement, we began to feel desperate for more prayers. My sister, Kathy, who lived in Wisconsin, had asked me several times to please let her post it on facebook. She was tirelessly texting so many groups of people trying to get as many prayers as possible. She kept telling us that she could reach so many more people if she could put it on facebook.

By Wednesday morning, just a day and a half after Seth's accident, Chris came to me saying that he felt very strongly that we needed to let Kathy put it on facebook. Private or not, we just needed as many prayers as we could get for Seth. He questioned, "If we keep it private, how will people even know to pray for Seth?" I understood his concern and agreed. That morning, I talked to Kathy and asked her to go ahead and post it. She made her first post right away.

Kathy Barth updated her status.
February 15 ·

I would like to ask all of my friends to please lift up my 21 year old nephew, Seth Alfaro, in your prayers. Seth fell about 25 feet through a roof late Monday and is in the ICU in a medically induced coma with swelling of the brain. Today the swelling is increasing and they are having trouble keeping his ICP (intracranial pressure) down. They just added another sedative which is working right now, but we really need prayers for the swelling to stop and begin to go down. We are really praying for a total and complete healing and that we get our precious Seth back. He is a young man of faith, full of life and creativity, with so many gifts to share. Please join me in storming the heavens for him and my beloved sister, Christine Faber Alfaro, my dear brother-in-law, Christopher Alfaro, and their whole family. We appreciate your prayers and support more than you know! THANK YOU!!!

Almost instantly hundreds of people saw it, and it was shared and spread to hundreds more. I was constantly sending the family detailed updates on how Seth was doing. Kathy would then post the updates as I sent them. Sometimes we would ask her not to post very sensitive things, always trying to protect Seth's privacy and dignity as much as possible.

Kathy's writing was so beautiful, heartfelt, and faith-filled that each post drew people, from near and far, into Seth's story. I would send her an update, and she would turn it into a beautiful message of faith and love, as well as a plea for anyone and everyone to offer prayers for Seth. So many people have told me how much her writing drew them into Seth's story and inspired their faith. For many people, it was the first thing they read in the morning and the last thing they read before going to bed at night.

People began immediately commenting on Kathy's posts about Seth's accident. We could not believe the number of people who began sharing the posts and praying for Seth. What surprised and amazed me most though was that they were all praying for complete healing, a total miracle for Seth. While I wanted a miracle, it was hard for me to pray for one and believe it would happen. I had begged God for miracles before and still ended up burying four of my babies. To see the faith of all the people on facebook gave me hope when I was weak. Their prayers and their comments really supported Chris and I and held us up.

Very early on we saw a post from one of Seth's friends, a friend that Seth had always tried to be a witness for by keeping his song lyrics clean, etc. This young man had changed his status from heartbroken to thankful. He spoke of how Seth had witnessed God to him, and then he began praying to God and calling others to join him in believing that Seth was going to be healed. As Chris and I read this, we began to realize that Seth's accident and present condition was way bigger than us and Seth, and that God could and would reach so many young people through this and use it to change lives.

Jonny Fiction was feeling thankful.
February 15 ·
changed this status from heartbroken to THANKFUL BECAUSE IM EXPECTING GOOD NEWS SOON
When i told u u needed to curse in our songs
"Bro we gotta keep it clean"
When i told u to get a song with swearing, you didn't want to cuz u knew deep down God would not approve, u showed me that u were faithful to your girl because of God and God gave u that control when most men could not do such a thing, smh i don't have words
Smh please God help my friend Seth Alfaro.
I know that You exist Father, I know that You know Seth Alfaro. Please forgive him for anything he has done and make him whole again. Let him come out of this coma and be stronger than before he went into this coma. It says that You Love Your children, and You said that your

mercy is everlasting so whatever happens, his family and the rest of Your children need him, and let anyone who reads this prayer say it with me if you know God is real and knows He can DO THIS, JUST BELIEVE WITH ME, JUST LET IT BE DONE AND IT WILL HAPPEN, seth alfaro IS GOING TO WAKE UP SO GET READY!

On this day, February 15th, Seth's intracranial pressures(ICPs) were very high. We were only two days in, and we had been told that he may not even hit the peak swelling for a couple more days. Doctors started the day telling us that they had many tricks in their bag which they could use to try to keep the pressure from the swelling down. But as the day progressed, the options were dwindling very quickly. At one point they had tried five different things to bring Seth's ICPs down and he wasn't responding. If the swelling continued at that rate for two more days, as was common, it would be extremely dangerous. Doctors told us they may have to knock him out completely which would temporarily paralyze him or they may actually have to remove part of his skull in order for his brain to have room to swell. Both of these options terrified us.

Kathy continued to post multiple times a day, asking for specific prayers based on Seth's particular needs at that moment.

Kathy Barth updated her status.
February 15 ·
The news on my nephew is not good. Please keep the prayers coming!!!!
LATEST UPDATE FROM MY SISTER:

They have had to work very hard to keep his ICP down. He is using up his options very quickly. If the swelling continues at this rate for 2 more days it could be bad. They can only give him so much of the meds safely. Then they will have to do much more invasive and risky procedures. Please have everyone pray that this is the peak of the swelling and that it stops now instead of getting worse for 2 more days like is common.

Please also pray for Chris and Chris and their family--for strength and peace and God's grace! Thank you!

Immediately, word of Seth's accident had traveled all over the world. We have a close friend, Marianne, who lives in New Zealand, and when she went to her church group to ask for prayers for Seth, someone stopped her and said, "Wait, are you talking about Seth Alfaro?" She already knew and was praying for him because of facebook. It was unbelievable to see how quickly and how far it spread through social media. It was literally like we were watching the Body of Christ all throughout the world rise up like an army in support and prayer for Seth and us. There were messages coming from all over the country as well as Spain, Italy, Lebanon, New Zealand, etc. People were all praying for a miracle for Seth, for complete, total healing! I can't stress enough how much their faith buoyed us. Their prayers literally created a wave of faith that held us up and kept us from sinking under the weight of it all.

Along with being continually covered in prayer, we had also been given many prayer cards, novenas, relics, blessed salt, holy oil, and Lourdes water. I would bless Seth over and over with both the holy oil and holy water every day, sometimes several times a day.

Friends had also mentioned to us that we should be seeking the intercession of Blessed Pier Giorgio Frassati. The first time someone mentioned it, I didn't really think too much about it. I had never heard of him and didn't know anything about him. But by the time 3 different people had mentioned him to us within the first couple days, I figured it wasn't a coincidence and we had better listen. We learned that the miracle that was earning him sainthood was the miraculous healing of a young guy who had fallen off a roof and was expected to be a vegetable the rest of his life.

We immediately began seeking Blessed Pier Giorgio Frassati's intercession for Seth. Our niece, Karianna, bought us a book about him and brought us a picture of him that we kept in Seth's hospital room. We asked Kathy to post on facebook to get the word out to seek Blessed Pier Giorgio's intercession for a miracle for Seth. At the same time, we had also been given relics of Venerable Solanus Casey by three different people. It was very clear to us that these two, Blessed Pier Giorgio Frassati and Venerable Solanus Casey were the saints whose intercession we should be seeking. The blessing of so many faithful friends and prayer warriors was overwhelming.

Two of our close friends, Tom Theoret and Matt Parlmer, both worked at Spectrum Health Hospital where

Seth was. They both came by to see us and Seth many times, always asking if there was anything they could do for us. It was always such a blessing to see them and a comfort just knowing they were there.

Not too many people could really come to the hospital. If they did it was just real quick because we couldn't visit in the room since there couldn't be any noise. When people would come, we would have to leave Seth's room to visit with them for a few minutes in the waiting room. When someone did come into Seth's room, it was just for a minute to see him and say a quick prayer.

It was shocking for people to see Seth completely lifeless, not even breathing on his own. It is something you really can't grasp until you see it. It was kind of lonely not being able to have our friends there much, so having Tom and Matt pop in daily when they were at work was a very welcome and comforting blessing. Since we really didn't want to be away from Seth's room for long, when people would inquire about coming to visit, my sister, Kathy, began asking that they visit the Blessed Sacrament to pray for Seth instead.

Many of Seth's friends wanted to see him though. We let his closest friends come one at a time. They could only be there for a few minutes at a time in silence. It was actually heart wrenching to watch. I have never seen so many young men cry. Some even doubled over in pain and disbelief, falling to their knees before they even mustered the nerve to enter Seth's room.

A few days after Seth's accident we were blessed to have a visit from a woman from our parish who had recently been through something very similar with her son, Noah. It was extremely helpful to meet with Sarah. Noah, who was close to Seth's age, had been in the very same ICU just six weeks before Seth. He had a serious brain injury from a terrible car accident. Sarah offered to come talk to us to give us some idea of what to expect through this. We were so appreciative of this because it was all so new and overwhelming to us, and we had no idea what to expect in the days that laid ahead.

Listening to Sarah's experience was hard. I know the ER doctor had indicated this would be a marathon, but I really had no comprehension of what that meant. As Sarah shared that it had been a week before they got any responses from Noah, and ten days before he was really awake, I was deeply discouraged. I just couldn't imagine having to wait a week to see even a simple response from Seth. My heart ached for him, to see him awake, talk to him, and know he was alright. It seemed unbearable to have to wait as long as Sarah did. I wondered how I could possibly wait that long not knowing anything. It felt impossible. I tried to cling to hope that maybe Seth's injury would not be as bad as her son's.

Sarah also showed us pictures of Noah all throughout his time in the ICU. Chris and I and Andrea had all quietly wondered if we should take pictures of Seth, but never said anything to each other. Seth was always so into pictures that we thought he may want to see them later, if he came through this. So after seeing Sarah's pictures of her son, we decided then to start taking pictures of Seth.

It felt a little weird taking pictures at first. As I took pictures of Chris at Seth's side, it was like deja vu. It brought me right back to the pictures we have of us in the NICU with our dying newborns. It was so hard to believe we were actually in this position once again, this time with our twenty-one-year-old son.

My mind and heart just couldn't process the fact that Seth was laying there in a coma and could die. It felt like we were going through some horrible family tragedy and Seth wasn't there with us. It just didn't feel right not being able to talk to him about what was going on. When our kids weren't there and I was sending them updates, I felt like I needed to send an update to Seth. And then like an unending nightmare, I would be brought back to the reality that Seth really was there. He was the one fighting for his life. Surreal, is the only way I can describe it.

They were long, scary, and sleepless days that blended one into the other. What sleep we got was just a couple of hours at a time reclined in a chair in the waiting room, or stretched across a couple hard straight-back chairs sat next to each other, or a quick nap at home when possible. There was one chair in Seth's hospital room that reclined almost to flat. So one of us would be able to sleep in that some nights, but overall we were not getting much sleep.

To our surprise, one day our friend, Tom, brought us an incredible gift. He was able to get an extra chair out of the hospital storage and had it brought into our room. It was one that could fold down to lay completely flat. That was an amazing help, because it meant that two of us could actually lie down to sleep at night. Before that, Michael, Andrea, Ethan, Chris, and I spent the nights sleeping in chairs. Though some of us could have left and gone home to sleep, we just couldn't leave Seth or each other.

The nurses were always shocked when they came into the room and saw the new chair. They wondered how we had gotten so lucky. It was very nice to have friends in high places! With Tom's help, we were able to have two people at the hospital at night while still being able to lie down to sleep. As the days passed this also made some of us more comfortable going home to sleep, knowing that whoever stayed at the hospital would be able to get some sleep too.

Typically it was Chris and I who stayed the night in Seth's room. Both of us being able to lay down and sleep at night became extremely important and helpful as the days went on. They were very long and difficult days. The fact that Chris and I could be there together and still get some sleep was a great comfort. I was incredibly grateful for that, because truthfully, I was very afraid to stay at the hospital alone. It was heart wrenching and incredibly scary as alarms would go off alerting the nurses to life threatening needs. For many days, every little detail was important to keep Seth alive.

The morning of Friday, February 17th, Chris and I were awakened very early, around 5:30am, by the sound of alarms going off alerting us that Seth's ICPs were spiking way too high, meaning the pressure in his brain was dangerously high. Usually if nurses tried to reposition him or had to touch him at all, it could cause his ICPs to go up, but this time no one else had been in the room or touching him at all. When Dylan, his ICU nurse at the time, came into the room, he noticed that Seth's CO2 level was too high. He said Seth must have been fighting the ventilator and not blowing out enough CO2, causing it to build up in his system, which in turn can cause the ICPs to spike. It was crazy to see how specific the levels of every single thing needed to be in order to sustain Seth's life. The situation corrected itself within about ten minutes or so, but it was a terrifying ten minutes. I struggled to stay calm and not panic in those moments as machines were beeping and nurses were emergently working to resolve the issues. I was extremely grateful that Chris and I could be there together most of the time. I don't know if I could have handled that alone.

While it was most often Chris and I who stayed overnight, Michael, Andrea, Ethan and Seth's Aunt Sarah also took some turns staying, so that once in a while Chris or I could go home to sleep and be with Caleb, Mary, and Peter. They still needed us too, but unfortunately didn't get too much of us during that time. In trying to protect them from the situation, we realized later that we actually caused them a lot of pain. Because we didn't talk to them about what was going on and include them in it, they felt very isolated and alone.

In hindsight, I wish I had given more to them, spent more time talking to them and listening to them about what they were going through, but regretfully, I didn't see their needs at the time. So unfortunately, we all continued the pattern of not really telling them much of anything. We wanted to protect them from it all, but in reality sometimes not knowing the truth and being excluded from it can be worse. In actuality, they were there, going through it too, and unfortunately were often misinformed and feeling very alone. In fact, friends and teachers at school would ask them how Seth was, and they didn't even know how to answer because they didn't know.

I am so grateful that Meg was with Caleb, Mary, and Peter. However, Meg, too, felt very alone and unable to express her emotions. For example, when she heard the news that Seth was in an induced coma, she was with the younger kids, so while she would have normally freaked out and cried, she didn't. She worked hard to hold it all in and stay calm and composed in front of the kids so as not to scare them. That sort of started a pattern for Meg of holding in all her feelings and emotions and trying to be strong for everyone else.

Even when Meg did get a chance to come to the hospital, she usually stuffed her own emotions down, trying to be strong for the rest of us. She watched in torment as Ethan stood over Seth crying and apologizing to him. It tore her apart to see such heartache, brokenness, and pain in Ethan, but she stood strong beside both Ethan and Seth. And as she stood there, she kept thinking, "If only Seth knew how much we loved him and needed him, he'd fight to come back to us." She desperately wanted Seth to know how much he was loved. He had distanced himself from the family so much in recent years that she was afraid he might not know how much he was loved and might not fight to come back. Meg has always been more like a daughter than a daughter-in-law, and she was an irreplaceable and invaluable support to each one of us in the midst of this tragedy. She constantly put our needs and feelings above her own.

Seth was deeply loved by family and friends alike. It was unbelievable and uplifting to see the number of people following Seth's story on facebook and sharing it and posting things about him trying to get more and more people praying. Early on Seth's cousin, Kieran, put a beautiful post on facebook about Seth asking others to pray:

"So many emotions have been racing around me this past week, for those who don't know my cousin Seth was in an accident and has been in a coma since Monday night, in that time we have had good news and bad news on what feels like a never ending roller coaster.
I know some people become uncomfortable when asked to pray for something or someone, but I'm asking anyone and everyone to put up a prayer for Seth. It doesn't have to be a long one, it can just be a quick "please help him heal" but I know that anything helps."

Kieran continued with a letter to Seth:

"Seth,
I know we aren't as close as we used to be, but I can't begin to tell you how proud I am of the person you've become, your tireless work ethic is something that amazes everyone who sees you. Your passion for the things that move you is incredible to witness, and your joy and laughter is contagious. I know you're strong and I know you're fighting, but just know you have a community fighting right there with you. I love you man!! Get well and know WE are praying for you.
This song has been my prayer for you the whole week and I just want to share it with everyone
'I have this hope in the depth of my soul, in the flood or the fire you are with me and you won't let go.'"

At the end of the post, Kieran added a link to the song, "I Have this Hope" by Tenth Avenue North. I had never heard the song before, but once I did, I listened to it over and over again. It became my theme song throughout the whole ordeal. We grabbed onto every bit of encouragement and inspiration people had to offer.

Truly, the support and faith of so many people held us up through it all.

We received unending support from the people of our parish, St. Thomas the Apostle Catholic Church in Grand Rapids, Michigan. Not only did they hold us in prayer, but they also totally took care of our family's physical needs as well. They immediately set up a schedule of people to bring meals to our home. It was unbelievable the amount of food we received. I remember one day going home to shower, and in the short time I was home three different people showed up at our house with meals. The love and generosity was overwhelming. Teachers and parents also pitched in to buy hot lunches for Caleb, Mary, and Peter, so no one had to worry about packing lunches, and the school also suspended our tuition payments so we would not have any extra financial burdens. Others offered rides for our kids whenever needed, while cards and calls offering support also flooded in.

Thanks also to Chris' brother-in-law, Dallas, from Hawaii, we did not have to worry about money at all. Dallas started a GoFundMe for Seth right away. The response was amazing and removed all worry over finances. The generosity and outpouring of love and support by family, friends and even strangers was completely overwhelming and humbling.

The love and support of our faith community was overwhelming, and the acts of kindness were too numerous to count and not just simple, one time things. Two of my close friends actually stepped in with a huge ongoing favor, for which I could never repay them. Since we didn't know how long Seth would be in the hospital, Lucyna and Casey completely took over my childcare business, watching all the kids in Casey's home. All of the parents of the kids were a huge support to us as well

75

and had been incredibly understanding and patient making temporary arrangements for their children since I had to leave so abruptly. However, as time went on, they would have eventually had to make more permanent arrangements for childcare. Realizing that, Lucyna and Casey stepped in and took over, so that I would not completely lose my business. I hadn't even thought about that. They were amazing and the kids loved them. All throughout, we were blessed by the support of so many, like Lucyna and Casey, who just acted on our behalf, enabling us to focus entirely on Seth.

I cannot adequately express how truly blessed we were to be continually surrounded by support on all sides starting with our own family, and including incredible hospital staff and nurses like Dylan, the constant support of friends, unending meals and support from the St. Thomas community and beyond, as well as prayers reaching across the globe. As difficult as it was, we knew Seth was in good hands, and we were too.

We knew that Seth was not only in the hands of incredible medical personnel, but he was also in the hands of God. As the days went on, he continued to be completely covered in prayer. Within days everyone was seeking the intercession of both Blessed Pier Giorgio Frassati and Venerable Solanus Casey. Many had also begun a rosary novena for Seth, inserting his name into the Hail Mary prayer as was suggested by our friend,

Carol Dills. After the name of Jesus, we would say, "healer of Seth."

Tyler F Antonides with Seth Alfaro.
February 17 ·
Alright guys, starting today we are beginning a Rosary Novena for Seth Alfaro. For those of you who do not know how to pray the Rosary, you can follow this link: https://goo.gl/Zbk4nM
However, with each Hail Mary bead we are asking you to repeat this modified Hail Mary:
"Hail Mary, full of grace. The Lord is with thee.
Blessed art thou among women, and blessed is the fruit of thy womb, Jesus, healer of Seth.
Holy Mary, Mother of God, pray for us sinners, now and at the hour of our death. Amen.
We are asking these intentions through the intercession of Blessed Pier Giorgio Frassati, and Venerable Solanus Casey. Solanus Casey always said to "Thank God ahead of time." So Father in Heaven, we thank you now for the gift of Seth, we thank you for healing him, and we thank you for bringing comfort and peace to his family.
The Novena begins today (February 17th) and will continue each day until next Saturday (February 25th). This Novena has worked miracles before, and we trust it will work for Seth as well. If you want to go deeper with helping Seth, I encourage you to join us in this daily prayer. Lastly, I just want to give a huge thank you to Carol Dills for organizing the Novena. We really appreciate it. Thank you all for the prayers. Seth is a fighter, but we're all in this together.

That Friday the Mass in the hospital chapel was even offered specifically for Seth. Our niece, Karianna's friend arranged it for us. Dave and Sarah as well as our children, Ethan, Caleb, Mary-Kate, and Peter all came for the Mass. Our dear friends, Tom and Carol, and their daughter, Grace, came too, and they took us to lunch after, while Dave and Sarah stayed with Seth. Even though Seth was in a coma, we still never left Seth alone without a family member with him.

The first few days were kind of a blur of emotions all over the spectrum, from total numbness at times to intense and overwhelming emotion at others. There were beautiful moments of grace as well as agonizing moments of fear. It was a rollercoaster ride, but we knew we were being held up by the body of Christ. We couldn't have managed it on our own. We felt all the grace and the prayers, and the fear did not overcome us. God was good to us in the prayers and support of the body of Christ.

CHAPTER SIX
- THE TRACHEOSTOMY -
God is Good... in the Waiting

On Thursday, three days in, doctors began talking to us about the need to put in a tracheostomy, so that they could remove the breathing tube. They explained that the longer the breathing tube was in, the more risk Seth would have of developing an infection like pneumonia. The breathing tube had also really been irritating Seth and was causing him to cough quite violently. Even though he was heavily sedated, he coughed so hard that his whole body would practically convulse.

The idea of Seth having a trach was very scary. It was something I never imagined one of my children ever having. And for Seth in particular it seemed like it might be especially harmful. Both Chris and I were concerned that it may damage his vocal cords. Seth loved to sing more than anything. It was his dream to be a famous rapper/singer someday. Regardless of the possible risks, at this point, we knew the trach was vital. The coughing and irritation brought about by the breathing tube was causing Seth's ICPs to continue to spike. It was crucial that the pressure in his brain be minimized as much as possible. Therefore, getting the trach in as soon as possible was imperative.

Around this time, any kind of movement caused his ICPs to spike. Nurses were having trouble even trying to reposition Seth to prevent bed sores, because every time they tried to move him even slightly, his ICPs would spike. So all his violent coughing couldn't have possibly been good for the pressure in his brain. Getting the tracheostomy in would help relax his body and in turn bring his ICPs down. It was a critical step for preventing further damage to his brain and his overall healing. However, it was very tricky. You see, Seth needed the tracheostomy in order to bring his ICPs down, but the ICPs were too high for him to handle the procedure. It was all a delicate balancing act and a process which required much patience as we waited hour after hour, day after day.

It was a long waiting game, a marathon as Dr. Gibson had told us. While the doctors kept talking about wanting to begin lowering the sedation medications so they could try to get any responses from Seth, they really couldn't until the swelling and pressure in his brain were reduced. It seemed that there were endless complications that kept him teetering between life and death and delayed our desire and hope of waking Seth up and seeing if we would ever get our Seth back. Every day felt like an eternity.

As we waited, Seth seemed to gain new prayer warriors each day, following and sharing Aunt Kathy's facebook posts. The following post was made by a St.

80

Thomas friend and mother of one of Seth's middle school classmates. She coined the phrase #sethstrong which then began to be used by many.

Stephanie Lancaster-Lavoie with <u>Kathy Barth</u> and <u>3 others</u>.
<u>February 18</u> ·

We were constantly surrounded by the love and support of many. I know many of the peaks throughout this time were directly because of all the people praying for us. We could feel the strength from them. They truly kept us afloat.

Saturday morning, February 18th, we got an encouraging report. Seth's CT scan looked better than before. This was very positive news. It meant that the brain must be past the peak of its swelling. The neurosurgeon was very positive about how the scan looked. He said the swelling was definitely down from before and that there was no sign of any need for brain surgery.

Based on the CT scan, the doctors planned to put the tracheostomy in at 1 o'clock that afternoon. Even though Seth was still having issues with his ICPs spiking, they figured they could probably medicate him even more heavily in order to help with that. Getting the tracheostomy in would set many positive forward steps into motion. With the tracheostomy in, doctors would be able to get the bolt out of his head on Monday, which would then enable them to get an MRI of his neck and head. The MRI would do two very important things. First, it would show if there was any damage to the ligaments in Seth's neck. If there was no damage, his neck brace could be removed, making him more comfortable. Secondly, the MRI could also give the doctors a better look at the damage to Seth's brain and a possible prognosis. After the MRI, the next step would be to begin to gradually lower Seth's sedation and try to wake him up.

There were obviously many steps involved, but with the brain swelling finally decreasing rather than increasing, things were looking up. It seemed he may have gotten through the most critical part and that things were finally going to begin progressing toward recovery. Surgery to get the tracheostomy was scheduled for 1pm. Getting the tracheostomy was truly going to be a huge step forward. We were excited.

There were, however, constant ups and downs, waves of joy and sorrow, hope and discouragement, peace and fear. By 1:15pm our hopes came crashing down. The surgeon told us that they were not going to be able to put the trach in yet. Seth's ICPs were still too high and too unstable. Doctors thought maybe they would be able to do it the next day, but we would just have to wait and see. Seth's ICPs continued to be unstable until late into the evening. Things weren't looking promising. The doctors weren't really too surprised by it though. They explained that even though he was past the peak swelling, his brain was undoubtedly still very swollen. We were on a seemingly never-ending roller coaster of peaks and valleys. We laid down to sleep that night tremendously disheartened.

My sister, Kathy, knowing it had been an exceptionally tough day for us, couldn't sleep that night. So at about 2am Wisconsin time, which is 3am in Michigan, she posted again on facebook asking for more prayers.

Kathy Barth
February 19 · Darboy, WI ·

For anyone who may still be awake (especially Seth's family and friends on the West Coast)...

Despite the good news I posted yesterday (Saturday) morning, Seth didn't have a very good day. The doctors weren't able to do anything they'd hoped because his ICP numbers were too high and unstable. I know this time of waiting is very hard.

Please pray his numbers come down and stabilize. Please pray he has a good night. Please pray Chris and Chris have a good night, too. Please pray for healing for Seth and for strength and courage for his family. Thank you, again, dear friends!

Kathy got some very interesting responses the next morning.

Amy Oatley A dream/vision I had last night around 3am. Whenever I awake in the middle of the night, I ask the Holy Spirit to fly me and whoever needs prayer to Jesus in the Tabernacle. I fell back asleep pretty sure and had this vivid movie-like picture of hundreds and hundreds of people streaming into Seth's hospital room and the Adoration chapel praying on their knees for Seth. When I awoke this morning, I wondered if it was real because how could hundreds and hundreds of people be allowed into his hospital room! Our Father is listening and loving. As you say, the waiting is hard, yet He is healing Seth in the waiting. Trust in Jesus even more. To Jesus through Mary ♥

Regina Kerwin Ricketts Oh my goodness!! I woke at three thirteen this morn and immediately saw myself with others in prayer for Seth. I said my rosary on my fingers (the way Carol Dills told me to inserting Seth's name in each Hail Mary). Then I went back to sleep. Powerful warriors at work.

When Chris and I awoke on Sunday morning, February 19th, we saw this on facebook. I remember thinking it was really cool, but honestly I didn't really grasp what it meant. Afterall, Chris and I were in Seth's hospital room the whole night. No one was there that we could see. We knew many, many people were praying for Seth, and that was a huge comfort. However, trusting that God was healing Seth in the waiting was getting really difficult. We were, frankly, sick and tired of all the waiting. Talking with our friend about her son, Noah, I had felt like waiting a week to see any kind of response would be nearly impossible. Yet, here we were on day six, nowhere near that. Afterall, the doctors were still having trouble just trying to stabilize Seth's ICP's.

Thankfully though, this particular morning the trauma doctors told us they were going to push to get the trach in. They no longer thought it made a lot of sense that Seth's ICPs were still spiking even without any stimulation. They said the longer the bolt is in, the less reliable the numbers are. They said it was time for the bolt to come out and start trying to wake Seth up, but that they couldn't take the bolt out until the trach was in. They needed it to monitor the pressure in his head during the procedure. They seemed ready to get going and get Seth moving forward toward recovery, which sounded great to Chris and me. We were more than ready to move forward, but the problem was that there were two different teams of doctors working with Seth: the Trauma doctors and the Surgical ICU doctors, and they didn't always agree.

Each morning both teams would assess Seth and tell us their plan of action, but nothing could be done until they met together and agreed on the plan. So while we knew the trauma doctors were going to push to get the trach in this day, it was the SICU doctors who would have to do the procedure. So we waited some more to see if the trauma doctors would be successful in getting the SICU doctors to agree to put it in. It had become normal each morning to hear two varying plans from the two teams of doctors and then have to wait to see what they would decide together as far as how to proceed with Seth's treatment for the day.

The SICU doctors agreed to put the trach in at 1pm. They were also going to put a peg feeding tube directly into his stomach at the same time. That way they could take the feeding tube out of his nose and relieve him of all the irritation caused by tubes going down his throat. It was their hope that this would successfully stop Seth's violent coughing.

At 12:15pm, Seth's ICPs were still unstable and his fever was going up. I was getting nervous that if things didn't settle down, they may not be able to proceed with the surgery. The nurses put heated socks on Seth's hands and feet because they were freezing cold. They thought that maybe his body temperature was going up in order to try to warm his extremities because they were so cold. They were hoping that warming his extremities would help keep his body temperature from going up any further.

At 1:15pm the doctors began prepping Seth for surgery for the trach and peg feeding tube even though Seth still had a fever. They told us the surgery would take about an hour. Michael, Andrea, Dave and Sarah were all there with Chris and me. We all waited together out in the waiting room while Seth was in surgery. I remember the mood was quite light. We were all so relieved and excited, feeling hopeful and like we were finally moving forward with Seth.

That hour while we all waited together during Seth's surgery was one of the happiest times we had had all week. We finally felt a little relief and joy. About an hour after they took Seth to surgery, the doctor came out to the waiting room to talk to us. Assuming the surgery was finished, we were anxious to hear how the surgery had gone.

To our utter disbelief, the doctor told us that she was unable to put the trach in. Our hearts sank. The surgeon went on to explain that Seth was desaturating, meaning his oxygen saturation levels kept dropping. "We think he may have pneumonia," she said. "We have started him on IV antibiotics and will need to wait to do the surgery." This was a huge and devastating setback. Just like that, the little joy and lightness we felt was completely obliterated and our hope instantly derailed.

At that moment, Chris literally felt like he had been sucker punched in the gut. It was like the wind had been knocked out of him. As we all headed back into Seth's hospital room, Chris literally felt as though he couldn't breathe. He took one step into the room, stopped, turned around, and walked out without a word. He didn't tell me where he was going or when he would be back. He didn't even tell me that he was leaving. He just left. He had never done that before… He needed air. He needed space. He needed hope. He needed strength… He always tried so hard to be strong for me and our children, but at this point he felt like he had nothing left to give us. He felt at such a loss and didn't know what to do. Not knowing where he was going, he just turned around and walked out the door of Seth's room. He walked down the hall, got on the elevator, went down to the first floor and walked out of the hospital. He continued to walk down the street and around the corner. He just kept walking with no destination in mind. Eventually he ended up on a park bench a few blocks away. He was confused and angry. He cried out, "Lord, I don't know what to do anymore. We've been praying nonstop..." He was feeling every emotion possible all at once. He didn't know what to think. Everything felt like it was in disarray, and he was completely depleted. Right then, by the grace of God, he happened to have reached into his pocket and felt his rosary there.

The rosary is Chris' consolation when he is lonely and his strength in times of trouble, and he knew this was trouble. Things were bleak. He looked back at the hospital and could see the room where Seth was and where Michael, Andrea, and I were, and he felt he just couldn't give us what he needed to give us. Weak and bewildered, he pulled out his rosary and did what he always did, what he had done, hour after hour, day after day, since the minute he heard of Seth's accident, he prayed. Amazingly, by the time he finished the rosary, he had recovered his peace and his strength once again. He knew then that he could go back into that hospital room and face the situation, ready to continue the fight and the vigil at Seth's side and be strong for his family.

At the same time that Chris was struggling, I was losing it too. When I saw Chris leave Seth's room, all I could think was how badly I wanted to run out of there too. I felt desperate to get out of there. We had been in Seth's room night and day, and I just couldn't take it any longer.

Knowing that Michael, Andrea, Dave, and Sarah were all there with Seth, I left the room too. Like Chris, I didn't have a clue where I was going or what I was doing. I just wandered, unable to face another moment in that ICU room. I struggled to hold it together. Eventually I found myself all alone in the hospital chapel, where I completely fell apart. Day after day I had to hold it together and be silent in Seth's room. I couldn't hold it in anymore. I knelt down, bent over, buried my face in the floor and sobbed out loud. I yelled out, "No God, please NO!"

I knew in my heart what I needed to do. I knew that God was asking me to surrender Seth to Him, but I couldn't. I did not want to! I was so afraid to. I had surrendered my children to God before, and I knew darn well that God's will and mine were often not the same. I could not bear losing Seth. I poured my heart out to God begging, "You can't take him from me...I can't lose him..." I wrestled with God, and I wrestled with myself... But before I left that chapel, kneeling on that floor, bent over, desperate, teeth clenched, fists clenched, tears streaming down my face, with every ounce of strength I had, I finally uttered those words, "Your will Lord, not mine, be done for Seth."

I have to admit, there was no sentiment or warm fuzzy feeling at all. It was purely a heart wrenching, conscious act, giving my will over to God. The very principle I had tried to teach Seth to live by, was testing and challenging everything within me. I didn't want to do it, but I knew I had to. I knew that ultimately true joy only comes in God's will. Although I had finally surrendered, it was not one and done. I had to pray constantly for the grace and strength to surrender my will and trust God's will for Seth's life, minute by minute, hour after hour, day after day. I had been praying the Surrender Novena, which is my favorite novena. But instead of just praying it once a day, I prayed it several times a day trying to let the words seep in and transform my heart.

The words of the novena are absolutely beautiful. I needed them to penetrate into the depths of my mind and heart. I have included the novena here. Hopefully it will be a comfort to you in difficult times as it has been for me.

The Surrender Novena

Day 1 Jesus to the soul: Why do you confuse yourselves by worrying? Leave the care of your affairs to Me and everything will be peaceful. I say to you in truth that every act of true, blind, complete surrender to Me produces the effect that you desire and resolves all difficult situations.

O Jesus, I surrender myself to You, take care of everything! (10 times)

Day 2 *Jesus to the soul: Surrender to Me does not mean to fret, to be upset, or to lose hope, nor does it mean offering to Me a worried prayer asking Me to follow you and change your worry into prayer. It is against this surrender, deeply against it, to worry, to be nervous and to desire to think about the consequences of anything. It is like the confusion that children feel when they ask their mother to see to their needs, and then try to take care of those needs for themselves so that their childlike efforts get in their mother's way. Surrender means to placidly close the eyes of the soul, to turn away from thoughts of tribulation and to put yourself in My care, so that only I act; saying, "You take care of it."*
O Jesus, I surrender myself to You, take care of everything! (10 times)

Day 3 *Jesus to the soul: How many things I do when the soul, in so much spiritual and material need turns to Me, looks at Me and says to Me; "You take care of it, then closes its eyes and rests." In pain you pray for Me to act, but that I act in the way you want. You do not turn to Me; instead, you want Me to adapt to your ideas. You are not sick people who ask the doctor to cure you, but rather sick people who tell the doctor how to. So do not act this way, but pray as I taught you in the Our Father: Hallowed be Thy Name, that is, be glorified in my need. Thy kingdom come, that is, let all that is in us and in the world be in accord with Your kingdom. Thy will be done on Earth as it is in Heaven, that is, in our need, decide as You see fit for our temporal and eternal life. If you say to Me truly: Thy will be done, which is the same as saying: You take care of it. I will intervene with all My omnipotence, and I will resolve the most difficult situations.*
O Jesus, I surrender myself to You, take care of everything! (10 times)

Day 4 *Jesus to the soul: Do you see evil growing instead of weakening? Do not worry; close your eyes and say to Me with faith: "Thy will be done, You take care of it." I say to you that I will take care of it, and that I will intervene as does a doctor; and I will accomplish miracles when they are needed. Do you see that the sick person is getting worse? Do not be upset, but close your eyes and say, "You take care of it." I say to you that I will take care of it, and that there is no medicine more powerful than My loving intervention. By My love, I promise this to you.*
O Jesus, I surrender myself to You, take care of everything! (10 times)

Day 5 *Jesus to the soul: And when I must lead you on a path different from the one you see, I will prepare you; I will carry you in My arms; I will let you find yourself, like children who have fallen asleep in their mothers' arms, on the other bank of the river. What troubles you and hurts you immensely are your reason, your thoughts and worry, and your desire at all costs to deal with what afflicts you. O Jesus, I surrender myself to You, take care of everything! (10 times)*

Day 6 *Jesus to the soul: You are sleepless; you want to judge everything, direct everything and see to everything and you surrender to human strength, or worse—to men themselves, trusting in their intervention; this is what hinders My words and My views. Oh how much I wish from you this surrender, to help you; and how I suffer when I see you so agitated! Satan tries to do exactly this: to agitate you and to remove you from My protection and to throw you into the jaws of human initiative. So, trust only in Me, rest in Me, surrender to Me in everything. O Jesus, I surrender myself to You, take care of everything! (10 times)*

Day 7 Jesus to the soul: *I perform miracles in proportion to your full surrender to Me and to your not thinking of yourselves. I sow treasure troves of graces when you are in the deepest poverty. No person of reason, no thinker, has ever performed miracles, not even among the saints. He does divine works whosoever surrenders to God. So don't think about it any more, because your mind is acute and for you it is very hard to see evil and to trust in Me and to not think of yourself. Do this for all your needs; do this all of you and you will see great continual silent miracles. I will take care of things, I promise this to you.*
O Jesus, I surrender myself to You, take care of everything! (10 times)

Day 8 Jesus to the soul: *Close your eyes and let yourself be carried away on the flowing current of My grace; close your eyes and do not think of the present, turning your thoughts away from the future just as you would from temptation. Repose in Me, believing in My goodness, and I promise you by My love that if you say, "You take care of it." I will take care of it all; I will console you, liberate you and guide you.*
O Jesus, I surrender myself to You, take care of everything! (10 times)

Day 9 Jesus to the soul: *Pray always in readiness to surrender, and you will receive from it great peace and great rewards, even when I confer on you the grace of immolation, of repentance and of love. Then what does suffering matter? It seems impossible to you? Close your eyes and say with all your soul, "Jesus, you take care of it." Do not be afraid, I will take care of things and you will bless My name by humbling yourself. A thousand prayers cannot equal one single act of surrender, remember this well. There is no novena more effective than this:*
O Jesus, I surrender myself to You, take care of everything! (10 times)

Prayer to the Blessed Virgin Mary: Mother, I am yours now and forever. Through you and with you I always want to belong completely to Jesus.

About this novena: The surrender novena was given to Fr. Don Dolindo Ruotolo by Jesus. Fr. Don Dolindo Ruotolo had extraordinary communications with Jesus throughout his life. He led a life totally devoted to God and our Blessed and Holy Mother Mary. He suffered tremendously throughout his life and in his humility, was able to hear the words of God clearly.

After this second failed attempt to put the trach in, Seth was immediately started on IV antibiotics for the pneumonia. Now it was even more uncertain when they would be able to do the tracheostomy. They would have to wait and see. More waiting… In her post, early that morning of day six, Amy Oatley had said that God was healing Seth in the waiting, but we couldn't see it, and we certainly didn't understand any of it. We were continually being asked to have patience and trust. As we struggled, the pleas for prayers continued, and we were constantly covered and strengthened by the prayers of the body of Christ.

Kathy Barth
February 19 · Darboy, WI ·
Seth's temperature is going up and his ICP numbers are still not stable. Please keep the prayers coming! For those of you who are Catholic, if you could offer up your Mass today for Seth, that would be wonderful! ALL prayers from everyone are greatly appreciated!

Kathy Barth
February 19 ·

> If anyone would like to join together in prayer tonight, my niece Meg, Seth's sister-in-law, is sharing this invitation.... Jesus says, "Where two or three are gathered in My Name, there I will be also."

Meg Alfaro
February 19 ·

For anyone who is interested I will be at the ministry center chapel at St. Thomas tonight around 7:30. Nothing fancy, I might play a couple songs. Maybe do a divine mercy chaplet. Feel free to join if you want. Love you
Seth Alfaro

Kathy Barth updated her status.
February 19 ·

> Today has been quite a roller coaster for Seth and for all of us. The doctors planned to do an important procedure this afternoon, but had to stop when Seth's oxygen levels dropped and they discovered he has pneumonia. That's probably the cause of his elevated temp. So, the procedure was again put on hold and what had seemed like a hopeful day turned discouraging. He is now on antibiotics and they hope to try again on Tuesday. More waiting.
> The good news tonight is that his temp is almost back to normal and his ICP numbers are lower and more stable. They are hoping to be able to take the bolt out of his head tomorrow. We thank God for every minute and every day He gives us, even the hard ones.
> Thank you, dear friends, for your continued prayers and support. Seth needs them, Chris and Chris and their family need them, Seth's doctors and caregivers need them, we all need them...and we all need to lift up Seth and each other so we can remain strong....strong in God's power and Seth-strong! Our love and thanks to you all!!! #sethstrong

It was an exhausting and emotional day. That night, Sarah and Ethan stayed overnight with Seth, so that Chris and I could go home together to sleep. This was the first time we had been home together since

95

Seth's accident. It was a very needed break from the hospital.

The next day, Monday, February 20, 2017, marked one week since Seth's accident, one week that he had laid there lifeless, one week since he had taken a breath on his own, one week since we had talked to him, seen him smile…

Seth's friend, Nate, had made a video of Seth skateboarding that night right before he went up on the roof that he fell through. Nate posted the video on instagram. I got instagram just so I could watch it. We all watched it over and over again. Seth looked so happy…Our hearts ached for him… We wanted him back so bad…

My sister, Kathy, was finally able to come from Wisconsin and arrived that Monday too. We had spent most of our adult lives within blocks from each other as we raised our kids. It was so hard for her not to have been at the hospital and with us that whole first week. But because she couldn't be with us, she was on facebook several hours every day rallying all the prayer warriors, keeping them informed and also responding to all their comments. I believe that was all part of God's plan, because all those prayers were so important, more so than we even realized at that time. It was hard for her to wait a week to come, but God is good even in the waiting.

CHAPTER SEVEN
- THE MRI -
God is Good... Regardless of the Prognosis

Things changed from day to day. Originally, we were told that the tracheostomy had to be in before the bolt could come out. However, since they had already attempted the tracheostomy twice and were unsuccessful, the trauma doctors decided the bolt should be removed first. They said the longer it is in, the more unreliable it is and the greater the risk of it causing infection in the brain. We were extremely grateful. It meant that things could still move forward even though they hadn't been able to do the tracheostomy yet.

That Monday, February 20th, the bolt was removed. That was an incredible blessing. Watching that ICP monitor had been so stressful. We had anxiously stared at those numbers on the monitor since the moment it was put in that first night. If we touched Seth or whispered something into his ear, we would watch those numbers to make sure the stimulation wasn't causing more pressure in his brain. So many times throughout the nights and days the machine would beep alerting the medical staff that the pressure in his brain was dangerously high. It was frightening. We were so happy and relieved not to have to think and worry about those numbers anymore!

Having the bolt out also meant they could do an MRI. As soon as they had the bolt out, they scheduled Seth's MRI for eleven o'clock that same night. They hadn't been able to do an MRI as long as Seth had that metal wire going into his head. Doing the MRI would allow the doctors to make sure that there was no ligament damage in Seth's neck, and if so, they would be able to take his neck brace off. The other purpose of the MRI was to better see the extent of the damage done to Seth's brain, which would give us some indication of how Seth may come out of this.

I was scared to death to have the MRI done. I was so scared that the results were going to be really bad. I was a nervous wreck that whole day in anticipation of it. My nerves were shot, and I was shaky and anxious. I remember Chris asking me why I was so nervous. Afterall, this was what we had been waiting for, and it would at least be a step forward. I told him that I was scared because I had a very strong feeling that the MRI was going to be bad, VERY bad.

As Chris and I talked, we realized that deep down we both felt that if God was going to give us a miracle, the MRI was going to be bad, so that God could reveal His glory through Seth. We sort of had this inclination that God was going to use Seth's accident to bring people to Himself, like He was going to do something miraculous. This gave Chris great hope going into the MRI, but I, on the other hand, was filled with fear. I was so afraid of how bad it might be. Every day for us was filled with peaks of hope and trust, and then valleys of fear and doubt. This was a peak for Chris when he felt strong, but a valley for me. I was petrified and felt extremely weak. I tried to hold on to hope for a miracle deep in my heart, but the reality of it all and what we may find out about Seth's outcome was overwhelming and terrifying.

About 10:30pm they began prepping Seth for the MRI. It was going to take one and a half to two hours. When they returned Seth to the room, they said he handled it really well. Typically, with someone in a coma it would be easy since they aren't able to move at all, but with Seth they were concerned about his strong cough causing movement during the test. By the grace of God, Seth did not cough at all during the MRI. Being that it was so late at night, we were told we would not get any results until the next day.

Early the next morning, Tuesday, February 21st, day eight, the doctors came in with the MRI report. You know it's bad when the first thing the doctor says is, "I'm so sorry." Those were definitely not the words we wanted to hear. They went on to tell us that Seth had diffuse axonal injury, which is also known as brain shearing. Brain shearing is actually described as shredding of the brain. It is one of the worst brain injuries you can have. When Seth first had his accident, the medical staff had given us a pamphlet which described all the different types of brain injuries. So we knew that this was one of the worst. They told us that Seth had brain shearing as well as brain bleeds scattered all throughout his brain and in his brainstem. This was devastating news. The fact that the shearing was also in the brain stem made it a very real possibility that Seth may never wake up. And beyond that, the doctors were no longer hopeful about what Seth would be like if he did wake up. It was the worst-case scenario.

Before the MRI, the doctors had tried to stay very positive. While they told us that no two brain injuries are alike, and that you can never really predict how someone will come out of them, they were always pretty positive and hopeful saying that because Seth was young and healthy, his chances would be better. They had originally talked about Seth going to Mary Free Bed, one of the best acute rehabilitation hospitals in the country, after he woke up. But once they got the results of the MRI, their tune changed, and they began talking to us about long term, lower functioning rehab centers, as if they expected Seth to spend the rest of his life in some sort of nursing home. We were absolutely crushed by the MRI report. As much as I was afraid and thought it was going to be bad, nothing prepared me for this.

At eight o'clock the same morning, immediately after giving us the MRI results, the doctors were finally able to take Seth to surgery for the tracheostomy and peg feeding tube. Things were finally moving forward, but what they were moving forward to was no longer hopeful. In fact, it was terrifying.

Chris and I decided right then that if our deepest fear for Seth was going to be our reality, we needed to talk to the kids about it and be totally honest with all of them about the results of the MRI and how Seth may come out of this. Up to this point, the younger kids still didn't really know how serious Seth's accident was and that he could have actually even died from it.

My sister, Kathy, having just gotten to Michigan the day before, came to the hospital early that morning, right as nurses were prepping Seth for surgery. We didn't want to tell anyone the results of the MRI, until we had talked to the kids first, but I remember being totally devastated and my eyes catching hers. All I said was something like, "It's bad. We need to go talk to the kids." She said she would wait there for Seth to get back from surgery in case we didn't get back in time. Unbeknownst to us, Michael had already headed to the hospital while we headed home to talk to the family. Michael stayed at the hospital and spent that time with his Aunt Kathy.

When we got home, everyone was there except for Andrea who lived in her own apartment and Caleb who was at his friend's house, since it was mid-winter break from school. Caleb's friend Danny's family brought Caleb to their house a lot during this time to help him and kind of distract him. We called them, and they brought Caleb home right away. Andrea also came right away.

Chris and I sat in our living room solemnly with Michael's wife, Meg and our two grandsons, along with Andrea, Ethan, Caleb, Mary-Kate, and Peter, all looking on anxiously awaiting what we had to say. We told them the results of the MRI and that it was a very real possibility that Seth may not even wake up or ever be the same. We told them that the doctors didn't know and couldn't predict what Seth would be able to do or be like. Together we faced the fact that we may never get Seth back the way we knew him. There were many silent tears streaming down each of their faces.

We talked about the value of every person not being in what they can do. Fighting the tears and the despair I felt inside, I talked to the kids about the fact that no matter how Seth came home or what he would be able to do, he would still be the same Seth and deserving of the same respect and dignity. Peter, our youngest at nine years old, hugged me as I cried. Peter, with the beautiful wisdom and faith of a child, looked up at me and said, "It's okay, Mom, because life is really about getting to Heaven." At that moment my heart was wrenched. His words were like a piercing arrow. I knew Peter was right, but I didn't want to accept it right then. My heart ached with a pain so agonizing and sharp that I felt I couldn't possibly bear it any longer. All I could think was, "Then take me home right now, Lord, because this is too painful, and I just can't do it anymore. It hurts too much!"

That was one of the darkest moments of my life, because in that moment I felt absolutely no joy at all in motherhood. I had already buried four of my children, but even through all of that, I never felt the complete hopelessness and darkness that I felt at that moment. I had extremely difficult times where I felt dead inside and completely void of emotion, but this time I felt a darkness that was so different. No matter how painful parenting could sometimes be, I always saw the beauty and joy in it, and that helped carry me through the difficult times. Life, new life, babies, children always brought me so much joy even in the face of death and grief. But at this very moment, I felt no joy, no good, no beauty at all. In fact, I remember looking at my two grandsons that morning, which normally always flooded my heart with joy, and instead feeling sorry for Michael and Meg. I actually thought to myself, "Oh Michael and Meg, what have you gotten yourselves into? Parenting is just way too painful."

It broke my heart and horrified me to feel this way. I had never before felt so negative about being a parent. For me, being a mother had always been one of the most incredible gifts and joys in my life. It's hard to explain the depth of the darkness I felt. I was overcome by the pain and could not feel any consolation or joy in life. It was definitely one of the lowest and darkest moments in my life.

After talking to the kids that morning, Caleb, Mary, and Peter begged us to please take them to the hospital and let them see Seth. They now knew the truth of the situation, and they wanted to see him and be with us and fully be a part of it all. Caleb and Mary-Kate were kind of hurt that we didn't include them in all of it sooner. Caleb actually felt guilty that he didn't worry that much and had been having fun at his friend's house. However, that was what we wanted for him. We wanted to spare the youngest three from all the fear and worry. We knew that we couldn't be there with them to help them process it all, so we tried to protect them from the fear, the possible nightmares, etc. I don't know if that was the right move or not. At the time, we didn't really make a well thought out decision about it, it just sort of happened that way. But now that they knew everything, we knew we were going to have to include them in it, and allow them to go through it with the rest of us.

We got back to the hospital just as they were bringing Seth back to his room from surgery. It was just before 10am. This time, the doctors were successful getting the tracheostomy and the peg feeding tube in. Seth looked so much better with all those tubes out of his nose and mouth and away from his face. He also had the neck brace off. He looked much more relaxed and peaceful and not nearly as frightening as before. It was so nice to fully see his face again. Seth's nutrition could now be given through the peg feeding tube in his stomach rather than through a tube in his nose. And the ventilator was still breathing for Seth, just through the trach instead of his mouth. The doctors told us that some patients only need the ventilator for two or three days longer once they get the trach in. However, for Seth, they said it would probably be more like two or three weeks.

Right around the time of the MRI, we received some really good advice from a friend, Julie Augustyn, from our parish. She suggested that we reject any and all negative news, results, prognosis, etc. in the name of Jesus and claim healing for Seth. She told us that's what she did when her husband, Brian, had a serious brain injury back in 2000.

This advice couldn't have come at a more perfect time. After getting the MRI results, we needed it more than ever. So we began rejecting his negative prognosis immediately. I especially did it any time doctors or anyone talked about the brain shearing. Whenever someone mentioned it, in my head I would say, "I reject it in the name of Jesus, and I claim healing for Seth." It was timely advice that we clung to and tried to continually follow. It ended up being a tremendous blessing, giving us a glimmer of hope in the midst of our darkest fears. It helped us stay more positive and try to begin living the miracle that everyone was praying for, regardless of the signs and prognosis.

Later in the day, we brought Caleb, Mary, and Peter to the hospital to see Seth. To us, he didn't look nearly as scary without the neck brace and all the tubes in his nose and mouth, but for them this was like nothing they had ever experienced before. When Caleb, who was fourteen, first walked into the room, he couldn't even look at Seth. He just kept staring out the window crying. Chris and I encouraged the kids to go close to Seth and talk to him. Caleb thought, "talk to who? That's not Seth! Seth's not there." Although it was extremely difficult for him, eventually he did make his way right up next to Seth. He didn't know what to say. Instead, a steady stream of tears just flowed down his cheeks. Mary and Peter never went close to Seth. Seeing his lifeless body was shocking and scary, and they didn't know what to think or do. It was hard to handle, and the sight of Seth that way stayed in their minds long after. Mary couldn't get it out of her head, especially when she tried to sleep at night. While it was a terrible and frightening situation that we had wanted to protect them from, Caleb, Mary, and Peter were thankful to finally be there with the rest of the family and be included in it. The first week had been lonely and isolating for them, but from this point on, they came to the hospital regularly.

There were no texts or facebook posts about the results of Seth's MRI at first. We did not make that public knowledge until we had spoken personally to each of our family members. And even then, we didn't fully disclose how grim the results really were. All throughout the day we called our parents and siblings one by one and talked and cried about the report and what it may mean for Seth's life. They were very hard conversations to have, but we received tender love, support, and consolation from both of our families. Their love and deep faith held us up and helped us to trust in God's goodness regardless of the prognosis.

Kathy Barth
February 21 · Grand Rapids ·
LATEST UPDATE on Seth -
As I shared in my post this morning, the MRI showed no damage to the ligaments in Seth's neck and they were able to take off his neck brace. In addition, they successfully did the trach surgery and inserted a peg (feeding tube directly into his stomach). He looks so much better with all the stuff off his face! All of these things are great things and steps in the right direction.

However, what I didn't share this morning is that the MRI showed more damage throughout the brain than what the doctors had first thought. There are multiple small brain bleeds throughout Seth's brain and in his brain stem. I didn't share this information immediately because Chris and Chris needed time to process what the doctors told them and to share it with their family.

We do NOT know the extent of the damage (or what may or may not be resolved in the coming days, weeks or months). We may not know that for months. What we do know is that the doctors expect a long road ahead and Seth needs your prayers and support more than ever--so do Chris and Chris and their family.

We are going to continue to storm the heavens and claim healing for Seth through the healing hands of Jesus, the Divine Healer. The doctors admit they do not know what will happen or what Seth's ultimate prognosis will be, only God knows the plans He has for Seth. So, we are going to ask everyone we know to continue to pray for Seth, especially asking for the intercession of our Blessed Mother, Blessed Pier Giorgio Frassati and Venerable Solanus Casey. And we are going to stay positive and work side by side with Seth through this journey.

The doctors' immediate plans are to remove all sedation tomorrow and begin to try and wake Seth up. This is our next hurdle. Please pray it goes well.

I ask you to be vigilant in prayer and patient with us. Chris and Chris really need to focus on Seth right now and, as much as they love all of you, are limiting visitors at this time to family only.

I will keep you updated as we learn more. Thanks, again, for your continued prayers for Seth. We really need them. We are grateful for each and every one of you and for each prayer offered on Seth's behalf. Let's storm the heavens and continue to pray for a miracle for our Seth!!!

CHAPTER EIGHT
- WAKING UP -
God is Good... in "Abraham Moments"

With the bolt out, the neck brace off, the trach in, and the MRI done, the doctors began cutting Seth's sedation medications. Eight days after that fateful night of Seth's accident, things were finally going to move forward toward recovery. But what that really meant, nobody knew. The thought of waking Seth up excited and petrified me all at the same time.

Doctors and nurses began to warn us about neurostorming. They said many people wake up from a brain injury very angry and violent, flailing around and yelling. We were told it is normal as the brain is firing and waking up, and that when you add to it the fact that Seth is twenty-one and a male, it is a recipe for disaster. We were also told by others who had been through it with a family member, that it is exceedingly painful and agonizing to watch and go through. Doctors told us that they try to adjust patients' medications as they are coming out of sedation in a way to help cut down on neurostorming, but it is still very common. So they put Seth's arms in restraints in anticipation of it. This all scared me to death.

As we began preparations for waking Seth from the coma, Chris and I decided to totally limit visitors to only family. The neurostorming sounded awful, and we literally had no idea what to expect. We really didn't know how Seth was going to wake up or what he would even be like when he woke up. We felt more strongly than ever that his privacy needed to be protected at this point.

Two days later, by Wednesday, February 22nd, ten days after Seth's accident, Seth was finally off all sedation medications. Now that they wanted him to wake up, the lights were all on and the blinds opened to let the sunshine into the room. Wow was that nice after all those days of sitting in darkness. As Seth came off the sedation medications, we and the doctors would try to get him to respond to simple commands just like we had the very first night.

Since he had been on such heavy sedation, no one knew how long it would take to get it completely out of his system. I kind of thought that Seth would just wake up all of the sudden one day, but instead his waking was painstakingly gradual. We would get a few small movements from Seth on command like a little wiggle of his thumb or toes. I mean the type of wiggle that is so small, you question if you actually saw it or not. He still appeared as though he were completely asleep. He was silent and motionless, other than very slight movements of his head and shoulders. Though it wasn't much, it was still good to see even the tiniest of movements after watching him lay so completely still for so long.

The first day that he was totally off sedation, Ethan actually got Seth to squeeze his hand. That was so exciting! We were elated! Later, he also wiggled his thumb on the right hand and a couple toes on his left foot. Chris and I and Ethan were all there to see it. It was crazy how happy a simple wiggle of a finger or toe made us. At one point, Seth even cracked one eye open for a split second. In those moments that we saw even the slightest movement, we had hope, and we clung to that hope. We talked about every movement over and over. We had to in order to stay positive. Because the reality was that we, as well as the doctors and nurses were intermittently all day long, twenty-four hours a day, trying to get Seth to respond to us. And most of the time there was no response at all. Truth is, there was a lot of nothing and a lot of dashed hopes each time. It was basically twenty-three hours, fifty-nine minutes, and several seconds a day of no movement, watching our strong, active, athletic son lay completely out of it, even though he was no longer on sedation medications. We clung to every bit of positivity we could because our reality was basically hour upon hour, day after day of virtually nothing but more waiting...

On Seth's first day off all sedation, we also had a visit from a consultant from Mary Free Bed Rehabilitation Hospital who came in to evaluate him. All along, the doctors had talked about Seth eventually doing rehab at Mary Free Bed, but as soon as they got the MRI results everything seemed to change. They no longer thought Seth was a candidate for an acute rehab center like Mary Free Bed. Instead, they began talking to us about long term, lower functioning rehab centers. However, we were not willing to give up on Mary Free Bed. We knew Seth needed to be there to get the best and most aggressive rehab possible.

When Dr. Ho from Mary Free Bed came in to evaluate Seth that day, I was not there, but thankfully Chris was. As soon as Chris heard the words "Mary Free Bed" and "evaluate," he knew it was imperative that he fight for Seth to get there. Not surprisingly, Seth didn't respond to Dr. Ho at all, so Chris knew he had to let Dr. Ho know who Seth was and advocate strongly for him. Chris confidently talked up Seth's progress and boasted of every little movement and response we had gotten from Seth. He knew that Seth was responding more than what the doctors had seen. Most of the time when we saw small responses the doctors weren't in the room. Since we were with Seth twenty-four hours a day, we would wait to ask for responses until we saw an eyelid crack or a slight movement of his head, figuring he might be awake then. Chris didn't want Dr. Ho to just read Seth's charts, see him lying there unresponsive, and just dismiss him. So Chris pleaded Seth's case, stressing every minute movement we had seen, as well as how strong, athletic, and otherwise healthy Seth was. He knew at that moment that he was Seth's only hope for getting to Mary Free Bed. In the back of his mind, Chris was a bit nervous that he may have bitten off more than Seth could chew, that maybe Seth wouldn't be able to handle the therapy at Mary Free Bed. However, Chris didn't let that deter him. He wanted to be sure Seth would have the best possible opportunity to recover.

Later that same day, Physical and Occupational Therapists came in to get Seth sitting up. They got him into a sitting position on the side of the bed, however he was completely asleep and limp. They totally had to hold his head and back up. While they were holding him up, I was able to wrap my arms around Seth and give him a big hug and kiss for the first time since his accident, but there was absolutely no response. I can't describe how empty that felt. It was like Seth wasn't even there, and it was unfathomable to think this could be all I may ever get back from my son. My heart was torn apart. I wanted my Seth back so bad. I imagined and ached for the day when he would be awake and hug me back. I hoped and prayed with all my heart that day would come...

The next day, Thursday, February 23, Seth continued to lay asleep and unresponsive most of the day. Our friend, Matt, who is an anesthesiologist, told us that it could take a couple days for Seth to come out of sedation since he had been so heavily sedated for so long. His body was basically saturated with it. That made sense, however, nobody really knew or could tell us for certain whether Seth's unresponsiveness was still from the sedation or from the brain injury. The doubt and fear constantly lingered over our heads. With each passing day, the uncertainty became increasingly more difficult for us to handle.

Though he hadn't woken up, Seth still continued to make progress. One way was through his breathing. They had been gradually turning the ventilator down so that Seth was breathing more and more on his own, and by around 1:30 that Thursday afternoon, they had taken him completely off the ventilator. Seth was breathing on his own with only a little oxygen support! That was miraculous progress. Doctors had expected him to be on the ventilator for two or three more weeks after getting the trach in. Instead, he was completely off it in only two days! Being that there was damage even in his brain stem, this was huge, and we were extremely grateful.

Kathy Barth updated her status.
February 23 ·
Latest update on Seth (2/23 pm) -
NO MORE VENTILATOR! After successfully breathing on his own for over 8 1/2 hours now, the respiratory therapist just wheeled the ventilator out of his room! Praise God!!!
That was a major goal met for today!
Now, we need him to wake up! So, please keep storming the heavens. He has definitely been more responsive today...he gave Michael a GREAT thumbs up when Michael asked him to, he's squeezed hands upon request and he's trying to open his eyes...we've seen little peeps of those beautiful eyes. So, please keep praying. He needs to wake up in order to be moved to an acute rehab facility. That is our next goal!
Again, we know there's a long journey ahead and we appreciate every prayer said, every sacrifice made, on his behalf. From the bottom of our

hearts, thank you, and PLEASE keep praying. We can't do this without you!

Lord Jesus, our Redeemer, heal Seth. Mary, our Blessed Mother, wrap your mantle of protection around Seth. Blessed Pier Giorgio Frassati, pray for Seth. Venerable Solanus Casey, pray for Seth. #allforhisglory #sethstrong

With Seth off the ventilator, he began to yawn. Believe it or not, this made us extremely happy. His yawns were huge. I don't think any of us had ever seen anyone yawn as huge as Seth was. It was actually pretty funny. We were happy because not only was it a movement that we hadn't seen from Seth since the accident, but it also made us feel a little of Seth's personality. He always made the funniest facial expressions. In his huge, overly dramatic yawn, we saw a little piece of Seth, and we relished it. In a very simple way, he was still making us laugh in an otherwise dark time. That was Seth!

Beside the progress with Seth's breathing, there was also another small miracle that same day. As Seth was lying there completely unresponsive, one of his doctors walked in the room and out of the blue said, "Seth, show me two." Chris and I both thought, "Yeah, right! Are you kidding? He barely even wiggled one finger." Seth didn't even appear to us to be "awake" at all. We thought there was no way he could do that. Then to our surprise, with eyes closed, still looking completely asleep, Seth very slowly and deliberately put out two fingers. We were all stunned and amazed! Not only did he follow a command to move a body part, but he also counted! It was a glimmer of hope in the middle of what felt like a desert of stagnant time. We clung to that glimmer, but it gradually dimmed as we continued to watch Seth lay there totally unresponsive for the rest of the day. Seth remained comatose, never even opening his eyes. The days were long, and it got increasingly difficult not to become discouraged.

On Friday, February 24th, Dr. Ho, from Mary Free Bed, came back again. Spectrum had sent him all of Seth's records to look over. Seth was still completely unresponsive for Dr. Ho. Even so, Dr. Ho decided he would take Seth to Mary Free Bed and give him a chance. That was another miracle! Dr. Ho's colleagues even questioned him, asking why he was taking someone who looked like a hopeless case. They didn't understand or agree with his decision. Dr. Ho told us that his decision was heavily based on the conversation he had with Chris two days earlier on Wednesday. While others did not think Seth was a good candidate for rehab at Mary Free Bed, Dr. Ho said after talking to his dad and seeing this strong and otherwise healthy young guy laying there, he just had to give him a chance.

This was incredible news! Mary Free Bed was known as one of the top rehabilitation hospitals in the country, and it was only seven minutes from our home. We were truly blessed. I am so grateful that Chris had the foresight and courage that day to advocate so strongly for

Seth. Dr. Ho told us that they would take Seth as soon as Spectrum was ready to discharge him. This was an amazing blessing and answer to prayer. Seth's Spectrum doctors told us they might be ready to discharge Seth to Mary Free Bed the next day!

In order for Seth to be discharged to Mary Free Bed, he would have to no longer have any significant medical issues. Seth was making good progress in that the respiratory therapists had completely weaned him off the oxygen, and he was breathing comfortably and keeping his oxygenation levels perfect without it. However, being the rollercoaster that it was, Seth had developed a new medical issue. He was no longer digesting his tube feeds. They were just sitting and building up in his stomach, so much so that he even started coughing some of it out through his trach site. This problem would most likely need to be resolved before he could be discharged. This was the next hurdle to be jumped.

All along, Kathy had been asking for specific prayers for each of Seth's needs in her posts. Over time, we started noticing a pattern. It seemed like every time we asked for prayers for a specific need, our prayers would be answered. So Kathy posted on Facebook asking for specific prayers for Seth's stomach to begin working properly.

Kathy Barth updated her status.

February 24 ·

Latest Update to Seth - (2/24 pm)

Seth's major accomplishment today was that he's been off oxygen since 1:00 pm this afternoon. The doctors are very pleased with his progress. Seth was moving more today and a little more alert, but he is not "awake" yet. He opened his eyes a little bit wider and seemed to know when people were talking to him. It's obvious that he's trying to come out of it. Please pray that he wakes up soon!

Also, in order for Seth to be transferred to Mary Free Bed, he must be medically discharged. In order for that to happen, his stomach has to start moving the food they are feeding him through the feeding tube into the intestines. Right now, it's just sitting there and the stomach isn't really working. They have started giving him a medication that will make his stomach contract. Please pray that the medication is successful and his stomach starts working properly again.

Every day, a little more progress. It's slow, but it's steady. Please keep up the prayers! They are keeping Seth and all of us, going.
#allforhisglory#sethstrong

Kathy Barth

February 25 · Grand Rapids ·

Latest update on Seth - (2/25 am)

The medicine seems to be working and Seth's stomach is starting to move food through. Chris was really encouraged...she said every time Seth has a hurdle to jump and we ask people to pray, they PRAY and he jumps the hurdle!!! We have an AWESOME GOD and amazing prayer warriors!

They have him sitting up in a chair again. Although his stomach is working better, it still is not as well as it needs to be. They are checking with Mary Freebed to see if they can handle the stomach issue there. If so they may send him today!!! Otherwise they will keep him here until the stomach issue is resolved . Please KEEP PRAYING the stomach issue is resolved!

So today we pray for his stomach and that he continues to wake up!

118

Thanks, again, for keeping him in your prayers! One step at a time....
Jesus, our Redeemer, heal Seth. #allforhisglory #sethstrong

Saturday, February 25th, twelve days after Seth's accident, was a great day for Seth and super encouraging for me. Seth sat propped up in the chair for quite a long time. He also had his eyes open much more, and we felt like he actually connected with us several times throughout the day. He occasionally even answered questions for us by squeezing our hands or giving us a thumbs up. He also seemed to thoroughly enjoy listening to his own music. Once in a while he even moved his hand to the beat. In the evening, I asked Seth if he wanted me to put on some of my soft prayerful music. He shook his head no just slightly. So I played his song, "Rollin' Dice" again. We were all enjoying it and talking about it. Seth looked super happy. I said, "Seth, you look so happy. You look like you want to smile. Can you smile for me?" He actually tried! Obviously, it wasn't his full normal smile, but we could tell he was trying, as the ends of his lips curved up ever so slightly. It was at times like this that I felt like he was going to come back to us. Chris and I, as well as Andrea, Ethan, Caleb, Mary, and Peter were all there and excited to see Seth starting to "wake up" a little and responding more. It was a beautiful day. I massaged his forearms just the way he always liked it, and we all took turns sitting next to him holding his hand. We were all able to interact with Seth

119

in some small way, which actually felt gigantic at that time.

Sadly, Michael had to work that day, so he and Meg were not able to be there. It was very hard on them, especially Michael. He had been at the hospital night and day waiting to see any sign of his brother Seth coming back. He was extremely disappointed and upset to have missed it. I told Michael not to worry, that he would get to see Seth the next day...

Seth's best friend, Tyler, also spent a long time there with all of us that day. He was a pretty amazing friend. He just sat there and talked to Seth for a long time, holding his hand and laughing about old memories, while Seth sat there silently, sometimes with his eyes open a little and sometimes with them closed. Tyler treated him exactly like he would have if nothing had ever happened. It was amazing how comfortable he was. It was heartwarming to watch him talk and laugh about all the silly and stupid things he and Seth had done together. He was an incredible friend to Seth. As he talked that day, Seth sometimes responded to Tyler by squeezing his hand and trying to pull it up to his chest. At one point, Tyler asked Seth to squeeze his hand if he had an experience of God in the coma. Tyler told us that Seth squeezed his hand really tight. I didn't know what that meant or exactly what to think about that, but it brought me great joy and peace knowing that God had him.

The next day, Sunday, February 26th, Michael came to the hospital so excited, hoping to see Seth a little more awake, but consistent with the roller coaster ride we had been on all along, as much as Saturday was good, Sunday was bad. Seth slept most of the day and was very unresponsive all day. The day before had been so encouraging. We thought Seth was coming back to us. We expected each day to get better and better. Instead, Seth was mostly unresponsive and lifeless again. After having had such a promising day, it was especially distressing and concerning.

I thought maybe Seth had worn himself out the day before. It seemed as though his brain just shut down again, which was unbearably hard to see. I wondered if that's what was needed for the brain to heal, but I really didn't know. Truth was, none of us knew. On days like this, it was hard not to worry and wonder if this was it for Seth, if this was how Seth would be forever. We would think, "Is this it for our active, passionate, full of life son?" Michael too was terribly disheartened and heartbroken to have missed the one time that Seth was somewhat awake and alert.

That Sunday was a hard day all around. Seth was having more issues with his stomach not functioning, and he had developed a fever again. On top of Seth's unresponsiveness and developing medical issues, my sister, Kathy, also had to leave to go back home to Wisconsin this particular day. She was my older sister and she had always looked out for me. She was very thoughtful and took care of us in simple little ways that we didn't even think about. For example, because Seth had such a high fever in the beginning, they kept his ICU room freezing cold. As a result, much of the time we sat there in winter coats, with hats and gloves on, and at night when we tried to sleep, we would freeze. Without hesitation, immediately after arriving in Grand Rapids and recognizing the situation, Kathy went out and bought us two comforters, so that whoever was staying the night in Seth's room would be warm. It was so simple and practical, yet none of us had even thought of it. It was unimaginably helpful! That's how Kathy has always been though. She has always taken care of me. It was very difficult for Kathy to leave that day, and equally as difficult for me to see her go. It was a tearful goodbye.

As the day progressed, Chris was having an extremely tough time holding it together. At dinner time, Chris and I and Michael had gone down to the hospital cafeteria to eat, while Dave and Sarah stayed with Seth. Chris couldn't even talk… He was so discouraged. I had been planning to go home that night and stay with the kids, but I decided to stay. I couldn't leave Chris that night. I knew he and I needed to be together.

That night, we held each other and talked and cried as we stood at Seth's bedside. I had never seen Chris so distraught… Usually Chris was really good at not letting his mind wander to all the "what ifs," but at this point

Chris was really struggling. Chris was always very good at not looking ahead and worrying about things, but after getting the MRI report, his worst nightmare was no longer a speculation. It was a very real possibility. And watching Seth lay there unresponsive and not really waking up day after day wasn't helping either. This definitely was not the life Chris had imagined for Seth, and it broke his heart.

Throughout this time, Chris' fear engulfed him, and he became unable to talk to anyone, even his parents and sisters in California and Hawaii whom he had been updating constantly on Seth's condition. He asked me to keep them updated instead, saying that he just couldn't talk to anyone. He felt his faith knees buckling under him. Through everything we had already been through with the deaths of our four babies, I had never seen him so overcome by pain and despair.

While Saturday had been a peak, Sunday felt like an insurmountable valley. We constantly had to fight the fear and discouragement, constantly surrendering Seth and ourselves to Jesus. Deep in our hearts, we hoped and prayed that Seth's being asleep, unaware, and unresponsiveness was still from the sedation he had rather than the extent of his brain injury. But unfortunately, no one could disprove our fear, because no one knew, only God.

Kathy Barth updated her status.

February 27 ·

Latest update on Seth - (2/26 late)

So, today was a hard day. As I shared earlier, Seth spiked a fever. He also had stomach issues again. In addition, he was REALLY worn out from all the activity he had yesterday, so he seemed less responsive and more groggy than yesterday. When you seem to take a step or two backwards, it's hard not to get discouraged. And so I am asking those of you who are still awake (sorry it's so late, I'm on Wisconsin time now) to ask Jesus to comfort Seth's family and give them peace and to continue to heal and bring Seth back to us.

We need to remain positive and prayerful, but sometimes it's hard to do that. That's when we turn to our family and friends for support as we have turned to you. Thank you, thank you, thank you for every prayer, every hug, every meal, every donation, every good wish. We do feel your love and support.

We are praying that the fever and stomach issues are quickly resolved so that Seth can be transferred to Mary Free Bed tomorrow. His temp was down to 99.6 last time I talked to Chris. Thank you, Jesus.

You are the BEST prayer warriors and friends we could ask for. Love to you all! #allforhisglory #sethstrong

Kathy Barth updated her status.

February 27 ·

Latest update on Seth - 2/27 am

Seth's fever is going up a little this morning and his respirations are randomly spiking. His nurse says respiration rates can go up when they have pain or discomfort. They are giving him some Motrin for pain. Please pray that helps.

Seth just had another bad feeding this morning, where he had too much that didn't digest. He seems to do good and then has about one feeding each shift that he doesn't. Obviously, the medicine they are giving him is helping, which is good, but we need his stomach to actually get going and back to normal function! Another prayer petition for today.

Also, we are hoping they will be able to transfer Seth to Mary Free Bed today, however we don't know if the fever, stomach issues, and now respiration spikes will delay that. Please pray that these are all resolved and they can move him safely and get started on his rehab.

Mostly, please pray that we stay strong and do not let the spirit of discouragement take hold. May God grant Chris and Chris, and their family, his strength and peace!

Thank you for continuing to support Seth and his family in this journey. They feel your prayer support -- it's what is keeping them going day after day. We are grateful beyond words!!! #allforhisglory #sethstrong

On Monday, we got a text from Seth's friend, Tyler. He shared with us his experience with Seth on Sunday when he stopped by to say goodbye to Seth before going back to college. He apparently stopped by while we were in the cafeteria and Dave and Sarah were with Seth. Tyler's text said, "I was holding his [Seth's] hand talking to him and his eyes were 'completely' open staring deep into my eyes. I'd make some small joke about an old memory and he'd pull my hand up and shake it (maybe as if to laugh, I don't know for sure). Then I laid one of my hands on his shoulder and prayed with him for about ten minutes just asking the Lord to heal Seth and to let His will be done. During this time Seth kept squeezing my hand and kept trying to pull my hand up to his chest. We only made it up to his ribs, but I could feel him trying. He also might have tried to bless himself at the end of the prayer, so that was cool. I could tell he didn't want me to leave because he reached for my hand as I was getting up. But I told him I had to go and gave him a gentle fist bump."

God continually gave us beautiful little messages and signs like this, and we tried to hold on to them and trust, but it became increasingly difficult as more days went by without Seth waking up. We had read about how bad brain shearing was, and the fact that even the brain stem, which controls consciousness, was damaged, really terrified us.

When Monday came, Seth's fever was going up, and he was visibly sweating. Andrea was so sweetly and gently wiping the sweat from his face over and over again. It was so beautiful to see the love and care she gave to her brother. Seth's respirations were also spiking, which they thought could possibly be from pain or discomfort, but Seth couldn't tell us. His stomach was also still not fully functioning properly. The medical issues seemed to be mounting rather than resolving. It was uncertain if Seth would be able to transfer to Mary Free Bed with these.

Still struggling considerably and unable to call and talk to anyone, in desperation, Chris reached out to our friend, Tom, through text. He said, "Tom, I feel like my fear is overcoming me. I don't know if I can do this. My faith knees are buckling. I don't know how much more I can stand. Please pray for me." When Tom received this text, he and his wife, Carol, had just pulled into the Church to pray for us. We were exceedingly blessed to have such faithful and prayerful friends.

Mid-morning on Monday, Sharon, an RN from Mary Free Bed, came in to talk to us. She told us there would not be a room available for Seth at Mary Free Bed until Tuesday or Wednesday. Any news of further waiting was always discouraging, but despite that, we were extremely grateful to have been able to talk to her that day. She gave us a lot of hope.

Sharon told us that the responses we had gotten from Seth were really good and encouraging, especially this early. We were stunned when she used the words, "this early." No one had told us that this was still early. What a relief! She was so positive. It lifted a huge weight off our hearts. Both Chris and I felt renewed and encouraged after meeting with her. Before she left, we asked her if Seth not waking up was still from the sedation in his system or from his brain injury. Like all the others, she couldn't answer that question for us either. No one could. We just had to wait… and trust.

After talking to Sharon that morning, we set up a tour of Mary Free Bed for that afternoon. The nurse who gave us the tour also stressed how early it was in the process and what a good sign that was. It was more hope to uplift our weary spirits. However, our emotions were still on a continual rollercoaster ride. They were all over the place from minute to minute. While we were very grateful to have the opportunity for Seth to be going to Mary Free Bed, it was also very overwhelming and frightening. I know I was not prepared for it. As we toured, and witnessed so much suffering, children and adults in wheelchairs with life altering conditions, I felt so overwhelmed and almost sick. I couldn't believe and accept that this could be Seth's fate. I kept thinking, "this is not the life I had imagined for Seth." My heart ached from the reality and uncertainty of it all. It was a constant battle for Chris and I to stay on top of the fear. We tried to stay positive, but we knew that according to the MRI report, Seth should not come out of this the same. We had read how bad brain shearing was, and the doctors no longer expected Seth to recover. So it was very difficult sometimes to hold onto hope.

While we were touring Mary Free Bed, Ethan stayed at the hospital with Seth. Reclining in the chair, Ethan dozed off to sleep. We were all pretty worn out and tired by this time, and Ethan was trying to complete his senior year of high school on top of being at the hospital daily. Ethan awoke to find one of Seth's friends, Brooke, sitting there with him. She explained to Ethan that she and Jake, another one of Seth's friends, had special tee shirts made as a way for family and friends to show their support. The shirts said "#sethstrong" on them. Brook left a full box of shirts at the hospital for us and our family. Then she and Jake sold others to Seth's prayer warriors and supporters far and wide. It is impossible to adequately express how touched we were by this and the constant outpouring of love and support shown for Seth and our family.

It had been a long day of ups and downs, and it wasn't over yet. At 10:30 Monday night, Seth was finally moved out of the ICU. For the first time since the accident two weeks earlier, Seth had no monitors on him at all. We had gone from three full screens of monitors to none. That was amazing and frightening all at once! The room they moved him to was so small that only one of us could stay overnight. We had always had two of us there together with Seth. I was a little scared to stay by myself, especially with no monitors and no ICU nurses constantly looking after him, but I knew Chris needed to get away and go home.

When Chris went home that night, Michael and Meg were there since they had been staying with our younger kids. The lights were dim in the living room, and when Chris walked in, Michael asked him, "Dad, how are you doing?" Chris had been trying to be so strong for the family, but he needed to leave the hospital that night because he felt like he was starting to break a little. When Michael asked him how he was, that heartfelt question and sign of love and concern from his oldest son just pierced Chris' breaking heart. Michael is such an incredible, loving, and devoted young man with a beautiful heart, and the way he asked was so sincere that it was like an arrow that chinked Chris' already cracking armor.

Tears started to roll down Chris' cheeks. He said to Michael and Meg, "What if this is the best it gets?

129

Seth is supposed to be waking up and there's no movement. We don't know if he's going to be in a wheelchair his whole life. I'm really afraid for him." Chris couldn't accept that Seth, who had been the best athlete in the family and so strong, was stuck in that hospital bed not even able to move. He couldn't do anything. He pleaded, "What if he never walks again? What if he never talks again?" In agony, Chris grabbed Michael and hugging him cried, "I'm so afraid for Seth. He has so many hopes and dreams, and he may never get to live them. He may never get to experience any of it." Then Chris' deepest feelings and doubts poured out. He started bawling in Michael's arms. He just couldn't contain it anymore.

Having finally released all of his pent-up emotion and fear, he said, "Michael, I know what God wants. He wants me to surrender Seth to Him. I just don't know if I can do it." Chris had already surrendered four babies to God. He was afraid that if he surrendered Seth, God would take him too. Chris did not want to let go of Seth. However, as much as he didn't want to, as soon as Chris expressed this, he knew in his heart what he had to do and what he was going to do. He said, "But Michael, I know I'm going to say 'yes.' That's what God wants, and I've got to do what He wants, but it is so hard." Chris knew that just as Abraham had to surrender Isaac and trust God with Isaac's life, God was asking him to surrender Seth and trust God with Seth's life. That night, right there in our living room with Michael and Meg, Chris finally surrendered Seth to God's will and purpose. This is what Chris refers to as his "Abraham moment."

The next morning, Tuesday, February 28th, Seth's fever was up to 102 degrees. It had been four days since Dr. Ho said he would take Seth at Mary Free Bed, and it was still uncertain whether Seth was medically stable enough to transfer there and whether or not our insurance would approve him going there. Fevers are pretty common with brain injuries. Often the body has trouble regulating temperature for the first couple weeks after a brain injury, but they needed to be sure that nothing else was going on. They decided to run several tests in order to rule out other possible problems. They did an ultrasound of Seth's legs to make sure there were no blood clots, a CT scan of his head, blood work, and a urinalysis. They needed to be sure he was medically stable before they could discharge him to Mary Free Bed. He was scheduled to transfer to Mary Free Bed at 2:30pm if all the tests came back good and the insurance approved the transfer.

All the tests came back good, but 2:30pm came and went and we still hadn't heard anything from the insurance company. Every day, we would get our hopes up for him to be transferred. We were anxious for him to get started with therapy. Yet, at the same time, we were afraid. Seth still wasn't really awake. How was he possibly going to be able to do therapy? At Mary Free

Bed, patients typically do three to five hours of therapy, five days a week. Chris worried that maybe he had gotten Seth in over his head. Dr. Ho said in some cases they will spread the therapy over all seven days of the week, doing only two hours of therapy each day. This is what he was planning to do with Seth at first, but even that seemed impossible for Seth. He was not awake! Chris feared he may have advocated for something that Seth wasn't ready for.

It's hard to explain the constant rollercoaster we felt like we were riding. One minute we would be confident and filled with hope, and the next we would be consumed with fear. Every little physical step forward brought us so much joy. Seeing any little sign of Seth's personality coming back gave us hope, but then the reality of the situation would hit us like a speeding truck. We'd be rejoicing that he squeezed our hands, "looked" happy, or his eyes were slightly open. That was all amazing after watching him lay without any movement at all for the past two weeks. It was truly incredible to see a little of Seth alive! But then, in the next instant, reality would come crashing in as we wondered if this would be it for Seth, if this was all we were ever going to get.

The reality was that his movement thus far was him wiggling his fingers or toes and moving his right forearm by bending it at the elbow. He couldn't even lift the rest of his arm up, and he didn't move his left arm or either leg at all. In fact they had to put special boots on him to hold his legs and feet in the right position. His eyes "open" were really only opened like slits. Sometimes I could look into his eyes and connect with him, and I knew he was in there somewhere. But then in the very next second, I could look into those same beautiful brown eyes and there was nothing. It was like he was gone. He was also completely silent. He never even tried to talk. It was all so hard to process and accept. Most of the time we just tried to be present in the moment and not think ahead. It was too overwhelming and frightening. When we did look ahead, our fear and grief would overcome us.

Chris stayed with Seth on Tuesday night, while I went home to sleep and be with our other kids. Wednesday morning, March 1st, sixteen days after Seth's accident, Chris called me at 6am all excited saying that Seth had been moving his right leg all night long and had even been sleeping with it bent and out to the side. It had been a week since Seth was taken off all sedation medications, and this was the first time he had moved his leg and the most movement we had seen since the day he last walked out of our house two and a half weeks earlier. Chris went on to tell me that Seth was also lifting his right arm all the way up and reaching up and feeling his hair. This was a first. Before then he had only been bending his arm at the elbow. We were beside ourselves with excitement! I was filled with delight as I woke the kids and quickly got them off to school. I couldn't wait to get to the hospital to see Seth "moving."

I drove to the hospital with so much hope. On my way, the song, "I Have This Hope" by Tenth Avenue North came on the radio. I was singing it out so loudly and just praising God! When I got to the hospital and saw Seth, there were lots of promising signs of him waking up more. He was almost "conversational." He shook his head no in response to a couple of questions. He opened his eyes when Chris asked him to. They were also opened wider than before. He kept squinting and blinking them as if he were trying to focus. He also responded to the light. When Chris turned the light on, he put his hand up and covered his eyes. Seth responded to the nurses too. He squeezed with both hands, moved both legs, and opened his eyes when asked.

Throughout the day, Seth continued to get more awake and responsive. He was continually using more muscles, lifting his arm, his leg, and even his head at times. When Michael came and was sitting at Seth's side, Seth reached out and put his arm around Michael! This was a moment Michael had waited for and prayed for in those long, lonely hours, days, and weeks of cold, darkness, and silence.

Later when Andrea was sitting with Seth holding his hand, he pulled Andrea's hand up to his lips as if to kiss it. He was so affectionate and seemed so grateful to have us there with him. All of us were so happy to see more of Seth coming alive that day. Even Caleb, Mary, and Peter were there along with Sarah and Seth's cousin, Regina. It was a tiny room, but we all fit and were rejoicing to be there together with Seth alive and a little more aware.

Seth was waking up very peacefully, without any neurostorming at all! This was quite unusual and such a blessing for him and us. But the more Seth was waking up from the sedation, the more restless and uncomfortable he seemed to be getting. When the nurse asked him if he had pain, he shook his head no. Then she asked him to squeeze her hand if there was something she could do for him. He squeezed her hand really tight, but none of us could figure out what he needed, and he couldn't tell us. It was heartbreaking for me not to be able to help him. Seth remained calm and peaceful though.

That night when the nurse was brushing Seth's teeth, he put his hand up as if to grab the toothbrush. So the nurse gave it to him, and he started to try to brush his own teeth. She looked at Seth and joyfully proclaimed, "He is so ready for rehab." The ambulance had been scheduled and set to transfer Seth to Mary Free Bed earlier that day at 11am, but we still had not received approval from our insurance company. They kept pushing back the time all day waiting to hear from the insurance, but it never worked. We were going to have to wait yet another day. This was more than disappointing to us. To be honest, it made us quite angry, but we just kept riding the rollercoaster of emotions. What else could we do?

We had to trust God's timing. Through it all, we continued to receive signs of God's love and care for Seth. One example is a text I received that day from my sister-in-law, Mary. Mary wrote: "One of my friends who has been praying for Seth e-mailed me this morning and said that when she prayed this morning, she saw this 'Mary (Our Blessed Mother) is sitting by his (Seth's) bed and stroking his head and Jesus is standing beside her.'" Then my sister-in-law wrote, "I thought 'that's nice.' But it just clicked in my head that you said that Seth was lifting his arm and feeling his hair - I'll bet he feels Mary's touch!!!"

Kathy continued to update everyone on facebook with Seth's progress as well as asking for more prayers. Through it all she expressed constant gratitude for all the amazing prayer warriors and continually gave all glory to God.

Kathy Barth
March 1 · Appleton, WI ·
Latest update on Seth - 3/1 pm
Well, the good news continues...
Seth has continued to be more responsive today. He will have moments when he is very lucid and will do what is asked or will answer questions with a head shake. Then he will quickly appear to be back asleep.
Friends who've gone through traumatic brain injuries say this is very common.

He is continually using more muscles, lifting his arm, his leg and even his head at times.

Today he put his arm around his older brother Michael in a hug and tried to kiss his sister Andrea's hand! Tonight, when the nurse was brushing his teeth, he put his hand up and she asked him if he wanted to hold the toothbrush. He didn't just hold it, he started brushing his teeth! The nurse looked at him and said, "He is soooo ready for rehab!" Please pray the insurance approval comes through tomorrow.

Tonight Seth seems to be uncomfortable. When the nurse asks him if he has pain he doesn't really respond or shakes his head no. But then she asked him to squeeze her hand if there is something she can do for him. He squeezed it very tight. We just can't figure out what it is he needs. Please pray we can figure out what he needs or wants. It is heartbreaking not knowing!

Please pray that Seth will be comfortable and can sleep well tonight. The more his body is waking up from the sedation, the more restless and uncomfortable he seems to be getting. Please also pray that he can go to MFB tomorrow. We really think he needs to get out of this bed!

Thank you all for your constant prayers! As much as we have begged, and continue to beg, for complete healing for Seth, we also need to offer up prayers of thanksgiving!

Thank you, Jesus, for answering our cries. Please continue to pour your healing power upon Seth. Mary, our Blessed Mother, please wrap your mantle of protection around him. Blessed Pier Giorgio Frassati, pray for Seth. Venerable Solanus Casey, pray for him. #allforhisglory #sethstrong

Even though Seth was not able to transfer to Mary Free Bed yet, Wednesday was still a peak day. However, as things seemed to go, later that evening when we got home, the valley of fear hit once again. Chris and I had both gone home for a while and were sitting at the table sharing some of the experiences of the day, how Seth had recognized Michael and Andrea and shown such affection for them. Then Chris spoke up and said, "I don't think Seth recognizes me." Chris seemed so heartbroken. I tried to encourage him and tell him that of course Seth would recognize him, but we really had no proof of that. Once again we just had to wait and trust.

At the hospital the next morning, Thursday, March 2nd, Seth showed me right away that he knew me. As I was sitting on the edge of his bed, he reached up and put his hand around my neck and pulled me to him and hugged me! For weeks I had sat at his side, holding him while he lay lifeless. Now for the first time, he was able to hold me back. No words can describe that moment. It was a moment I had feared may never come. God is so good!

When Chris was coming that morning, I said a little prayer that Seth would somehow show Chris that he knew him. As Chris walked into the room, I said, "Seth, Dad is here." Seth immediately looked like he was going to cry and reached his right arm out to Chris to hug him. There was no doubt that he knew his Dad and wanted him! Later in the day when I hugged Seth again, he turned his head and kissed me on the cheek 3 times! Our Seth was coming back! He also reached out and hugged both his nephews, David and Christopher. He definitely recognized and loved us all. We rejoiced and reveled in every single sign of our Seth coming back to us and his visible love and appreciation for each of us.

Kathy continued to share Seth's progress on Facebook in her beautiful, faith-filled way that gave all glory to God while encouraging and inspiring each reader, themselves, to continually grow closer to our great God!

Kathy Barth updated her status.
March 2 ·
Latest update on Seth - 3/2 am

Sometimes there are just no words to describe the emotions or intense gratitude flowing from your heart....

Today there are no words...
This morning, Seth's mother Chris was sitting on the edge of Seth's bed. Without any prompting, Seth reached up and put his hand around her neck and pulled her to him and hugged her!!!

There are no words....
A hug from the son you feared might never wake up.
Oh, thank you, Jesus!

Thank you, Jesus, that Seth continues to wake up and we see more and more of him each day!

Our prayers for today continue to be that the insurance approval comes through and Seth is able to be transferred to Mary Free Bed so he can begin therapy.

We also ask prayers for Seth's Dad, Chris, who is getting sick. Please pray he will get better quickly and that Chrissy and the whole family can stay well and strong. Also pray for protection over Seth so that he doesn't catch anything.

I said there are no words. I take that back. Because now I'm shouting, "Thank you, Jesus!!!" while tears of joy flow.

Seth has a long road to healing and there will likely be many mountains or obstacles to surmount along the way, but in that hug we can feel God reaching down and hugging not only Seth, but each one of us.

As we continue to pray for Seth and all those we are lifting up in prayer, let's take a moment today to hug the special people in our lives. For we know now the power of a hug!!!

May God bless you all. We thank you, our dear friends and prayer warriors, that you are standing by Seth's side as he walks this journey. May God thank you in ways far beyond what we can say or do.

Thank you, Jesus!!! ALL FOR YOUR GLORY, LORD!!! #allforhisglory#sethstrong

While Seth was waking up more and more, he would still sleep most of the day and even had his eyes closed a lot when he was awake. But even so, we were continuing to see gradual progress. For example, Seth moved his lips as if to talk for the first time since his accident. There was no sound, but at least he tried to lip something. Up to this point, he had never even tried. It seemed as though more and more of his brain was waking up. It seemed our prayers were continually being answered.

Finally, that Thursday, day seventeen, another huge prayer we had been waiting for was answered. Our insurance approved Seth's transfer to Mary Free Bed! It had been almost a week since Dr. Ho first told us they would take him. While we had been impatient and frustrated with the constant delays, especially waiting for the approval from the insurance company, we later realized that it was all God's perfect timing. Before this time, Seth would not have been awake enough to even try to do therapy. But by the time the insurance approval had come through, Seth had actually been starting to wake up and be ready for rehabilitation. Seth was headed to one of

140

the top rehabilitation hospitals in the country, giving him the best possible chance at rehabilitation. God is good in our "Abraham moments" when we surrender ourselves to His timing and His plan.

CHAPTER NINE
- A NEW REALITY -
God is Good... in Transition

Seth was transported by ambulance to Mary Free Bed on Thursday, March 2nd, seventeen days after his accident. He handled the move very well. Lying in his bed he even reached up and shook his nurse's hand when he got there. He was put on the fourth floor with other brain injury patients.

From the looks of things, it seemed Seth was the worst off of anyone there. Since he was awake but not fully aware of where he was or what was going on, he had to be monitored very closely. They had alarms set on his bed in case he ever got to the point of trying to get up on his own. He was considered high risk for falls because he couldn't stand or even sit on his own. They also had a camera in his room that was aimed directly at his bed, so they could see him at all times. They monitored him 24/7, so that he wouldn't pull his trach out. If he even reached toward his neck, they would talk to him over the speaker, and tell him not to touch his trach. It's strange to think that our twenty-one-year-old son had to be watched so closely, but Seth really was not at all aware of what was going on, and at that point we had no idea what he knew or understood.

The move to Mary Free Bed was exciting and scary all at the same time. It was exciting to take this new step forward with Seth, but at the same time, I was nervous and fearful of all the unknown in our new reality. The doctors, nurses, and therapists at Mary Free Bed were all exceptionally kind and helpful though.

We had to get accustomed to things very quickly, as the first night we were already given Seth's therapy schedule for the next day. He was scheduled to have two and a half hours of therapy including physical, occupational, and speech therapy. It was like his work schedule, and every bit of his energy needed to be saved for his therapy. We wondered how he would be awake and aware enough to handle it. Dr. Ho told us that we needed to limit visitors to just family and only a couple at a time. He told us we needed to keep Seth's room quiet and the lighting dim so he would have as little stimulation as possible. All of Seth's attention and energy was going to need to be focused on his therapy, and the rest of the time he would need to have very little stimulation so that he could rest and sleep.

Seth kept trying to pull his trach out. One time when they talked to him over the intercom to tell him not to touch it, he looked right at the camera and gave them the "ay okay" sign with his right hand. The techs laughed out loud over the intercom. Along with the expression on his face, it was very funny. We all laughed. We were always filled with joy when we saw even the smallest signs of Seth's humor. Seth's whole life he had always been so goofy and made us laugh, and we all desperately wanted that back.

Seth grabbing at his trach became a problem, though. It could be extremely dangerous if he were to pull it out. So the nurses put a large padded mitt on his hand, which prevented him from grabbing anything. He hated that mitt. He kept looking at Chris and me, whichever one of us was with him at the time, with a desperate look. He would look us right in the eyes and hold his mitted hand up as if to say, "please take this thing off!" He was so frustrated, and the look on his face was pitiful, just pleading with Chris and me to take it off him. He tried every way he could to get it off...putting it between his legs or in his teeth to hold it as he tried to pull his hand out of it. He wasn't able to get the mitt off. However, he did figure out how to turn it around, so the padding was on the back of his hand instead, therefore enabling him to grab things. We realized then that Seth certainly had not lost his determination!

Seth had always been a very determined and passionate person. In fact when he was nineteen, he had the word "passion" tattooed on his left forearm. It was a tattoo that Chris and I never wanted Seth to get, but somehow in the midst of what Seth was going through, it had become something that embodied an important part of Seth's personality that we hoped he would retain. We ended up making the word "passion" Seth's personal

144

passcode at Mary Free Bed. No visitors were allowed in to see Seth unless they knew his passcode. As much as Seth's tattoo had once irritated us, it had now become sort of endearing. We were acutely aware that Seth was definitely going to need that passion to get through all that lay ahead.

Dr. Ho ordered that a nurse tech be with Seth 24/7 since Seth was not fully aware of where he was or what he was doing. Someone from our family was always with Seth too, but Dr. Ho wanted us to feel comfortable if we ever had to leave the room. He also wanted us to be able to sleep at night without worrying about Seth. One of the first nurse techs assigned to stay with Seth was a young girl in her early twenties. She talked and talked nonstop. At this point Seth could not talk and was completely silent. She had no trouble filling the void. After a while, she looked at Seth and said, "Most of my patients usually tell me I talk too much. I bet when you can talk, you'll be telling me to be quiet too." Seth didn't bother to wait until he could talk. He looked right at her and without hesitation, put his finger up to his lips as if to say, "shhh." The expression on his face was priceless. Yep, Seth's personality was definitely starting to come through in little moments like this. We relished each and every moment.

Even though Seth had cameras on him and a nurse tech with him 24/7, he still managed to pull his trach out one night. Chris was there with him that night. Both

Chris and the nurse tech had been watching him carefully, but in one swift motion Seth reached up and yanked it out in a split second! Thankfully, the nurses responded super fast and got a new one put in right away with no harm done. It became obvious that the sooner Seth could get that trach out, the better. During the days, respiratory therapists had been doing some short breathing trials with Seth's trach capped off, but like most things, it was a process which would take some time.

When Seth first lay in the ICU, he was so muscular, but after nearly three weeks of lying in a bed, his muscles had atrophied so much that he was a mere shadow of what he once was. He was so weak and frail. I remember massaging his calves and being shocked by how small they were. They felt about the same size as his thirteen-year-old sister, Mary-Kate's calves.

The first day of therapy was mostly just in Seth's room. He wasn't mobile at all. Nurses had to use a mechanical lift to move him from the bed to the wheelchair because Seth couldn't support himself at all. They also had to get him a special wheelchair that would allow him to lay back and support his head because he couldn't hold it up on his own or even support himself in a sitting position.

Seth was quickly progressing in therapy. The first day of therapy, physical therapists couldn't even hold Seth in a standing position at the side of his bed for more than a few seconds, but by the second day, they already had him up "walking," trying to retrain his brain. It was clear, they weren't going to waste any time. One therapist had to completely hold Seth up using the gait belt around his waist, while Seth leaned on a tall, padded walker. The other therapist moved Seth's legs for him. Seth could move his right leg a tiny bit on his own. It took painstaking effort, but he was doing it. However, he could not move his left leg at all. The therapist had to completely move it for him.

Sadly, I wasn't there to see Seth "walking" for the first time, but Chris recorded the whole thing for me on his phone. After watching Seth lay lifeless in a bed for so long, this was absolutely amazing! That night, after only two days at Mary Free Bed, this was the text I sent to my family: "It is so surreal when I actually step back and try to process the fact that Seth is going through all this and has to relearn so much, but we praise God for every positive step in the right direction. Based on the results of his MRI, and watching his progress, I do believe we are watching a miracle unfold!"

Therapists noticed right away that Seth had what is called left side neglect. He couldn't use most of the left side of his body. He would even turn his head slightly to look at us out of the bottom right corner of his right eye, rather than his left. His left arm was stuck bent up to his chest with the muscle constantly contracted, much like a stroke victim. The left side of his mouth didn't move as much as his right, and it was even the weakness in the left side of his vocal cords that made him unable to talk. He was also unable to eat or drink, because the left side of his throat was too weak for him to even swallow.

The left side neglect became the focus of much of his therapy. Occupational therapists spent a lot of time massaging the muscles in his left arm trying to get them to relax. They also had us gently trying to straighten his arm as often as we could. They asked us to sit on his left side as much as possible as well, in order to force him to use his left eye. Our oldest son, Michael, had a Physical Therapy Assistant degree, so he and his wife, Meg knew that left side neglect could be very bad, and it scared them a lot to see Seth like that. The rest of us were kind of blissfully ignorant about it and how bad it could be.

Although Seth was becoming more alert each day, he still would constantly drift in and out of sleep and awareness. He would seem wide awake one second and then be sound asleep the next. It was so hard to get used to how his brain would just shut down when it was tired. It was always very disheartening to see him drift in and out of awareness even when he was awake. For example, on one of the first days of therapy, his speech therapist had him following several simple commands like give me a thumbs up, point at mom, etc. Seth followed each command quite quickly without hesitation, but then when she asked him to try to make some sounds, he did nothing. She asked him to try to say "hi." It looked like he didn't try at all. He just sat there with a blank stare, as if he didn't understand and his brain couldn't even process what she was asking. Moments like that were crushing. While watching his progress was joyful, it was also extremely nerve wracking not knowing how much he would actually be able to do.

Seth definitely knew and recognized all of his family. And he was becoming more emotional and very affectionate with us. One day Chris wasn't able to see Seth because he was sick and didn't want to expose Seth to it. The next day when Chris showed up, Seth almost cried and reached right out to grab Chris' hand. Seth seemed genuinely appreciative of our being there with him.

As Seth became more aware of his situation, his sadness grew. We had almost three weeks to get used to the idea that Seth may never be the same. So we rejoiced in every little step forward. But Seth was just waking up to a new reality. Even playing his own music had become a source of sadness for him. It seemed the realization that he was not able to do those things anymore was sinking in. He couldn't even talk, much less sing.

With Seth being unable to talk, we couldn't even figure out what he was thinking and feeling or what he needed. We tried to tell Seth that we realized how difficult it must be for him. We continually tried to assure him that the therapists were going to help him walk and talk and do all the things he loved again. Seth was obviously sad, but he handled it with great grace. Though discouraged, he remained patient and peaceful, which was not necessarily typical of his personality. God's grace in him was very evident.

Transitioning into therapy and this new reality continued to be filled with peaks and valleys. Our present reality was filled with the unknown, which constantly loomed over our heads. We clung to the hope of a miracle, but no one really knew or could predict how Seth would come out of this. Only time would reveal the impact of Seth's brain injury. We were continually up and down between hope and fear from minute to minute.

I remember early on, one of Seth's nurses at Mary Free Bed telling us that Seth would be okay, but that he would be a different person, and we would just have to get used to that. She said it so matter of factly, that it actually made me angry. I think she was trying to help, but that was in no way encouraging for us. We didn't want that to be our new reality. It was honestly one of our biggest fears. We desperately wanted our funny, talented, creative, musical, passionate, full of life Seth back, as we had always known him.

Fortunately, we were able to see small signs of Seth's humor coming out quite quickly. Even his therapists could tell just by his motions and expressions. One day his physical therapist, Kelli, asked me if Seth was a funny guy. When I told her yes, she wasn't surprised at all. Though Seth was silent, she said she could tell there was a big personality inside him! She was definitely right. We were excited to see that big personality coming out in humorous little ways. We couldn't wait for the day we would get to hear him laugh again. We hoped and prayed that day would come. Chris would say, "When we hear Seth laugh, then we'll know he's really back!"

Therapists also noticed Seth's determination right away. They said most people with left side neglect would typically just ignore their left side, but Seth was not okay with the fact that his left side wasn't working. He was determined to make it work. He would lift his left arm with his right arm and make it move. For instance, when Seth had an itch, instead of just itching his face with his right hand, Seth would use his right hand to lift his left hand to his face and make it do the itching. The therapist said he displayed incredible drive and determination to get better and not accept anything less.

By Sunday, March 5th, only Seth's third day of therapy, when the physical therapists came into Seth's room, he started to try to sit up like he was going to just jump out of bed on his own and get going with therapy. Obviously, he wasn't able to get up on his own, but he was driven to try. Though his body was weak, his will was strong. However, after only a few steps trying to walk in therapy, he was completely fatigued. His physical therapists sat him down in the wheelchair for a rest. He sat there looking so sad and discouraged that he couldn't just get up, stand and walk. Something we all take for granted every day was now so difficult for him. It was hard for Chris and me to watch him suffer that way.

The same day in speech therapy, Laurie, his therapist, asked him yes and no questions. Seth didn't even know if he had graduated from high school or how old he was. That was hard to watch. We were on such an emotional rollercoaster of ups and downs. I was heartbroken that he didn't remember certain things about himself, but then in the next minute I would be encouraged by more progress. As the session went on he actually tried to say yes or no to some questions. He made a tiny whisper with the word "no." That was incredible considering that just one day earlier he couldn't even process how to make a sound. Only one day later, he was doing it! He was literally changing on a daily basis right in front of our eyes. Next his speech therapist had him try to say "hi" and "bye." He could mouth the word hi, but not bye. He would purse his lips together to make the "b" sound but couldn't finish the movement. The second time he tried to do it, he got really sad and shook his head "no" because he couldn't do it. We could see his frustration with not being able to do the simplest things that he's been doing his whole life, the kind of things that we normally never even think about. At one point during the session he mouthed, "more than anything," but we couldn't figure out what he wanted more than anything… He was trapped inside his body and couldn't communicate what he was thinking or feeling with us. I can't imagine how difficult that must have been for him. My heart ached for him.

Therapy continued that day with Occupational Therapy next. His Occupational Therapist put four blocks on the table in front of Seth. They had the four letters of his name on them. She asked him if he could put them in order to spell his name. He looked at them blankly and then slowly and pointlessly pushed them around the table using the back of his right hand, as if he didn't even know what the letters were for. My emotional rollercoaster ride plunged to a new low at that moment. My fear overcame me as I wondered, "Is this it for Seth? Is this Seth now?" There were many moments like this. Each day was long, difficult, and exhausting for Seth, and emotionally draining for Chris and me as well as Michael and Andrea, since we were most often the ones attending therapy with him.

Kathy continued to update everyone on facebook with Seth's progress as well as asking for prayers for his specific needs. We purposely tried to have her highlight and focus on his positive progress rather than the disappointing and difficult parts of therapy. We wanted to protect Seth's privacy and dignity as much as possible. Kathy did a beautiful job of rallying the prayer warriors and giving all glory to God in each new step along the way.

I'd like to ask for specific prayers today to help Seth battle against sadness and discouragement. While we are all SO grateful that he is alive and actually making wonderful progress, we have to imagine what this is like for Seth. He woke up and suddenly can no longer do things that we all take for granted. We had weeks to consider all of this. He just woke up to it. As he becomes more and more aware, he is getting very sad, frustrated and discouraged that the things he could do and wants to do, are now such a struggle or impossible for him.

On one hand, this is actually wonderful news, because we realize that Seth truly knows that this is not his "normal." But, it is very sad and frustrating to Seth, and seeing his discouragement and sadness is really hard for his parents and family. Please continue to lift them up in prayer, too, so that they can stay positive and help keep Seth's spirits lifted up.

Also, please pray they are soon able to take the trach out. It is really bothering him. He actually pulled it out last night and they had to quickly put a new one in. Fortunately, he did well with it capped this morning and we are hoping they will soon be able to remove it.

They can really tell that Seth wants to work hard and get going in his therapy, but it is, of course, exhausting and very hard. Still, today was better than yesterday and we rejoice as we continue to see daily improvement!

Nights are hard for him. He just can't get comfortable and is very fidgety. If you happen to wake up during the night, please pray for him.

Thank you, again, for all of your prayers, dear friends. We really need them as this journey continues. Praising God for answering our cries....
#allforhisglory #sethstrong

Originally Dr. Ho thought Seth would most likely not be able to handle the typical three hours of therapy, five days a week. He thought they would have to give Seth less hours of therapy seven days a week instead. However, Seth was improving so rapidly that by only the

4th day of therapy, he was scheduled for not the typical three hours of therapy, but four hours!

With Seth settling into Mary Free Bed, Chris returned to work on Monday, March 6th. This was extremely hard for Chris. He wanted to stay with Seth. He had been at Seth's side every day since the accident. It was a difficult transition for Seth too. Whenever Chris was gone, Seth would wonder where he was and want him to come back right away. He would tell me to call Chris and tell him to come back. I tried to explain to Seth that his dad had to go to work but would be back after. Seth missed Chris a lot and would get down when he was gone.

Knowing Seth's stay at Mary Free Bed could be quite long, we had to figure out a new normal for our lives. Michael and Andrea, like Chris, tried to resume their normal work schedules, and Michael and Meg moved back into their own home. Their young sons, Christopher and David, had been starting to get out of sorts having been away from their home and their normal routine for so long.

At the same time, therapists told us that patients who have family members with them in therapy tend to heal and recover much better. So we sort of made a schedule for everyone, making sure someone was with Seth at all times. I was with Seth most days. Michael had Wednesdays off, so he stayed overnight with Seth on Tuesdays and then did his therapy with him on

Wednesdays, so I could have a little time at home. Then on Friday and Saturday nights and throughout the weekend Andrea would stay with Seth along with either Chris or me. It was always extremely difficult for Andrea to leave Seth on Sunday nights, even though she still came back basically every evening after work. Working or not, her heart and thoughts were always with Seth.

As Seth transitioned into life at Mary Free Bed, we tried to limit extra visitors like Dr. Ho had requested. Even Seth's younger siblings didn't see him for the first few days, so that he could get settled and be rested and focused on therapy. However, we did make a couple exceptions for friends who had traveled a long distance to be there. One of Seth's friends, Brett, came all the way from Florida to see him. When he came, he gave Seth a cross, which had been very special to him.

We also allowed Tyler and a couple of his friends, who had come from college across the state, to come in and pray over Seth while he was sleeping. We never wanted to turn down prayers. Tyler's friend, Joe, even brought a first class relic of St. Camillus. This relic was extremely special to Joe's family, yet they allowed Joe to bring it and leave it in Seth's room for the remainder of his time at Mary Free Bed. To see the beautiful faith of these young college students and the generosity of Joe's family was uplifting.

Seth's Aunt Sarah and Uncle Dave came to visit Seth at Mary Free Bed for the first time on Sunday night,

March 5th. After having seen Seth lifeless in a coma day after day, they were thrilled to see Seth up and dressed sitting in a wheelchair. When Seth saw them, he reached out his hand to them and smiled at them. That alone was more than they had seen from him the whole time. Seth very visibly expressed joy in seeing them.

Kathy Barth updated her status.
March 6 ·
Latest update on Seth -
I thought I'd share, with her permission, this text from my sister-in-law, Sarah Faber, that I received last night.
"Dave and I visited Seth, Chris and Chris tonight. It was so nice to see Seth sitting up in a wheelchair, dressed and out in the family waiting room! He recognized us and reached his hand out and even smiled! It was so beautiful to see. Unbelievable progress from one week ago and I'm sure one week from now will be that much better! Praise the Lord! Obviously he has a long way to go, but THANK YOU, JESUS!"
I was with Seth just a week ago and I can assure you that this is MIRACULOUS progress from where he was just 7 days ago. God is good and He is answering our prayers!
Please, please, keep up the prayers...for Seth's mental, emotional and physical aspects of his recovery...and that his strong determination will shine through and really help him on this tough journey.
He is really struggling with "turning on" his voice. For those of you who know Seth well, you know how important singing is to him. Also, not being able to communicate is very hard. He is really trying to communicate things to them, and it's frustrating on his part and his family's. He's trying so hard!!! Please pray he has a breakthrough with communication this week!
I'd also like to ask for prayers for Seth's family, particularly his parents and siblings who are all feeling the strain and fatigue of being apart for 3 weeks now. Seth has 2 older siblings, and 4 younger ones still living at

home. This has been so hard on all of them and I know they can all use our prayers.

As always, your prayers--both in petition and thanksgiving--are SO important and SO appreciated. We can't thank you enough. And we can't thank Him enough!!! #allforhisglory #sethstrong

The next evening, Monday, March 6th, Michael and Meg brought Mary and Peter to see Seth. Unfortunately, Ethan and Caleb weren't able to visit because they were sick. The same night Seth's cousin, Anna, and her husband, Andrew, also came to visit. Seth clearly recognized each person and seemed genuinely happy and uplifted to see everyone. They, in turn, were all amazed and encouraged to see Seth's progress in such a short time. We had a nice visit in the family lounge, which was right next to Seth's room. It was a perfect place for us to have visitors and be together as a family.

As time went on and Seth was allowed more visitors, Mary Free Bed became our second home, and that family lounge was like our living room. We gathered there together as a family pretty much every evening. Even Meg and our grandsons, Christopher and David, were able to be there too. In many ways it had become our home away from home, and we were thankful to all be together again.

Seth's frustration over his inability to communicate with us was growing. He wanted to talk so badly, but just couldn't. The vocal cord on the left side was still too weak. He could sometimes get out a tiny whisper, but not enough for us to understand. He was constantly, all day long, trying to tell us things, but we couldn't understand him no matter how hard we tried. He was visibly very discouraged, but he showed no anger at all. God's grace was obviously abundant in him, as he stayed calm and displayed great patience, something he rarely did growing up. It was evident that everyone's prayers were holding him up.

Our faith has always been extremely important to us, and we knew that ultimately that was the thing that would get us through this ordeal. Even Seth with his limited awareness and ability seemed to be finding comfort is his faith. He had shown us some small signs of it. For example, every day in the ICU, I blessed Seth on the forehead with both Holy Water from Lourdes, France and Holy Oil. Now at Mary Free Bed when I blessed him with one of them, he put up two fingers, as if to remind me that I needed to bless him with a second one also. I was amazed by this because most of the time I had blessed Seth he was in a coma and seemingly unaware of it. It was awesome to know that he was aware and desiring of these blessings. One day he even tried to reach up as if to make the sign of the cross when I blessed him. It was always uplifting for me to see little signs of Seth's awareness of things and acceptance of his faith.

I remembered how in the ICU I would sometimes become very afraid that if Seth came through this, he may end up being angry with God. Those long days at Seth's side, I prayed that God would be present to him in his coma. So as Seth was becoming more awake and aware of his new reality, any sign of his faith brought me tremendous peace and comfort. It was evident in his transition thus far that God had heard our prayers and had been watching over Seth all along. I was relieved and grateful for that. However, nothing could have prepared any of us for what was to come...

CHAPTER TEN
- A SPIRITUAL MIRACLE -
God is Good... Wow!

Tuesday, March 7, 2017, is a day I will never forget. It started out like any other day. First thing each day Seth would have what is called OT (Occupational Therapy) Dress. OT Dress is when occupational therapists would shower Seth and get him dressed for the day, gradually working with him to become independent with dressing and hygiene again. This particular day though, he didn't have OT Dress. Instead, one of the nurse techs gave Seth his shower and got him dressed. As a twenty-one-year-old, having to be showered and dressed by someone was extremely difficult for Seth, and this time, Seth was very upset by it.

Immediately after that, Seth had speech therapy. Noticing that Seth seemed a bit uncomfortable that morning, his speech therapist, Laurie, asked him if he had pain. Seth gently beat his chest as if to say yes. The therapist asked him if he had pain in his chest, to which she didn't get a clear answer. Holding a chart with numbers on it, she asked Seth to rate his pain on a scale from one to ten. Since Seth was unable to effectively communicate, she gave him a pen and asked if he could write what his pain level was. I watched and waited very curiously, knowing that just two days earlier he didn't even recognize the letters in his own name when given four blocks. I thought, "How could he possibly write?" but to my utter amazement, Seth took the pen and wrote "My ego is a 9½." It was inconceivable that Seth had just written a complete sentence. I just wanted to cry… both tears of pain for Seth's pain and embarrassment, and at the same time, tears of joy because not only was he writing, he was also using adult thinking! And to think that just two days earlier, he couldn't even put wooden blocks in the correct order to spell his name. This was astonishing, absolutely miraculous!

I was in awe, but that wasn't all. Seth wrote more. Next, he wrote asking for his glasses. Typically, he wore contacts, but hadn't used anything since he had come out of the coma. He actually remembered he had glasses and recognized that he needed them and wanted them! Unbelievable!

I rushed to Seth's room to get his glasses for him. When I returned, Seth's speech therapist showed me her white board saying, "Look what Seth just wrote." I looked down at the white board. In Seth's own writing, it said, "My God is Good" and was signed, "Seth Alfaro." I couldn't believe my eyes. I was awestruck. I knew right then and there that something had to have happened to Seth while he was in the coma. I mean, think about it. Seth was a twenty-one-year-old guy who had just woken up in a hospital unable to walk or talk or do anything for himself. He wasn't even able to go to the bathroom on his own. He had been unable to communicate with us for weeks. I knew this would not typically be the first thing he would want to tell us in this situation!

On top of that, he had none of the neurostorming and anger they had warned us about. To be honest, anger would have been more typical for Seth, even without a brain injury. Yet there he was, helpless in a hospital, but completely at peace, telling us that God is good. Right in the middle of his pain and suffering, he was giving glory to God. It was definitely not Seth's normal. It was supernatural. I couldn't help but wonder what had happened to him!

Laurie then asked Seth if he wanted to pray the "Our Father" with her. He shook his head yes. He mouthed the whole Our Father and then tried to say, "I love you, God." Laurie was so impressed. She said he was an inspiration to her. He was an inspiration to me too. It was unbelievable!! I was in awe at what I was witnessing. Thoughts and questions were racing through my head... What happened to Seth in his coma? How is he proclaiming "God is good" in the middle of all this? Is it possible that he saw God? I didn't know what to think or feel, but I had a new hope.

Kathy Barth
March 7 ·
Latest update on Seth - 3/7/17
We have a true cause for REJOICING!!!
I am going to share a text and photo I just got from my sister, Seth's mom.

163

"Miracles are happening! Seth still cannot talk which is extremely frustrating for him. So his speech therapist had him try writing. This is one of the things he wrote! In the middle of his pain, he is giving glory to God! His therapist asked him if he wanted to pray the Our Father with her. He shook his head yes. He mouthed the whole Our Father and then tried to say, "I love you, God." His therapist said he was an inspiration to her! No doubt, God is at work!"

Look at the photo below. If someone you know doesn't believe in miracles, show them this. Yes, our GOD IS GOOD and Seth's love for God is as strong as ever! Thank you, Jesus!!!! #allforhisglory #sethstrong

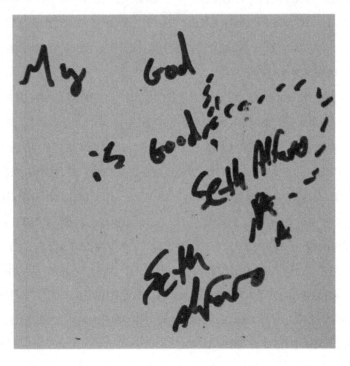

After that speech therapy session, Seth was frantically trying to tell me something all day long. He could only make occasional, tiny whispers, which were almost impossible to understand. He would move his lips so fast trying to tell me things, but I could not understand

any of it. I gave him a pen and paper hoping he could write more. He kept writing "promise land" over and over. I asked him if he saw the promised land or God while he was sleeping. I couldn't get a clear answer. So I asked him if he could write what he saw while he was sleeping in the coma. He shook his head yes. I was so curious and excited. Seth slowly started to write "I… s-a-w… a-l-l… o-f…" Leaning over him to see, I hung on every letter, every word as he wrote. My heart was pounding. I wanted to know what Seth saw… But then, Seth's last word was a jumble of letters all on top of each other. I couldn't read it at all! He tried and tried to write it, and I tried and tried so hard to read it but couldn't. This was big, and I am such a curious person. I wanted to shout, "what did you see Seth?" But what good would that do? He was doing everything he possibly could to tell me. He was trapped and unable to communicate. As frustrating as it was for me, it had to have been a hundred times worse for Seth.

Eventually, we gave up, and I said, "Seth, someday you are going to be able to tell us what you saw and all about your experience while you were sleeping." He mouthed, "I hope." He obviously had some sort of experience while he was in the coma, and it was becoming very frustrating to us and to him that he couldn't tell us about it. He did not rest or sleep all day because of it. We wanted to know what had happened to him in the coma, and he really wanted to tell us, but it had become apparent that, like most things, we were going to have to wait yet again.

Still, March 7th was an incredible day all around. Besides giving us a clue that he had some sort of spiritual experience while in the coma, Seth was also completely lucid the whole day. His mental function all day was totally miraculous! At one point he asked me (and I actually understood what he was trying to say) what had happened to him. This was the first time he ever inquired about what had happened. I explained to Seth that he and Hunter had gone up on a roof to watch the sunset, and when he was jumping down onto a lower roof, he fell through it. To my surprise, Seth's first concern was how Hunter was. He didn't seem angry about it at all. Rather, he seemed grateful for his life and genuinely concerned about everyone else involved.

Later that night, Dave and Sarah, along with Seth's cousin, Katherine, and her husband, Michael, who was Seth's boss, came to visit. Seth broke into a huge smile when he saw Michael. He had really loved working for Michael. Seth tried and tried to communicate with them, but they just couldn't understand him. That was hard. Michael and Katherine told Seth that their kids really missed him. They asked Seth if they could bring the kids to see him. He shook his head "no" and then showed his muscle, or lack of it, indicating "not til I'm strong again." Apparently, he didn't want them to see him that way.

Seth didn't nap or rest all day that day. He just wanted so badly to communicate with us. That night we were talking about God giving him his voice back, and he mouthed, "that's all I want." We asked for specific prayers for God to give Seth his voice back and for peace and patience for Seth until then. Like so many small miracles that had been happening all along the way, the peace came almost instantly. Seth relaxed and quit trying to talk about it anymore. He appeared to be totally at peace.

A huge help for Seth to be able to talk would be for him to be decannulated, which is to have his trach taken out. It had been capped off since 9am, and they were going to try to keep it capped off through the night. They needed to be absolutely sure he could breathe through his mouth without any problems. The rule was that it had to be successfully capped off for seventy-two hours without any breathing problems before he could have it removed.

At the end of the day, Seth's brother Michael came to the hospital to stay the night and the next day with Seth. Going home together with Chris on this particular Tuesday night was a perfect end to a beautiful day. For the first time, I felt like I had Seth back, not just for a brief moment, but all day long. My heart was full.

After hearing about the incredible day Seth had, Michael was looking forward to spending some time with Seth on Wednesday. Seth was scheduled for five hours of therapy that day. To our dismay, Wednesday ended up being a much harder day for Seth. He had been so mentally with it the whole day before that now he was very tired and kept zoning out mentally. We were slowly learning that this was completely normal for brain injury patients. But that didn't make it easy. It was devastating and disheartening to watch. I finally thought I had Seth back, only to wake up and find him gone again. It was emotionally heart wrenching to continually go back and forth between "having Seth" and "losing Seth." In a very real sense, that's how it felt. It was hard for me to accept. Just the day before, I felt like I had Seth back, and now I felt like I had lost him again. I hated those times when I would look into Seth's eyes and see and feel nothing. My heart sank into the pit of my stomach and it made me feel sick. It totally crushed me every time. I didn't think it was something I could ever get used to. I hoped and prayed that I wouldn't have to. Only time would tell...

It was an extremely difficult day for Michael too. While Seth had been progressing, there was still such a long way for him to go, and it was very painful for Michael to watch Seth go through all of this. It was so hard for him to have Seth physically there, and at the same time not really there at all. At one point during the day, Seth had soiled himself and his bed. Knowing the nurses needed to change him and clean him up, I stepped out of the room to maintain Seth's dignity and privacy.

There were two nurses in the room trying to clean and change both Seth and his bed. Michael told me they left Seth sitting naked in a chair while they cleaned his bed. Seth sat there seemingly dazed, but most likely very embarrassed and humiliated. Michael felt they treated Seth as though he wasn't even there. Watching his twenty-one-year-old brother go through this, literally tore Michael's heart apart.

I remember Michael came out to me in the hallway visibly very upset. He looked like he wanted to scream. He cried out to me, "I can't take this anymore. I just want to run away from it all." He kept saying, "that's my brother in there, naked and dazed and unable to care for himself at all!" It was so deeply painful for Michael to see Seth this way. He just couldn't accept and come to terms with the fact that the frail, dazed, young man in that room was his once strong, capable, brother, Seth. He had so much heartache and grief that he didn't know how to process.

We didn't want any of Seth's friends to see him this way. We wanted to preserve his dignity and protect him from embarrassment. We didn't allow any of them to visit until Seth, himself, wanted them and said it was okay. However, the outpouring of love and support still continued. Even though they couldn't see Seth, two of his friends came to the hospital and dropped off checks of money they had collected for him. The continual love amazed and humbled us.

Seth's therapists had told us that it would be helpful if we put pictures of his family members up on the wall. They said that not only would it be good for Seth, but that they would also be able to use the pictures to ask Seth questions and help reorient him to his life. Peter printed individual pictures of each member of our family and labeled them with our names, ages, and relationship to Seth. He had: Dad (53), Mom (49), Michael (27) brother, Meg (24) sister-in-law, Christopher (3) nephew, David (8 months) nephew, Andrea (23) sister, Ethan (18) brother, Caleb (14) brother, Mary (13) sister, and Peter (9) brother.

As I was hanging the pictures on the wall of Seth's hospital room, Seth was sitting in his wheelchair right next to me. He would reach with his right arm and grab the next picture off his bed and hand it to me. His right arm was still the only one he could use. I was super happy that he was actually helping me. I put all the pictures of the family up with the Divine Mercy picture of Jesus at the top. When it was finished, Seth looked over at it and mouthed the word "beautiful." It was becoming increasingly apparent that Seth was different, strikingly different from the guy who when told he should get to know his younger siblings flippantly responded, "Naw, I'm good." There was no doubt in my mind that he had been touched by God in some way while in his coma. He seemed to have a newfound appreciation for his family, as well as a peace and humility that he didn't have before. It was truly beautiful to see in him, remarkable actually. He was helpless in a hospital, yet he was so obviously grateful for his life, his family, and every bit of help that people had been giving him.

As Seth was looking at the pictures, he pointed to the ones of Ethan and Caleb with a puzzled look on his face, as if to ask where they were. I told Seth that they were home sick. He seemed distressed that he had not seen them. Neither of them had been to Mary Free Bed yet because they had been sick. They still hadn't really seen Seth awake and aware. Hearing about all of Seth's progress, they couldn't wait to get there and see him. And Seth was anxious to see them too.

While Ethan was excited to see Seth, he was also kind of nervous. Afterall, they had just had that big fight the night before Seth's accident. To be honest, I was a little nervous too. Seth had been so affectionate and loving and appreciative of all of us, and I was hoping and praying that even though he and Ethan had fought, Seth would be openly loving and grateful for Ethan too, but I wasn't sure what to expect.

When Ethan got to Mary Free Bed, Seth was laying in his bed. He was happy to see Ethan and motioned for Ethan to give him a hug. As they hugged, Seth whispered faintly to Ethan, "I love you. You are a hard worker, and I am proud of you." As hard as Seth was to hear and understand, Ethan heard those words

171

clearly. They were the exact words that Ethan needed to hear to bring healing to his heart. Seth's words instantly brought Ethan to tears. Here Seth had a brain injury and was still so out of it, and yet his first words to Ethan had more clarity than anyone could have ever scripted. God had very obviously touched Seth's heart.

Growing up, Seth had often called Ethan lazy, so there were no more perfect words that he could have spoken. They were, I believe, directly from the Holy Spirit. The two of them sat and talked for a while. Seth did not remember the fight they had the day before his accident. However, as soon as Ethan mentioned that they had fought, without even knowing what he had done, Seth immediately apologized to Ethan. That didn't usually happen. Ethan told Seth how bad he felt about the fight and the things he had said to Seth and how afraid he was that Seth would die without them ever having another chance at a close relationship. Seth looked at Ethan and said, "Well, you'll have it now!"

Tears filled my eyes as I stood by and watched this exchange, this reconciliation between them. It was beyond anything they could have done, said, or accomplished on their own. Something supernatural definitely had to have happened to Seth while in his coma. He was a changed young man... How? Why? What? We didn't know, but we cherished every moment with awe and wonder. There was something so beautiful, so pure, so peaceful about him.

What was happening to Seth spiritually was beyond comprehension. Our hearts were erratically rejoicing and breaking all at the same time. Our emotions were up and down like a yoyo. It's hard to explain, but I'll try. One would think that with all of Seth's amazing progress, we would be filled with joy. Much of the time we were. In many ways we were riding a wave of faith and celebrating each new step, but sometimes the reality of the situation would hit us without warning. The facebook posts were all so positive and uplifting, giving glory to God for every positive step, which was intentional and beautiful. And when we saw people outside of the hospital like at church, they were all celebrating and rejoicing over all the good, which was what we wanted. But I have to admit, that was sometimes hard for us, because nobody saw what we saw. Yes, Seth would "walk" for a few minutes with lots of assistance, but the rest of the day we were watching him in a wheelchair or a hospital bed, wearing a diaper, not even able to go to the bathroom on his own. There was a lot of grieving going on in our hearts and probably his too. But if so, he couldn't tell us.

There was so much Seth could no longer do. He couldn't even swallow. A baby is born with that ability, yet Seth could no longer do it. I remember holding my eight-month-old grandson one day and thinking, "Oh my goodness, he has more control over his arms and legs than Seth does." That was a heartbreaking reality. And sometimes Seth was lucid and alert, and then other times his brain would just shut down. Often when he would do therapy, Seth would actually be very dazed looking. There was a blank, empty look in his eyes, almost like he wasn't there. It took every bit of his brain power and concentration just to do a small task, like picking up one foot to try to move it forward. It was terrifying to see him like that. It was something that no one else ever saw, except us, his family. So it was just a constant rollercoaster of emotions on every level. We were excited about the task he was doing and at the same time disheartened by the empty look in his eyes. I worried and wondered if Seth would "come and go" like that forever? We didn't know. No one knew. While I knew I was witnessing little miracles every day and rejoiced in those, there were moments when my fear would overcome me, because I never knew at what point the progress might stop and that would be how Seth would be left forever. It was a strange dichotomy in which we were grieving and rejoicing at the same time. It was a constant, daily struggle.

This was especially difficult for Seth's older siblings, Michael and Andrea, to deal with. It was agonizing for them to see this childlike version of their brother while knowing he was a twenty-one-year-old adult. There was sort of an odd blending of child and adult in Seth. He had the innocence of a child and yet at times the comprehension of an adult. In many ways we had to take care of him and treat him like a child, despite the fact that he was an adult. And things changed from minute to minute. Andrea never felt like she could get too excited about the good moments, because she didn't want to get her hopes up. Yes, he was taking steps forward, but the reality was that he was starting from zero. So one positive step forward was still a million steps backwards from the brother she desperately wanted back. Instead, she felt like she always had to be prepared for the present version of Seth to be what he would be like forever. She tried to be careful not to expect too much and instead be okay with whatever version of Seth we had at that moment. She was grieving Seth so much inside, but never felt like she could show it. She felt like if she grieved the version of Seth that was no longer there, she wasn't being appreciative and thankful for and accepting of the version of Seth there at the present time. She felt as though somehow her emotions of sadness and grief were selfish, and that she needed to just be thankful. So consequently, she buried a lot of her emotions as the days went on.

The array of emotions we all felt were extremely confusing. While we all continued to ride this turbulent rollercoaster of emotions, the days to follow took us on an even bigger, crazier ride than we ever could have imagined. The next part of this story is hard to explain and even harder to process in my heart and mind. I have thought and thought about how to write it. I feel called to try to walk you through it as closely to how we experienced it as I possibly can.

You see, we were taken on a spiritual journey we never expected. All those hours, days, weeks that we had begged God to save Seth's life, God was actually doing so much more. It is a journey I never could have imagined, but ultimately it is the reason for the writing of this book. It is a journey I believe God wants you to take as well.

I will outline the events of each day as it happened. I invite you to walk it with us in the pages to follow. So buckle up! As you read it, allow God to open your heart, speak to you, and stir up in your spirit His words and His all-consuming, unconditional love for you. I believe God wasn't just saving Seth, He was also saving you and me. He had each one of us in mind when He chose to spare Seth's life. Wow! Our God truly is good!

CHAPTER ELEVEN
- ONE DAY AT A TIME -
God is Good... in the Middle of Suffering

<u>*Thursday, March 9, 2017*</u>-

Seth had only been at Mary Free Bed for 1 week, and not only was he able to do the typical three hours of therapy, he had actually surpassed that and was doing five hours of therapy a day. He was doing so well, that they even added another physical therapist to work with him an extra hour every day. The fact that in a week's time he went from basically still being asleep to doing five hours of therapy in a day was absolutely amazing. We were literally witnessing small miracles like this on a daily basis.

After OT Dress, Seth's day began with Speech Therapy, which not only dealt with his speech but with his swallowing and eating as well. At this point, Seth was begging for a drink of water. His mouth was sooooooo dry! He was no longer able to swallow properly, a simple function that we innately and naturally do even as babies in the womb. The left side of Seth's throat was too weak for him to swallow properly, so consequently any liquid in his mouth would run down the back of his throat uncontrolled, making it a dangerous risk for him to either choke or aspirate. Even when they brushed his teeth, they had to use a suction toothbrush, so that he wouldn't accidentally swallow some water and aspirate. With each passing day, his mouth got more and more dry, and all he wanted was some water. However, a simple drink of water was not a simple request for Seth. There were many steps involved before he could have water. His speech therapist needed to first do a video swallow study to make sure that when he swallowed, the food or liquid would go down his esophagus rather than his windpipe. However, that wasn't so simple either because ideally, he should have his trach out before doing the swallow study. So unfortunately, like most things, it was all a process which meant more waiting... Wait for the trach to be capped successfully for seventy-two hours. Then wait for him to be decannulated. Then do the swallow study. Then, maybe, depending on the results, he could have a drink.

While having to wait for a drink was discouraging for Seth, the rest of speech therapy went well. Laurie said Seth's breath support, sequencing, swallowing, and all the little details she looks for were really improving. Seth even found a little voice at times. We were also beginning to understand Seth a little if he mouthed words slowly within context. Laurie was pleased with his improvements and told us she would check with respiratory to see if his trach could possibly come out early. She also let him try a few bites of applesauce. It wasn't water, but it was something.

Seth also had occupational therapy each day, which usually consisted of working with his left arm, trying to relax the muscle, which was still constantly contracted, and other muscles that needed to be strengthened, as well as his eyes. Outside of therapy, there were many little things that we were told to do with Seth to help with his recovery. Things like: keep stretching his left arm; keep orienting him to time, place, date, and what happened; do prayers and rote speech with him; sit on his left side so he would have to use his left eye; stretch his neck, gently moving his right ear to his right shoulder.

In physical therapy they had Seth "walking" in the zero-gravity harness, which held most of his body weight for him. He still could not stand on his own. However, he was walking much faster than before and was actually moving his left leg by himself. He didn't have much control as one foot would often cross over the other. It was very uncoordinated, but it was definitely a huge improvement, especially in only one week of therapy. Seth told Kelli, his physical therapist, that he wanted to run! And he told his nurse that he wanted to be home in two weeks. He was ambitious and definitely had not lost his strong determination, something we all admired in Seth.

In each therapy session, usually the therapists' first question for Seth was if he had any pain. Miraculously, Seth was completely spared from physical pain. He never even had a single headache, which is unheard of with even a simple concussion, much less such a serious brain injury. When Seth was asked if he had pain, he usually put his hand to his chest as if to say his ego hurt. I was so grateful that Seth didn't have to suffer physical pain, but as a mother it crushed me to see him suffer in any way.

The last therapy Seth had scheduled for the day was with the psychologist, Dr. Blackbird. When she came in to see Seth, he was very alert. She talked to him about his singing and voice and encouraged him saying it should come back eventually. Seth kept folding his hands to signify that he is praying it will. She said, "You seem like a man of faith," and Seth mouthed, "For sure." She gave him a stone that she had gotten from Israel. It was obviously very special to her. Seth took it, kissed it, and raised it up to Jesus. Dr. Blackbird then asked Seth how he was doing emotionally. He mouthed, "Good. It sucks, but it's good."

Seth was very attentive and pleasant throughout the session, and I think Dr. Blackbird really enjoyed meeting with him. He told her "Thank you very much," before she left. This was another experience that I just held and pondered in my heart. It was Seth, but a very peaceful and grateful Seth, right in the middle of a situation that "sucked," as he had said.

Throughout the day between therapy Seth would take naps, or we would take Seth for walks, pushing his wheelchair through the halls of Mary Free Bed, stopping at windows to look at the busy city below or the beautiful Cathedral next to Catholic Central where Seth had attended high school. We also continually tried to communicate with Seth through any means possible. Unable to actually talk yet, we still had him try to write things for us. This particular day he wrote, ***"You're wounded no more."*** When I asked him who said that to him, he mouthed, "God." In everything Seth did, he had an inexplicable peace like nothing I had ever seen in him before.   I had a growing curiosity about his coma experience. I was convinced that something beautiful had to have happened to him.

That evening, Caleb, finally feeling well, came to see Seth for the first time since he had been at Mary Free Bed. He was amazed by the difference in Seth. Most of our family was there, and Seth's friend, Nate, came too. We all had a great time together. Nate brought Seth a card from another one of his friends. As Seth opened it, he acted like he was looking for money in it. When he found no money, he threw it over his shoulder with the funniest expression. He couldn't even talk, yet he had us all laughing so hard. It was such a relief to see Seth's humor emerging! We longed for that joy he had always brought us throughout his life. This was the first light-hearted, fun evening we had had together in, what felt like, a very long time.

It had been a long and busy day for Seth and an emotionally draining one for me too. All in all, it was a good day. Most of the time I rejoiced in Seth's progress, but then there always seemed to be those moments when the reality of what he couldn't do would hit. I mean, he had been a phenomenal athlete with super speed, and we had been reduced to celebrating the slightest movement of his left leg. It was all hard to accept and overwhelming. I remember crawling into "my bed," which was the couch in Seth's hospital room, late that night after Seth was asleep. Tears rolled down my cheeks as I sent a text off to a couple of my dear friends. It read, "I am so weak and tired and often just want to run from the weight of this cross, but I know it is not by my strength but by God's that we will all make it through this." I held onto that thought as I cried myself to sleep.

Friday, March 10, 2017-

Things seemed to change daily. Instead of having to wait for the trach to be out in order to do the swallow study, Laurie, his speech therapist decided to go ahead and do it with the trach still in. At 8:30am, she did the FEES swallow study. She inserted a scope through his nose down into the back of his throat. She then examined his swallowing as he tried different liquids and soft foods. She also examined his vocal cords to make sure there was no swelling.

Fortunately, there was no swelling, but as she had suspected, the reason he couldn't talk was because the left side vocal cord was too weak to meet up with the right side in order to make the vibrations necessary to make sound. Laurie was confident that the left side would eventually strengthen and come back, and she was pleased with his swallowing and everything else she saw. As a result, she decannulated Seth right then! Seth's trach was out, just like that, when we had been told that it could be a few more days. Another little miracle!

The day continued with an hour of OT, a half hour working on his left arm and a half hour working with his eyes, and two hours of PT. With the trach out Seth could begin to make a little sound and actually talk in a very faint whisper almost immediately. This was huge. We could finally sort of communicate with him.

Throughout the day, between his therapy sessions, Seth tried to explain to us what things were like for him. He said it felt like he was drunk, that his memories and thoughts were all jumbled. He said it didn't feel real. It felt like a movie to him. It also became clear to us then that he had no sense of time at all. The fun time we had laughing with the family just the night before, Seth thought had been about two weeks earlier. It was beginning to make sense to us why Seth would get so upset and miss Chris so much when he had to go to work. Even though he would only be gone for work, to Seth it felt like Chris had been gone a very long time, possibly even weeks.

During Seth's last hour of physical therapy that afternoon, they worked on his balance while standing and also holding himself up in a sitting position. He still could not stand on his own but was doing much better with sitting. While working on this during PT, Seth told his therapist, Starr, that *he was gonna be on top of the world with God.* This was an interesting statement from Seth, and I wasn't really sure what he meant by it. Then later on in the session, he told her, *"I gotta find a good girl at youth group, but I got no 'game' with the girls anymore."* His mannerisms and goofy half smile were so funny. He had Starr and her assistant, Tess, laughing a lot.

I say half smile because all of his muscles on the left side of his body were weaker than the right, so only the right side of his mouth curved up into a smile. He always made us laugh with his huge smile on the right side of his mouth and his right eyebrow that he would lift super high up! Growing up, Seth always made the funniest facial expressions. We were elated to see that hadn't changed. His humor was very obviously coming back, and he still loved making people laugh just like he always had before.

Though he was kind of joking around with Starr, there was also a humble innocence in what he was saying. She also noticed how considerate he was. When she asked him how he was doing, after he answered, he turned and looked at her, asking, "how are you?" Starr was struck by his genuineness. She commented, pointing out that Seth was not self-absorbed like many twenty-one-year-olds. She was impressed. It was becoming more and more evident that he had been changed, and his faith seemed to be important to him once again.

Seth's talking was still just a very faint whisper, but we were at least beginning to understand some things he said. At one point in the day, he told me, *"I begged God for my life. I've never begged or pleaded or prayed so hard for anything."* I wondered when and how he had begged God for his life. Afterall, we had witnessed him unconscious and in a coma since his fall. So how? Was he with God? Did he see God? We couldn't get the answers to these questions. Whispering was difficult for him, and understanding was difficult for us. My heart was full of wonder and questions, but I had to be patient and wait, pondering it all in my heart.

It was Friday night, which meant Andrea was coming to spend the weekend with Seth. She and Chris usually stayed overnight with him on the weekend since they didn't have to work. It gave me a break and an opportunity to sleep at home with the other kids. That night Andrea was telling Seth how amazing it was that he was doing so much therapy and how all the therapists wanted to work with him because he was so motivated. Seth shocked us with his response. He looked at Andrea and whispered, *"I don't feel motivated. I feel depressed. Motivation is a choice."* His words totally caught us off guard. In fact, we were shocked by them. Seth had been working so hard in therapy, and handling everything about his situation with so much peace and had such a positive disposition, that we didn't even realize he was depressed. His words and attitude displayed incredible wisdom and grace in the midst of his suffering.

Seth had always been a very disciplined person. When he put his mind to something, he would accomplish it. His statement made us sad to realize that he felt depressed, but at the same time, his statement about motivation being a choice gave us joy. It was characteristic of Seth's disciplined personality, and every piece of Seth that we could see resurfacing encouraged us and gave us hope. While it was a blessing to see that part of his personality, I think we all knew that there was also something more going on. God's grace and strength in Seth were indisputable.

When I went home that night, I spent two hours talking to my sister, Kathy on the phone. Trying to share with her this incredible and renewed spirit we were witnessing in Seth.

Saturday, March 11, 2017-
Chris and Andrea were with Seth this morning. Chris said Seth was completely alert and trying to talk nonstop. In OT Dress Seth put his shirt on unassisted! That was tremendous progress. After that he went right to speech therapy where they had him try eating applesauce again. As Seth ate it he proclaimed ecstatically, "Applesauce is SO GOOD!!" over and over

again. He was so happy to actually eat real food. It had been almost a month since he had eaten anything. The speech therapist upgraded his diet to a soft pureed food diet and honey thickened liquids rather than tube feedings. Seth still couldn't drink water or regular liquids because they ran down his throat too quickly for him to swallow properly, but the honey thickened liquids moved slowly enough for him to handle safely. And Seth quickly discovered that he loved honey thickened cranberry juice. He couldn't get enough of it!

Kathy Barth updated her status.
March 11 ·
Latest update on <u>Seth</u> - 3/11
"Applesauce is SO good!"
According to Seth! He is also getting to drink a type of nectar this morning. Water is still too thin for him to handle, but he is getting to drink something. And he is fully awake and alert this morning and "talking" (in a whisper) up a storm. Praise God!!! Seriously, to God be ALL the honor and glory for His miraculous healing power!!!
I had the privilege and blessing of talking to my sister, Seth's mom, for two hours last night (something that she can't normally do because when she's at the hospital she's always with Seth and they are limiting any side conversations that are not directly with Seth). She asked me over and over to convey to you their DEEPEST GRATITUDE -- and Seth's gratitude!!! He can't believe that so many people are praying for him so intensely....even people he's never met. From the bottom of our hearts, "Thank you!!!!!!!" She also wanted me to ask you not to stop. There's so much work that needs to be done yet and they know they can't do it without being covered in God's grace.
A few days ago, I asked you all to pray for peace and patience for Seth. At that time he had been frantically trying to "tell" them something for two days and no one could understand what he was trying to say. He was

not at peace, he couldn't sleep, and everyone was so frustrated because they couldn't understand or help him. Once everyone started praying for peace and patience, he totally relaxed. When they told him not to worry-- that someday soon he'd be able to tell them everything--he accepted it with a peace and grace that was evident and from God alone. He has totally received the peace and patience we prayed for!

Every time we have prayed for something specific, God has answered our prayers!

And so now I ask you to pray for Seth's left side. It is the weakness on his left side that is preventing him from talking and swallowing and balancing and walking. The left side needs to catch up to the right side. It is getting stronger, but it isn't there yet.

The other thing she wanted me to share with you is that our SETH IS REALLY BACK, only stronger, with an intense awareness and gratitude to God for saving his life and a greater appreciation for God, his faith, and his family. She said it is truly BEAUTIFUL to see! He may not be able to walk or talk or swallow or do things we all take for granted, but he is so kind and loving and so absolutely grateful. The entire staff at MFB loves him. And for these answered prayers--that his personality and faith and love for God and family are all intact and stronger than ever--we are the MOST GRATEFUL of all.

To just say, "Thank you!" seems so inadequate. May God bless you as you have blessed us! You all have our prayers for your families and intentions. Let's keep storming the heavens and watch God's miracles continue to unfold. Jesus, loving Savior, thank you! Please continue to pour your healing love on Seth! #allforhisglory #sethstrong

Even though it was the weekend, Seth still had four hours of therapy. He was progressing so quickly that they didn't want to stop. After speech therapy, he had an hour of occupational therapy, in which he worked on sorting cards with his left hand and following targets with his eyes.

After OT, Seth got to eat lunch for the first time. Andrea fed Seth his lunch. It was soft pureed food, but Seth enjoyed every bite. He made us realize it was a blessing that we shouldn't take for granted. Andrea became Seth's "food helper." She helped him fill out his menus for his next meals, and when it was mealtime, Seth looked for Andrea to help him. That was always one of those moments that caused confusing emotions in my heart. It was beautiful to watch the love with which Andrea helped him and the gratitude with which Seth received her help, but at the same time, it was heartbreaking to watch Seth having to be fed. While he continued progressing rapidly, there were always those moments of fear, wondering how far Seth would progress and what kind of life he would end up having.

I brought Caleb, Mary, and Peter to the hospital with me since it was a Saturday. They loved being able to see Seth and be there with us whenever possible. Caleb, Mary, and Peter got to watch as Seth had his physical therapy. It was amazing for them to see his progression in only one week. This day, he walked through the hallway of Mary Free Bed without a walker or harness, just with a PT and a PTA on either side of him to support him. They also had him try a few steps backwards and side to side. At the end, they even helped him walk up and down a few stairs.

We knew in our hearts that we were watching a miracle unfold. We rejoiced in every step he took, and we had Kathy continually post all the progress, witnessing to the incredible glory of God. As everyone celebrated the miracles, they also picked up momentum praying for the next step. The faith of the body of Christ was palpable and it created for us what I like to call a wave of faith that supported us and held us up above the water in the difficult moments when we felt like we were sinking.

Along with Seth's other progress, Seth's voice was also getting a little stronger, and we were able to understand him most of the time. Seth could finally communicate with us, and let me tell you, all day long from start to finish, he filled our ears with words like no other...

He told us that *he looked up and saw all the machines and heard them beeping and that he bartered with God for his life, for even just 30 more seconds.* Seth told us that *his whole life belonged to God now.* *"I live all for Him for the rest of my life,"* he said matter of factly. Then he went on to tell us that *he saw everyone in his room praying for him.* *"I saw everyone. I don't even know who, like hundreds that overflowed into 5 different rooms."* We realized that he was describing exactly what Amy Oatley had seen in her dreamlike vision at 3am, the early morning of day six. We tried to ask Seth who he saw, but he really didn't remember specific people. He said there were people he knew as well as people he didn't know. The things he was saying were unfathomable, but he spoke, still a whisper, with such conviction, humility, and love. It was undeniable that while his body laid in the hospital bed hooked to machines keeping him alive, he had been in the spiritual realm. He had been in the presence of God.

As the day went on, we got other bits and pieces of his experience. *"I almost gave up,"* he said. *"I could have faded. I was down so low. It would have been easy to give in and give up and just fade away. So easy to die, so hard to stay and fight. But I saw everyone sad. I begged and pleaded for every second, for just 1 more minute, 30 more seconds. I am so thankful for every second He's given me."* And then again later, *"I could have died so easily, but I was aware of all the love."* Seth told us *he was aware of the love and prayers 24/7, and that it was all the prayers that gave him the strength to fight to come back to us.*

Throughout the day, Seth continued to go on about his coma experience every chance he got. It had become clear that he had an out of body experience. While we prayed beside his seemingly lifeless body, he was with God. He went on, *"I saw my body. I saw myself and I could have just faded. But I told myself, 'No. I'm not going out this way.'"*

"I would be happy if I could always see how God sees... the beauty, the love, the peace." These were incredible things to hear come out of his mouth...So heartfelt. So true. So humble. *"I wasn't the best guy*

191

before. I was immature. You couldn't just have a heart to heart with me. Now you can." It was obvious, Seth had been touched by God, and he had been changed. He wanted to share it all with us. His words just continued to flow with such peace and such ease. *"All I heard and felt at first was God. Eventually I heard the beeping of the machines."* As Seth continued, we were so intrigued and in complete awe, wanting to hear more and more. I remember I didn't want to forget any of it. So I grabbed a journal that friends had given us, and I began to write everything Seth said.

"I don't know what God looks like, but I know what it's like to be loved by God." Wow! This was coming from Seth, my rule follower, whose faith growing up had often been a bunch of dos and don'ts, rules that as Seth got older, he thought just held him back. I used to tell Seth that he was missing out on the best part of his faith, that is, the love relationship with God. I don't think he ever really understood what I meant. So imagine my surprise as Seth is telling me that he *knows what it's like to be loved by God!* I was awestruck, and I was sure he now understood it in a much deeper way than I ever did. My heart was on fire. I don't even know how to describe what I felt. This was like nothing I had ever experienced in my life. Our son was sitting there telling us firsthand what it was like to be with God. It was so unbelievable and yet so believable, because we could see it in Seth. He was so genuine. We

experienced the indescribable peace that only comes from Christ. The beauty of it all shone so brightly in Seth. It feels impossible to adequately convey… I might as well just let Seth's words do it.

Seth continued, *"I saw the world like God sees it. He doesn't want us to just pray because someone is dying. He says, 'I am here all the time.'"* God said to Seth, *"Look how they all pray because you are injured, but I am here always."* When Seth told us this, I felt like it was a direct message to us and all the prayer warriors. People all over the world had been praying for Seth. In Scripture, God tells us to persist in prayer, and to ask for what we need. He obviously heard our prayers and answered them, but through Seth, God was telling us that He wanted more. He wants a relationship with us, and He is always present and waiting for us! Wow! I was stunned and overwhelmed. I knew God was speaking directly to me and to each of us through Seth.

Our son had almost died, and we had watched in fear while he lay lifeless for weeks. Yet, almost a month later, here he is telling us that during that time he was walking and talking with God. I didn't know how to even begin to comprehend everything Seth was saying, and he wasn't stopping. He continued, saying, *"I saw all the people who were praying for me, and I saw all the people who weren't and who didn't care. It hurt! But I knew that I had been one of those people."* In the middle of a "fog" from a brain injury, he had such clarity and conviction about himself and how he had been living. As the day went on, the words just kept coming. We listened intently, trying to soak it all in. *"I was aware of all the love. I don't remember it all. I wish I did, but I was aware of the love."* He felt the love of all the people praying for him, and the love of God. He told us over and over again that *God's love was more amazing than anything he had ever experienced before.* He went on to say, *"I didn't have to see God, I felt him so close to me."* And he reiterated the power of prayer, saying, *"If all those people hadn't prayed for me, it would have been so easy to just fall asleep and die."*

It was an unforgettable day, and even Caleb, Mary and Peter had been there most of the day to hear it all. I remember so vividly the three of them standing in front of Seth's wheelchair that night, saying goodbye to him. He looked at the three of them and said, *"My whole life is God's. I live all for Him for the rest of my life."* I wish I could have captured the looks on their faces as they stared intently at him, just completely stunned. While he was quite helpless in a wheelchair, he had become our teacher. Mary remembers clearly Seth telling them very seriously to *never forget that we live for God, not ourselves.*

We were in awe and totally blown away by everything Seth had told us. I didn't know how to process all the emotions I was feeling. My heart felt overloaded, like it was going to burst. My spirit was on fire, just burning within me. I wanted to explode, and tell everyone, but it was completely overwhelming. I wondered how I could even begin to convey all this to our extended family and all the prayer warriors.

I remember going home that night and being completely emotionally spent. I sat in the big comfy chair in our living room and just laid back trying to process and sort through it in my mind. It was clear that Seth was truly a changed young man. God was good right in the middle of his suffering. I was beginning to think that what had seemed like our biggest tragedy may actually be unfolding as one of God's greatest blessings!

So there I sat contemplating all of this, when Caleb came into the living room with a pressing question. Caleb is one of our deepest thinkers, and I definitely was not prepared for his question that night. He asked me, "Mom, knowing all that you know about all the spiritual experiences Seth had with God while in his coma, if you could go back to the night of the accident and make it never happen, would you? Or would you keep it this way?" Wow. What kind of question was that? And what fourteen-year-old thinks like that? My mind was blown. Caleb, eyes and heart wide open, waited for my response.

I honestly didn't know how to answer him. I was so emotionally exhausted and confused. I couldn't handle it right then. I mean, yeah, I knew this was an incredible blessing and I felt an unexplainable joy so deep in my heart, but at the same time I was also still terrified.

Afterall, I was still watching my active, athletic, full of hopes and dreams, twenty-one-year-old son in a wheelchair, being fed by his twenty-three-year-old sister, Andrea. Yes, we rejoiced when he walked up a few stairs with assistance that day, but the reality was that when he got to the top, he wasn't even aware enough to know to turn around without them directing him to. My heart was broken and rejoicing all at the same time. I had so many conflicting emotions that I couldn't even begin to understand. It's humbling to admit, but at that moment, I couldn't answer Caleb's question. I knew what my answer should have been, "No, I wouldn't change a thing. If this is God's will for Seth, then so be it." But I'll be honest, I wasn't there at that point. While God had answered one of the greatest prayers of my heart for Seth, that he would know God and be in relationship with Him, I wanted Seth completely physically healed too.

I had verbally surrendered Seth to Christ over and over again, but my will was obviously not completely conformed to God's. It's terrible to think that while I sat there with my heart totally on fire, ready to burst, I was still afraid. Something beautiful and powerful was happening in my soul that I didn't even understand, and yet at the same time, physically I was exhausted, weak, and fearful of all that may lie ahead for Seth. God was undoubtedly showing me that He is good even in the middle of the suffering, but I still struggled to trust Him completely.

Caleb's question really humbled and challenged me. I wrestled with it, because at this point Seth had little to no physical talents or abilities. Yet spiritually it was like we were seeing the beauty of a purified soul. I can't adequately describe it, but honestly, I think it was the most beautiful thing I have ever witnessed. It was impossible to process. My heart was bursting with joy and yet, still broken. There was much to ponder. Although my emotions were all over the place, I went to bed that night with my spirit on fire and a renewed hope.

Sunday, March 12, 2017-
When Seth realized it was Sunday and he was missing Mass, he was very upset. He kept wanting to get out of bed, saying he had to go to Mass. People needed his prayers, and God was expecting him to be there. We had to convince him that he was not able to and God totally understood. We stressed to Seth that his job right now was to recover, but that he could still pray and offer up his suffering for the people who needed prayers. Seth asked me to make a list of powerful prayers he could pray. We came up with the St. Michael the Archangel prayer, the Chaplet of St. Michael, the Hail Mary, the Chaplet of Divine Mercy, the Memorare, and the Rosary. It was awe inspiring to see this desire in Seth to pray and be close to God.

Even though it was Sunday, Seth still had physical, occupational, and speech therapy. While he didn't really have physical pain, Seth's helplessness and inability to do anything for himself continued to cause the majority of his pain. He told Andrea, *"When everyone has to do everything for you, it's impossible to keep your dignity."* It was always a bit surprising when he would make comments like this because this constant suffering was not displayed in his behavior. He carried it all with overwhelming grace and gratitude. *"Thank you very much"* became a phrase we heard spoken by Seth all the time to every individual who assisted him in any way.

Brain injuries are very different from any other type of injury. The brain needs LOTS of rest and sleep to heal. When Seth's brain needed a break, it would seemingly just shut down. I know I have said this before, but I simply can't describe the apprehension and horror I felt as a mother watching Seth continually go in and out of awareness. He could be completely alert one minute and then look like he was gone or asleep the next. And then a little while later, he could say something so profound that it just stunned us.

This particular Sunday, Seth said to Andrea, *"You can gain a world of success but if you have no real people beside you, it means nothing. But if you have just a few good people by your side, the smallest things can be amazing."* This perfectly exemplified how Seth was living now. Though he had lost almost everything, he was more appreciative than I had ever seen him. He genuinely appreciated us, his family, and every moment he had been given. This was definitely very different from the young man who had fallen through that roof. The young man who wanted the world and all it had to offer, whose idea of success was fame and fortune.

It's impossible to even begin to explain how beautiful and inspiring it was to see Seth this way. God was so good right in the middle of the suffering. While still not physically healed, in many ways, the Seth that Chris and I felt we had "lost" the year before his accident, was back. When Chris was hugging Seth, he said, "Seth, I prayed so hard for you." Seth replied, *"I know Dad. That's why I came back."* No more special words had ever been spoken by Seth to Chris. At one point as Chris was talking to Seth, the hairs on his arms stood up as he realized that he was actually part of a miracle! He knew then that not only was he witnessing a physical miracle, but a spiritual one as well. Chris realized that while he had been praying so hard for God to save Seth's life, God was doing so much more. He was saving Seth's soul.

Seth seemed to have been enlightened in so many ways. Here he was, needing to be reminded what day it was and other simple things like that, but then in the same conversation he would say things with incredible wisdom. I just continued to journal everything he said. This day he had me write down possible song titles for when he could write and record songs again. We talked about him writing songs about his experience with God.

He said, *"I won't be able to write lyrics about this experience. I would have to use metaphors because it's not something I can explain. It is an experience. I hope I don't forget."* Seth didn't know if he would ever get his singing voice back or not, but he didn't seem worried at all. It was like he had total trust in God and was completely surrendered to His will.

Andrea loved spending the entire weekend with Seth. It was always extremely difficult for her to have to leave him on Sunday nights and go back to work on Mondays. Andrea has always been an exceptionally giving person, and she gave every spare moment she had to Seth during this time. There was no other place she desired to be. She was also always a very strong, independent, and hard working person. She held much of her emotion in, and just did what she had to do. It was both beautiful to watch her care for Seth so lovingly and attentively all weekend and heartbreaking to know her pain as she left on Sunday nights.

Monday, March 13, 2017-

Seth's day began with OT dress at 7:30am and his last therapy session did not end until 4pm that afternoon. It was a very long day for a guy with a brain injury who supposedly needed a lot of rest and sleep. He had been progressing so much that the therapists didn't want to miss any opportunity to work with him. So even though he had an offsite appointment, he was still scheduled for four hours of therapy too.

After breakfast, Seth was transported by ambulance to Spectrum Health for an appointment with the original trauma doctor who worked on him in the ER. This was the first time Seth had been out of the hospital. Dr. Gibson was amazed to see Seth alert and communicating with him. Often ER doctors don't get to see the outcome of their patients. Dr. Gibson told us it made his day to see Seth looking and doing so well.

After that outing, Seth told us he felt like God had flipped the script on him. He had flipped the roles. Seth was now the one in the wheelchair that people had to wait for as he was loaded in and out of the ambulance. He was now the handicapped guy, the type of guy that Seth used to get frustrated and impatient with. It was eye opening and humbling for him.

We found out later that when Seth would look at himself in the mirror at Mary Free Bed, he felt like he didn't even know who he was looking at. He said it felt like everything he once was, was gone. He would stand looking at himself in the mirror thinking, "Who am I?" Then he would answer himself, "Oh, I'm that kid, the guy in the wheelchair, the guy people will stare at. I'm a Mary Free Bed kid." It was a very surreal and painful experience for him. Yet, he handled it all so gracefully that we didn't even realize he was dealing with all that at the time.

Later that day, Seth told us more details of his experience with God. It was clear that he had been in the spiritual realm. He referred to himself and others he was apparently with as being *spiritual people*. He told us *they were out on a field crying because they could relate to "their" pain.* I didn't know who's pain he was talking about. He said, ***"We could feel what they felt and see what they saw. I could feel their pain. I don't ever want to forget that feeling."*** He went on to say, ***"When I looked at people who weren't crying, I thought how much do they really care? How much does that 12% of prayer really mean?"*** We weren't sure what he meant. He had told us that he saw all the people praying for him and crying for him. I wondered if he saw us crying and felt our pain? He went on to say, ***"How much you cry, how much you pray in church, shows how much you care. Never let me forget how much I feel God when I'm praying. I feel Him right here with me. He is right here crying. God is crying. When I'm praying, I can just see Him and feel Him right here."*** Seth had felt so close to God, and he did not want to forget it. He was adamant about us not letting him forget these experiences.

Seth repeated things many times throughout the days, like you do when you are really excited or amazed by something and you don't know how to adequately describe it. He said there was no timeline for how things happened. So Seth just kept sharing things as the memories came to him. One of the themes he repeated the most was *how amazing God's love was, how there was no other experience that could even come close to comparing with it.* This was extra impressive coming from Seth. He was our adventurer. He always had to be moving and experiencing something. He wanted his whole life to be about experiences, not ordinary experiences, but the biggest, best, and most exciting ones. He assured us many times over that *there is nothing on this earth that can compare with God's love and all that God allowed him to experience.*

I listened in awe. It was inspiring and overwhelming all at the same time. I didn't know how to process all that he was saying. He talked of God's amazing love. He talked of God crying. Why was God crying? I had never thought of our all-powerful God as crying. What did Seth mean? Did he and "they, the spiritual people out on that field" see and feel God's pain? I didn't know. It was a mystery, but something in my heart was burning and fanning a flame. Seth told us everything with such sincerity and total conviction. His faith was palpable, and it was stirring up something in my spirit.

"Don't put a chance or percentage on someone's life or situation," was another thing that Seth said to us during our conversations that day. It was another thing I didn't fully grasp. Did it have anything to do with the 12% of prayer he had mentioned? If we didn't take the

time to pray for someone or something, were we taking a chance with their life or their needs? These were questions that circled in my mind. Seth had also talked about how much *it hurt when people didn't pray for him, and how he knew he had often not prayed for people as he should have.* This clearly had an impact on Seth. It was clear that his eyes had been opened wide to truly examine how he had been living.

Seth continually stressed God's presence with us and how much he felt God. He said over and over, **"God is right here, right now."** It was visible when he prayed too. If we asked him to pray for someone in need, he would stop right then, close his eyes, and pray. It was never long, but appeared as if his heart was totally in it. He often was brought almost to the point of tears. It was obvious he was talking to God who had become very real and personal to him. And he told us over and over, **"You have no idea the power of prayer. Prayer does so much more than you know!"** This was another theme that Seth constantly reiterated. While we often had to be patient and wait for things to become clearer, there was never any doubt in our minds that Seth's experience was real.

Seth continued to progress at record pace in therapy. However, his short-term memory had been pretty badly affected by his injury. As a result, he often could not see his own progress and would get down and disappointed. We tried to encourage him. I started listing off to him all of his progress so far. It was amazing. After only a week and a half at Mary Free Bed, Seth had progressed and changed significantly more than we even realized until we paused and reflected on it. When he first got there, they had to use a lift to move him from his bed to his wheelchair, he couldn't even hold up his own head and couldn't sit without support. By this day though he could sit up with no back support. He only needed one person to transfer him from the bed to the wheelchair. He held his head up all the time and could move from lying in bed to sitting on the edge of the bed by himself. He no longer had a trach, was eating and talking, could lift his left arm above his head, itch his face with it, etc; and when he was walking in PT, still with help standing, he was able to move his left leg without assistance. He also could look at us with both eyes. Before he would mostly only look at us out of the bottom right-hand corner of his right eye and would connect with us for only a few minutes and then close his eyes and shut down, often looking dazed, like he was not there, and he would only respond to us some of the time. In comparison, by this time, he was able to have full conversations, and had a normal wake and sleep cycle instead of going in and out of it all day long.

As we listed all these changes and accomplishments for Seth, it really made me realize how far Seth had come and how fast he was changing. While I would have moments of fear for Seth's future, I knew I was witnessing a miracle. I felt as though I was riding an unfathomable wave of faith as both physical and spiritual miracles were unfolding right before my eyes.

By this time, Seth was working so hard in therapy and sharing his coma experiences so much that he was having a hard time turning his mind off. He told me that watching movies and listening to his dad's voice helped him with this. Chris had to be out of town for work this particular night, so Seth talked to him on the phone. When he got off the phone, he said, *"Dad's voice is so comforting."* Seth missed Chris a lot when he was working. Seth said to me that night, *"Dad's voice is so soothing and comforting. It helps me. He might think I'm not listening, but I am. I just can't retain it all right now. But I love Dad so much. If he weren't here, I think I would have died. I know I didn't always spend the time. I was always gone. I need to show people I care about them by spending time with them."* His experience with God gave him incredible clarity about his life and how he had been living. Such wisdom seemed to continually flow from his lips. It was a lot to take in and grasp. I just kept writing the words down and held them in the journal, as well as in my heart.

The days had been so full and overwhelming between the constant therapy and Seth's newfound voice and the telling of his experience, that it took a couple days for me to fully convey to the extended family all that Seth had been sharing with us. My sister, Kathy, did an amazing job then spreading it to all the prayer warriors in the most beautiful way, celebrating every miracle and giving all glory and honor to God. Lives were being touched and significantly impacted by Seth's experiences with God, his genuine love for God, and his continued miraculous physical recovery.

Kathy Barth at Mary Free Bed Rehabilitation Hospital.
March 13 · Grand Rapids ·
Latest update on Seth Alfaro - 3/13 - 1 Month
Today officially marks one month since Seth's fall. A month that has drastically changed Seth's life, and hopefully, in a good way, has also changed ours as we have witnessed God's miraculous power and love.
I promised I'd share more with you about Seth's spiritual journey thus far and the miracles God is working in Seth's life.
Seth has said so many times since waking up that it would have been so much easier to just "close his eyes," and fade away and die, than to stay and fight. He felt all the pain, but he saw all of us who needed him and all those who were praying for him and he fought to come back.
He remembers seeing what he calls a "video" of him falling (no one taped him falling) and remembers begging God for his life--even 30 seconds more. He says he's never begged for anything more in his life. He didn't beg for himself, because it would've been easier to just let go. No, he begged for us--those who needed and loved him. He remembers begging for his mom. He didn't "see" God, but he heard His voice and felt His tremendous love for him. He said he felt surrounded in love 24/7.
During the night/early morning of February 19th (the beginning of day 6) I couldn't fall asleep and was praying for Seth. I really felt I should post asking anyone who was still up to pray for Seth. His ICP numbers had been high all day and I felt he needed prayers. This was 2:00 am my time, 3:00 am Michigan time.
The next morning 31 people had replied to my middle of the night post including one woman who wrote this:
"A dream/vision I had last night around 3am. Whenever I awake in the middle of the night, I ask the Holy Spirit to fly me and whoever needs

prayer to Jesus in the Tabernacle. I fell back asleep pretty sure and had this vivid movie-like picture of hundreds and hundreds of people streaming into Seth's hospital room and the Adoration chapel praying on their knees for Seth. When I awoke this morning, I wondered if it was real because how could hundreds and hundreds of people be allowed into his hospital room!"

Another person I have never met confirmed the same thing, adding this post:

"Oh my goodness!! I woke at three thirteen this morn and immediately saw myself with others in prayer for Seth. I said my rosary on my fingers (the way Carol Dills told me to inserting Seth's name in each Hail Mary). Then I went back to sleep. Powerful warriors at work."

While in his coma, Seth saw/experienced this EXACT SAME SCENE!!! He said he saw his room overflowing with people praying for him, spilling out into five other rooms, all praying for him. He saw people he knew and people he didn't know...All praying for him. He SAW us praying for him. He FELT the power of our prayers. And he said he continued to fight to come back because of those prayers! He wants you to know that YOUR PRAYERS made the difference.

Do not let anyone EVER tell you that prayers are not powerful, because they are!!! We may not always get the answer we want, but God does answer. And sometimes, like now, we get even more than we've asked for.

Conversely, do not put off praying for people in need. Do not let other things "get in the way" of praying for those who need us. For, just as Seth saw all those of us who were praying for him, he said he also saw those who weren't. He saw all the people who didn't stop and pray and it hurt. He said it hurt more because he realized that he used to be one of those people--someone who said, "Yeah, I'll pray, but then let other things get in the way, and didn't pray." And he said that will never be him again!

When Seth found out yesterday was Sunday, he tried to get out of bed to go to Mass. Obviously, that was not possible, but he said he had to go because "all of the people who are suffering need him there" and need his prayers.

This young 21-year-old man has done more than "wake up" in the last month as we prayed for...he's had a real awakening! Your prayers have impacted Seth far beyond his physical healing. He has been very touched by them and can't quit talking about it.

In Seth's own words, that he shared with his younger siblings, "I live for Him now. I am His. Every minute is a gift from Him."

Seth still needs our prayers for continued physical strength and healing, but I can't help but want to spend today, on this one month anniversary, on my knees in thanksgiving! We have an amazing God who saves us, heals us, and loves us beyond our wildest hopes and dreams. To HIM be all the honor and glory forever! #allforhisglory #sethstrong#beyondourhopesanddreams

Chris and I were constantly astounded by the love and prayers of so many people, even strangers. Reading the Facebook posts and comments, we could feel and experience the joy and faith of the people, which elevated our spirits and our hope. Here is one of the Facebook comments in response to Kathy's March 13th post:

I would be one who doesn't know Seth, but once hearing his story, myself and my husband pray for him every day. I check every day for his updates. I cry at every one I read, with hope and joy knowing he is moving forward. I truly believe in the power of prayer and miracles do happen. My birthday wish yesterday was praying for Seth's left side. Will continue to pray. Sethstrong!

The love and commitment of the body of Christ for a young man they didn't even know was astonishing and very humbling for Chris and me.

The day ended with a great visit with Seth's Aunt Sarah and Uncle Dave, who were so happy to see that

Seth's sense of humor was alive and well. Of course he had them laughing a lot. They left uplifted, saying it was amazing and inspiring to talk to Seth and incredible to finally hear his voice again!

Being out of town for work, it was difficult for Chris to not be able to see Seth that day. Yet he was continually blown away by all he had heard. His heart was filled to overflowing with gratitude for the physical and spiritual miracles unfolding in Seth and the outpouring of love and prayers we were receiving. This was Chris' text to extended family that night: "'And they will know they are Christians by their love.' I am truly blown away by the love of strangers. I wish I could hug them and all my family of believers right now. It is because of them and you all that Seth is here today."

Tuesday, March 14, 2017-

Dr. Ho came in to see Seth first thing this morning. Dr. Ho was completely amazed by Seth's progress! He told us that Seth's injury was so serious that the doctors thought he would need to go to a long term, lower functioning kind of rehabilitation facility. He said that the doctors at Spectrum Health hospital really questioned why he was willing to take Seth to Mary Free Bed. Dr. Ho said that based on the injury that he saw on the MRI and the responses he saw from Seth, he didn't have a reason to bring him to Mary Free Bed. However, when Chris told him about the responses that we had gotten from Seth, Dr. Ho decided that he wanted to give this otherwise healthy young guy a chance. This was the first time we realized how much all the doctors were against Seth going to Mary Free Bed. It was hard to hear. Yet at the same time, we realized what an incredible gift Dr. Ho had given us by going against his colleagues recommendations and taking Seth as his patient. We will remain forever grateful to Dr. Ho.

Seth had another five hours of therapy. In speech therapy, he even got to try swallowing some water! He didn't pass yet, but he was still extremely happy to have gotten even just a tiny amount of water. It was inspiring to see how thankful he was for such small things that I know I take for granted every day.

Seth continued to work on swallowing safely. He had to completely learn how to swallow. Have you ever thought about the mechanics of swallowing? I certainly hadn't until I was in therapy with Seth. Did you know we hold our breath when we swallow? It makes total sense, but I had never thought about it. In fact, when I would try to follow the steps as they were teaching Seth how to swallow, it would mess me up. We typically don't ever have to learn how to swallow. We do it naturally, without thinking. It is another one of those things that we take for granted every day. Seth couldn't just take a drink without thinking. Everything he did took thought and lots of effort, and yet he was grateful. Just having that little bit of water, he said, was amazing. It was the first time he had water in a month. While Seth didn't pass the water trial, he did pass the nectar-thick liquid trial. They are thinner than honey thickened liquids, which made him only 1 step away from water!

As I have mentioned, Seth had always been a phenomenal athlete. It was something he took great pride in. On this day, he must have been thinking about that, as he said specifically that he should tell athletes, ***"Don't ever take what you have for granted. Just look at me. You could lose it in a second. Everything is a gift. One second I was popular, had good status, could get beautiful girls, and the next second I was in a coma fighting for my life, and now sitting here helpless in a wheelchair."*** Those were some pretty powerful words, but it was what he said later in the day that really blew me away. As he was laying in his hospital bed, he looked at me and said, ***"I'd rather be here doing God's will, than at home with everything, but not in God's will."*** This was the exact point I had tried to get across to Seth the night before his accident, that in God's will is the only place he would ever be truly happy or fulfilled. I had never envisioned anything like this though. Seth was in a hospital, unable to even walk or care for himself, yet he had more joy than I had ever seen in him. He didn't just accept the words I had spoken. He was actually living those words right in the midst of the greatest suffering of his life. Clearly Seth profoundly understood it in the depth of his soul and had completely surrendered

212

his will over to God's. It was beyond anything I could have ever imagined or hoped for. God truly is good right in the middle of our suffering!

With Michael and Meg back in their own home, Ethan had picked up a lot of the slack at our home. He carried a lot of responsibility as an 18-year-old trying to finish his senior year of highschool in the midst of this family crisis. It was a blessing that Ethan's school, Catholic Central, was across the street from Mary Free Bed. In fact, we could see it out the window of Seth's room. Ethan would come over most days right after school and spend time with Seth, before going home to have dinner with Caleb, Mary and Peter. After eating, the kids would pack up the rest of the food and bring it to the hospital for Chris and me to eat. As I said before, Mary Free Bed had become like our second home, and the family lounge next to Seth's room was like our living room. We gathered there together as a family pretty much every night.

All of our dinners were still being provided by the people of our parish, St. Thomas the Apostle Catholic Church. It was incredible how long St. Thomas parishioners took care of us. We were blessed beyond words by the faith, love, and kindness of our community. It was humbling and overwhelming. Ultimately, it was our faith and the love and prayers of our faith community that had gotten us through and were continuing to get us through this ordeal.

As Seth was progressing, he was allowed more visitors. This particular night, Seth's cousin Kaitlin, who had seen him almost every day in the ICU, came to visit with Seth. It was amazing for her to see the difference in Seth.

Kathy Barth
March 15 ·
Latest update on Seth Alfaro - 3/15
Last night, Chris asked me to share with all those who are praying what the MFB doctor who first evaluated Seth in the hospital said to them yesterday. He said everyone in the ICU was very surprised he agreed to take Seth to MFB for rehab. They all figured that Seth would need to go into a long term care facility. The results of his MRI were bleak--the prognosis uncertain and not at all positive. And, this doctor really didn't see any of the responses we had gotten from Seth, so he really had no reason to take him. But, he listened to what the family had seen and said he saw this young man lying there and just wanted to give him a chance. So he agreed to take Seth to MFB and our hearts were all lifted...our prayers renewed. That is the power of prayer!
This same doctor told them yesterday that Seth's progress is amazing him and everyone at MFB--every day! Like I said before, it is beyond the scope of what they normally see. They are as amazed as we are! What an awesome God we have.
And, while God has been at work mending together Seth's physically broken parts, He has been at work doing so much more.
I'd like to share my daughter Kaitlin's post from last night. She texted me just SOOO excited and said, "Mom, I am SO happy! I'm here visiting with Seth and he's back--only better than ever before. My heart is overflowing!"
I just read her Facebook post and I can't think of a better way to share this miracle with you...
"Hey there everyone. I wanted to thank you all again for the prayers you have lifted to heaven for my cousin and our family. The past month has been a rollercoaster. I was able to stop by and see Seth today and I

214

cannot convey how happy my heart is. It was so good to hear him talk, see him smile and hear him laugh. He was telling jokes, teasing his siblings and I felt like I was truly seeing him again for the first time since the accident. It was nice to have Seth "back" and stronger than ever. Sure he may be physically weaker but he is showing so much strength with his resilient and rediscovered love of the Lord.

Seth specifically asked us to put on the song "Tell Your Heart to Beat Again" [by Danny Gokey] while I was there. He said it really speaks to what he has been going through. We had a lovely little praise and worship session. I can't wait until he is back on the guitar and leading praise and worship as I know it will take on so much more of a new meaning now. Keep up the prayers my friends."

If you have a couple of minutes, please listen to this song. I had goosebumps! It perfectly describes Seth's journey, and quite possibly, some of our own journeys. Jesus, Healer of all, continue to heal Seth and THANK YOU for healing us in ways we don't even realize we need. #allforhisglory#sethstrong #beyondourhopesanddreams

The song Kaitlin referenced, "Tell Your Heart to Beat Again" by Danny Gokey meant a lot to Seth. It had been meaningful to him before his accident. It had inspired and encouraged him when he was trying to come back to his faith. At this stage in his recovery at Mary Free Bed, it had new and powerful added meaning for him. The words were so fitting and relatable to his life. The first verse starts out saying, "Shattered, like you've never been before. The life you knew in a thousand pieces on the floor. Words fall short in times like these. This world drives you to your knees. You think you're never gonna get back to the you that used to be." Then the refrain picks up with, "Tell your heart to beat again…" The rest of the words were just as beautiful and relatable for Seth. He played it over and over in his hospital room, as it filled his heart with hope.

Since it was a Tuesday night, Michael was staying the night with Seth at Mary Free Bed. Seth had been having trouble sleeping. He had been dreaming a lot and his sleep had been very restless. As a result, he wasn't feeling well rested in the mornings, which made it tough with so much therapy scheduled for each day. We asked for prayers for a good night's sleep.

Wednesday, March 15, 2017-

Michael spent the day going to therapy with Seth. It was a typical busy day with occupational, physical, speech, and recreational therapy. Therapists continued to work with him orienting him to time and date. By this point, Seth was pretty lucid most of the time he was awake, but tended to get more confused when he was tired.

In recreational therapy, they thought Seth may like to try to play the guitar. It seemed to be more of a disappointment to him, as he just didn't have enough control over his left arm and hand to play it. It was another realization of all that he had lost and could no longer do. His journey was continually filled with ups and downs, highs and lows.

Seth was eating soft foods, but the reality was that it was hard work. Even mealtime was therapy. Swallowing was still not completely natural, and getting all of his food down when he swallowed was still an issue. At lunchtime, his speech therapist evaluated his eating. He was instructed to eat slowly. He was told to take small bites and swallow each bite twice, put his fork down and take a drink between each bite. This was so frustrating to Seth. He was a young guy, who just wanted to eat normally. On a positive note though, Seth trialed (a term used by the therapists when Seth tried something new) a little water at lunch and actually did well!! It was a constant rollercoaster ride of joy and frustration!

Throughout the day, Seth continued to share his spiritual experience with Michael. He told Michael, *"God sees everything."* Michael got out the journal and began to write these things down as Seth shared. Seth then commented saying, *"The more I see on earth, the less I see of the spiritual realm."* This was extremely bothersome for Seth. He told us frequently that *he didn't ever want to forget what he saw and how he felt.* He repeatedly said, *"Don't ever let me forget."*

Seth continued to share his coma experiences. He told Michael that *he went with God to a baseball field where a player was laying on the ground, injured. It seemed to Seth that this player had no one to pray for him or care for him, like he was a "nobody" in the world's eye. He said they prayed for him and that God knelt down next to him, bent over him, prayed and cried for him.* Through that it was clear to Seth how much God loves us and hurts for us in our suffering. He said, *"He cries over us for our pain. I could see like He saw and feel what He felt."* Wow! God cries over each of us for our pain?! He actually hurts with us, and Seth experienced it. He felt it, that overwhelming love and pain that God feels for each of us...

Things that Seth had told us two days prior were beginning to make more sense. The field with the injured player must have been the field where he and others in the spiritual realm had been. Two days earlier he had talked about there being others out there with him on that field. He had referred to them as "all of us spiritual people." He said that *they, himself included, were all crying because they could relate to "their" pain.* Maybe "their" referred to suffering people because he said, *"We could feel what they felt and see what they saw. I could feel their pain. I don't ever want to forget that feeling."* He also said *he could feel Jesus' pain for us.* Whether it was Jesus' pain or suffering people's pain Seth had felt, he was adamant that he did NOT want to ever forget it. He knew God was good even in the suffering. I'll admit, it was a lot for us to take in and try to understand, but one thing was clear: God loves us more than we could ever imagine! Seth repeatedly described God's love as "amazing" and the whole experience as "crazy!"

With another five hours of therapy, Seth was very worn out and tired. Though everyone was so excited about Seth's progress and eager to work with him, Dr. Ho finally instructed his therapists to cut back Seth's therapy time to four hours and schedule a short nap time for him in the afternoons.

Thursday, March 16, 2017-

Two weeks after getting to Mary Free Bed, Seth can finally have WATER! In speech therapy Seth trialed brushing his teeth normally with water for the first time! He also trialed using a straw, but it was difficult to control the speed of the fluid coming in and swallow in time. So he still was not allowed to use straws, but he was upgraded to thin liquids and could drink water now, as much as he wanted. That was huge!! Seth had wanted water for so long, and now he could finally have it! Even though Seth had been able to drink other thickened liquids, nothing quenches thirst and a dry mouth like water! Such a simple thing, yet such a gift. Water - another one of those things we take for granted every day! Many of Seth's prayer warriors made a commitment to pray for Seth every time before they took a drink. That was so cool. Again we were astounded by the extraordinary love of Seth's prayer warriors, both friends and strangers alike.

Earlier on at Mary Free Bed, Michael had promised Seth that as soon as he was allowed to drink thin liquids, he would bring him a Monster, which was Seth's favorite beverage. I wasn't sure if energy drinks would be good for Seth at that point. It didn't seem like a good idea to me. His therapists didn't think it would be good either, so unfortunately the guys' plan got nipped in the bud right away. He and Michael, of course, joked about how Michael could smuggle it into the hospital for him. Seth's favorite type of Monster had been sitting in Michael's refrigerator in anticipation of this day. Apparently, it would just have to wait a little while longer.

March 16th was another day I don't think I will ever forget. Right around lunchtime, the hospital minister came to Seth's room wondering if he wanted to receive the Eucharist. Being that he was now able to eat some foods, he was allowed to have a small piece. However, the Speech Therapist and the Nutritionist were both there waiting to work with Seth right at that same time. They were both very kind and patient, and told us that Seth could go ahead and receive. So the hospital minister said a short prayer and gave Seth the Eucharist. Then she gave me the Eucharist. I was feeling really rushed because people were waiting to work with Seth. So after I received the Eucharist, I closed my eyes, bowed my head and said a hurried little prayer. I quickly made the sign of the cross and opened my eyes so that we could get moving since people were waiting. Then I turned and looked over at Seth. He was teary-eyed and at the same time appeared as if he were in complete ecstasy! I knew right then that something big was happening to him. He told me later that *the minute the Eucharist touched his tongue, he was right back with God again, just exactly like it was when he was in the coma.* He said, *"I realized then that is what it's like every time we receive Jesus in the Eucharist, we just don't see it."* I was stunned when he said that. I was immediately humbled. I had received the Eucharist so habitually and hurriedly, that in my heart I wasn't even recognizing the true gift of Jesus. I was deeply convicted. I realized how regularly I miss the miracle and the gift because I am too distracted. Time after time I have received the body and blood of my Lord and Savior, and yet I am occupied, thinking about everything else.

Later that day, Seth shared even more about his experience while he was in the coma. Seth told us that *he didn't know if he would have gone to heaven or hell if he had died.* I asked him if God told him. He said, *"It was like I could choose. But I felt like I wasn't that good of a person. I saw in an instant all the times I could have chosen him and whether I did or didn't. So then I felt like I didn't deserve Heaven. I couldn't hide anything from Him. In that moment, I didn't feel God's mercy. I felt the weight of all my sin. There were no excuses. We need to choose God now in this life, so he has a reason to choose us then."*

That afternoon, Seth met with Dr. Blackbird, the psychologist, again. While he was talking to her, he mixed up some facts that he knew. This made him quite upset later when he realized it. It was frustrating and embarrassing for him, but it was completely understandable with a brain injury. Things he had known before his accident were all mixed up in his head due to the injury. But they were gradually coming back and getting clearer. I tried to explain to him that he need not be embarrassed and that as his brain healed, the things he knew before would become more clear in his mind and memory. I went on to say though that his spiritual experience may actually become less clear and vivid the further he gets from it. Sadly, less than a week after he began to be able to tell us about it, he said it was already fading. He told me, *"It's already getting less clear. I don't ever want to forget."* He would tell all of us not to ever let him forget it. If only we had some control over that.

Seth never ceased to astound us by the things he said. Much of the time we were rendered speechless. I mean, imagine your twenty-one-year-old son saying this, ***"It's hard to say this, but this really is a blessing. It seems weird... I am laying here, can't walk, can't eat pizza... How can that be good? But the gifts God gives are greater than anything else we could ever imagine."*** He went on to say, ***"I've always wanted my life to be full of experiences. What God let me see, is an experience like nothing I have ever seen and one that most people never have."***

What made all of this even more convincing and inspiring is that Seth wasn't just saying all this because he had been healed. At the point that he was sharing these experiences, Seth was in a wheelchair, unable to walk or even stand on his own. He was only just beginning to be able to eat some foods and was being fed by me or Andrea most of the time. He had to be showered and dressed by others. He was a 21-year-old, not even able to go to the bathroom on his own. He had no idea what his life was going to be like or what the future held for him. Yet, he considered it a blessing. It was hard to fathom, but by his words and actions, he was continually witnessing to the truth that God is good even in the middle of suffering.

Anyone who had the privilege of seeing Seth at this time was inspired by him. His cousins Kaitlin and Karianna were back again to visit him. And his Uncle Dave and Aunt Sarah continued to be almost daily visitors at Mary Free Bed. Everyone was amazed by not only the things Seth said, but also the peace that he exuded. Even Dave and Sarah's two youngest daughters who still lived at home, Rebecca (who had grown up in the same school and class as Seth) and Regina, loved going to see Seth. They kept wanting to go back because they were so inspired by Seth and all that he was saying. No one could deny the truth of it all. It was palpable. You could feel it. Seth was so genuine and full of conviction. Yet all the while, he was still so Seth. He was the same guy we all knew and loved and still knew how to keep us all laughing!

The day started like any other day except that Seth was allowed to brush his teeth with a regular toothbrush and water! It's crazy how huge such simple things become after having lost the ability to do them. Each little step forward was cause for rejoicing and filled our hearts with joy and gratitude.

What started out as a "normal" day changed quickly during Seth's speech therapy session when Ethan called from school. He had just gotten the news that one of his classmates and friend had died in a car accident the night before. This shook Ethan to the core. Between this and Seth's accident, it had been a very emotional couple of months for Ethan and a serious wakeup call to the reality of life and death. It was a lot for him to handle all at once. Ethan left school early and came to Mary Free Bed to spend the day with Seth and me.

The news rattled me as well. It hit so close to home. I couldn't stop thinking about this young boy's mom and the nightmare she was living. For over a month now, we had been fighting for Seth's life, but instantly her fight was over. She had no fight. Her son was gone. My worst nightmare with Seth was suddenly her reality. My heart was broken for this poor family. I was humbled once again and filled with an even deeper appreciation for Seth's life and the miracles we had been recipients of on a daily basis.

We continued to be blessed by Seth's progress. In speech therapy, Seth trialed eating an open face sloppy joe, which he handled really well and enjoyed! Laurie upgraded his diet to the next level of foods. They were still rather soft foods, but no longer pureed. Seth was excited to eat real foods!

In physical therapy, Seth practiced walking with family assisting him instead of therapists. It's crazy to think that in just two weeks he had progressed from being unable to even stand or move his left leg to walking with us assisting him. He did so well that now we were allowed to walk with him, holding his gait belt, in the hallways without a physical therapist. This gave Seth greater freedom. We were also allowed to help him in and out of bed and his wheelchair. This meant that he would no longer have to wait for a nurse to go to the bathroom because we could take him. At this point, Seth could do it all on his own, except for needing someone to hold the gait belt to keep him steady as he walked and stood. A gait belt is a specific type of belt which was put around Seth any time he was getting out of bed. Caregivers could hold onto it in order to help steady Seth and keep him from falling while standing or walking. Our new ability as family members to help Seth to the bathroom, got interesting when only Andrea or I were there. But by this point in the journey, Seth didn't really care anymore. He had accepted that if this was his reality, he better just suck it up and make the best of it.

He preferred his family helping him over waiting for the nurses. So both Andrea and I had to take Seth into the bathroom at times when none of the guys were there. We would just hold on to his gait belt and turn the other way, giving him as much privacy as possible. Seth was so humble, and his good attitude, constant appreciation, and humor helped to put us at ease.

Seth's ex-girlfriend really wanted to see him. She had come to see him in the ICU, but once Seth had woken up we only allowed people to come if and when Seth wanted them. Seth decided he wanted to see her, though I think he was a bit afraid. He told me, "Once she sees me she won't want to come again because I'm not 'normal' yet." I understood how he might feel that way, but it broke my heart. Fortunately he was wrong about her reaction. She was super understanding and accepted him as he was. For Seth, that had to have been a huge relief and step forward toward recovery.

Saturday, March 18, 2017-

Seth was only scheduled for one hour of therapy on this day. He was finally getting a well-deserved and needed break over the weekend. Even so, we were still privileged to witness his progress as he walked up and down the whole hallway of Mary Free Bed four times during that hour of therapy! And the best part was that he walked part of it completely unassisted! No one was holding on to him! That was something to celebrate as we had worried so much that he may never get out of that wheelchair. There are no words to describe the joy we felt. What a gift.

Today, Brian, a friend from our parish, came to visit. Brian was someone Chris and I had prayed for seventeen years earlier when he had been in a serious car accident and sustained a traumatic brain injury. His wife, Julie, was the one who had told us while in the ICU to reject all negative prognosis and test results in the name of Jesus and continually claim healing for Seth instead. We had been following her advice ever since that time. One day during Seth's hospitalization, our son, Michael, had run into Brian at church. Brian told Michael that he would be happy to talk to Seth any time if he would like. Seth liked the idea and this was the day we had set up for a visit.

Brian came and sat with us, sharing his experience with Seth. He started off by telling us that he had no memory of his accident or recovery. What he was telling us was based on what others had told him about it. Brian had been through much of what Seth had, and more. Talking to Brian was such a tremendous comfort to Seth. There is so much about a brain injury that no one else can see, feel, or understand. So talking to someone who did understand was extremely helpful. Hearing all that Brian had come through, which was similar to what Seth was currently going through, brought a sense of relief. Seth had known Brian his whole life and never knew that he had a brain injury. This gave Seth a lot of hope that maybe he, too, could one day look and act completely "normal" again. It was an incredibly blessed visit, and Brian became a great resource for Seth. There was one particular thing that Brian told Seth that really stuck with him. Brian said, "You will look and act normal long before you feel normal." Something about that really struck Seth, and in his heart, he held onto that truth.

Sunday, March 19, 2017-

Seth's voice was gradually getting stronger and lower, more like his normal voice. Again, since it was Sunday, he only had one hour of therapy. His occupational therapist, Kate, took him on a long walk in the wheelchair to the Adoration Chapel in Lacks Cancer Center, a neighboring hospital which is attached to Mary Free Bed. When we got there, Seth got up and tried to genuflect with Kate holding onto him. It wasn't pretty. It was sloppy and very uncoordinated, but he tried. We stayed and prayed for a while.

More and more with each passing day, Seth became saddened by his situation and was beginning to grieve all the loss. He had such incredible, supernatural grace. But the longer he was left in the physical world, the more he had to grieve the loss and figure out how to deal with it all. It had been much easier on him and all of us when he had all that supernatural grace and peace. It was hard to watch him suffer as he began to grieve all the loss. It was obvious that the further he got from the spiritual realm, the harder it got for him. He told us, *"The longer I am 'here,' the more I forget and the less I see and feel God."* This was very upsetting for Seth.

To give you a little idea of the grace present in Seth, here is his instagram post this particular afternoon even though Seth was feeling seriously discouraged at the time: *"Almost having my life stripped from me has been one of the most life changing experiences I have ever had. Even through the suffering and pain, it's weird to say but it's truly been a blessing... I'm very lucky to have such a good friend like Tyler to help me through it."* Even on difficult days, Seth was still so grateful for everything and filled with an extraordinary supernatural grace. It was sometimes unfathomable because we could see his suffering and frustration, and yet he would still say things like this. It was remarkable and uplifting. There was no denying that God is good even in the middle of the suffering.

Earlier in the week, Seth had asked us to call Fr. Jim. He really wanted to tell Father all about his spiritual experiences before he forgot them. Fr. Jim had agreed to come this Sunday afternoon. As things seem to be with God, it was perfect timing because Seth was feeling very down about his memory of the experience fading and not feeling as close to God.

Seth began by telling Fr. Jim about how he had experienced God, but that he was starting to forget.

Father was not surprised at all. He talked to Seth about St. Teresa of Calcutta and how she once had a powerful experience of God but knew that it couldn't last. She knew that in order for it to last, she would have to die but that God still had work for her to do on earth. Fr. Jim told Seth that *he was allowed to see with his spiritual eyes and feel with his spiritual senses,* but since God decided to send Seth back, he would have to see and feel through his physical body and senses again. He explained that we cannot see the spiritual realm with our bodily eyes. He told Seth, "It was a gift, but now you need to release it back to God and ask Him to help you remember what He wants you to remember and trust Him to give it back to you when you need it."

As Seth described certain parts of his experience, I was very curious how Fr. Jim would respond. Seth told Father about how *he could actually feel people's prayers for him and that was what gave him the strength to fight to come back.* It evidently made total sense to Fr. Jim as he proceeded to explain to Seth that prayer is not words. He went on to say that prayer is active energy that flows from the person to God and then from God to others. That was exactly what Seth had felt.

Seth also told Father about *God praying and crying over the injured boy on the ball field who had no one to pray for him.* I really wondered what Father would say about that because I kept wondering why God prayed. Afterall, He is God. Fr. Jim so matter of factly

230

said, "Yes, God will do it Himself if He has to. However, He wants us to join Him praying for others." Seth continued telling Father about the reality of heaven and hell and how *he felt judgment in an instant.* He stressed that *we need to decide how we want to live and live that way now.* He went on, *"The spiritual realm is right here."* To which Fr. Jim responded, "You're absolutely right." My head was spinning and my heart bursting as Fr. Jim confirmed everything Seth was saying.

As they continued to talk about the spiritual realm and the physical realm, Seth told Father what it was like the first time he turned on his phone after the accident. He said, *"It was a culture shock going from the spiritual realm to social media. It was shocking how everything was all about me, me, me."* Fr. Jim emphatically responded, "Yes! And the more of 'me, me, me,' the less happy people are."

Fr. Jim seemed very excited about all Seth was telling him, and he had sound direction for Seth. He said, "Seth you have a chance to remake yourself into the man you want to be." He insinuated that it was a rare opportunity that not everyone gets. He repeatedly brought up the truth that Seth would have to forget because he couldn't live in both the spiritual and physical realms at once. He said, "You will have to perpetually decide to live by faith, but now it is based on what you know, not a guess." Eventually, Seth would have to live by faith again, just like the rest of us. However, Father told him that the scriptures may come more alive to him now, and that at times he may, just out of the blue, feel prompted to pray for someone. Fr. Jim directed Seth saying, "You don't even have to know who, just stop whatever you are doing right then and pray for them."

Their conversation went on for quite some time. Chris and I and some of the other kids were in the room, but we didn't say much. We mostly just sat, listening silently as Seth shared with Father. We never doubted that Seth's experiences were real, because we had experienced the presence of God so strongly in Seth. But still, it was an added blessing to witness the joy in Fr. Jim as he listened intently to all Seth was saying, while they discussed it together. I can't even begin to explain how awe-inspiring it was to hear Fr. Jim pronounce, "Seth, you have seen what the Saints have seen and reported." We had received a miracle beyond anything I could have ever imagined or hoped for. Fr. Jim told Seth that what he saw and experienced was a gift and would take a lifetime to unpack. He told Seth it doesn't have to be all at once. It becomes more clear each day that it was a gift not only for Seth, but for all of us, and it definitely will take a lifetime to unpack this incredible gift.

Seth was very uplifted by his time with Fr. Jim. It was perfect timing, lifting Seth out of the discouragement he had been feeling. It seemed to give him a new understanding and strength to accept the fact that his memory of the experience would have to fade, that he would have to begin to fully see and feel with his physical senses again, as difficult as that may be.

Later that night Seth got to see his Aunt Kathy again. She and her husband, Keith, had come back to Michigan for another visit. This was the first time she saw Seth since he had woken up. Last time she saw him he was in a coma. She was overjoyed. The following is her facebook post that night.

Kathy Barth updated her status.
March 19 ·
Latest update on Seth - 3/19
I told Seth that I would be writing today's update with tears streaming down my face. Tears of joy and gratitude. Yes, I told Seth--in person-- and he answered me. I hugged Seth and HE HUGGED ME BACK!!!
The last time I saw him and told him goodbye, he was laying in a bed, unable to respond, or open his eyes. Today, he conversed with us for an hour and a half--in almost his FULL voice--sharing his story, his faith, his struggles, his hopes, his fears, and over and over again, his TREMENDOUS GRATITUDE.
I know I've said it before, but this time I heard it directly from Seth himself...your prayers kept him alive!!! He stressed that over and over again--he is alive today because of all of our prayers. And he is extremely grateful!
He explained that he was SO close to dying, and would have, if he hadn't felt our prayers. He said it would have been so easy to just let go and die, but he felt our prayers inside him and surrounding him, and it was those prayers that kept him fighting to stay alive even though it was so hard to do.
He wants us to know the power that our prayers have...for him and for all those we pray for. Never stop praying, never think our prayers don't matter, never think our prayers don't count.
I have so much more to share with you, but for tonight, Seth would like prayers that he is able to sleep better. He was very tired when we left and

233

is not looking forward to his five hours of therapy tomorrow. He has been having trouble sleeping--both staying asleep and getting restful sleep that isn't filled with bad dreams of accidents. He would really love to be able to sleep through the night without dreams and without waking. Getting good sleep is very important for him since he needs to be rested in order to do all of his therapy. So, if we could all pray for that, he would really appreciate it.

He mentioned my posts several times. He is very grateful that so many people are following his story and are praying for him daily. He is amazed and overcome with gratitude that even total strangers are praying for him. Today, he went on Facebook and started accepting friend requests of the new prayer warriors in his life. He said that he would like it if people who are friend requesting him would include a short message saying they are praying for him or how they have heard about him. There's so much more to tell--my mind is spinning--but please be assured of Seth's gratitude and ours. Today I received one of the best hugs of my life and one of the greatest gifts I've ever been given--I got to witness a true miracle before my eyes. Thank you for your part in that. Thank God for answering our prayers! May God grant Seth and all of us a restful night. #allforhisglory #sethstrong #beyondourhopesanddreams #thepowerofprayer#hugs 🩶

Monday, March 20, 2017-

As my sister said in her post, Seth had been having a lot of trouble sleeping well. Between that and several hours of therapy each day, Seth was worn out much of the time. Today therapists discovered that Seth had been a coffee drinker before the accident. It never dawned on me that this could have an impact on Seth's energy level. It turned out that two cups of coffee in the morning before therapy woke him up and gave him more energy throughout the day. This became a daily routine which helped Seth significantly. In fact, one day we were a little behind and he didn't get his second cup of coffee before therapy. In our haste, I quickly handed Seth my cup of coffee as Laurie was wheeling him out the door of his room for his speech therapy session.

Later that day, Seth was still very tired and said, "I feel like I only had one cup of coffee." I assured him that he had two cups because I had given him mine. Then it dawned on me that my cup of coffee was decaf. Seth was right. He did only have 1 cup of coffee with caffeine. Seth really seemed to be very in tune with his body. Many of the nurses and therapists commented on how self-aware Seth was throughout his recovery. This was quite amazing, especially with a brain injury. Because Seth had a brain injury, there were times when we or his therapists would question what he was saying, but most of the time, like this time, he proved us wrong.

This same day in occupational therapy, Seth worked on tying his shoes. It was a lot of work. This is a vivid example of just how much Seth had to relearn, and how everything he did throughout the day was therapy, whether he was in a therapy session or not. He was doing great, but he had a long way to go. While we rejoiced in every positive step forward, it was difficult sometimes for Seth to accept all that he had lost and how difficult the simplest of things had become. It was another one of those things that we do every day and never even realize that it is a gift to be able to.

At lunchtime Seth trialed eating regular french fries and a deli sandwich with his speech therapist, Laurie. He passed, and his diet was upgraded to all regular foods! Because of this, his physical therapist planned a field trip to McDonalds for lunch the next day. Seth was looking forward to eating a big mac and fries!!

Seth's Aunt Mary, my brother Mike's wife, was in Grand Rapids for a visit from Portland, Oregon. She and Mike had been praying nonstop for Seth throughout this time. They had just moved to Oregon in 2016 for Mike's job. Before that we had lived only ten minutes from each other and had raised our families together. It was so different for us not to have them around as we went through all of this with Seth. We had always been near each other to help and support one another through the good and the bad times. I'm sure it must have been very difficult for them also not being able to be with us physically, even though I know they were with us in spirit.

I couldn't wait to see Mary and actually give her a hug in person! It was such a blessing to see and visit with her. As Seth shared his experience with his Aunt Mary, we learned something new. He said that when he first woke up from the coma *he had a clear vision of what God's plan for him was and what he wanted to do with his music and sharing God's message with people.* It was like God showed him what his purpose was in being sent back. This was the first time we had heard anything about this. He had never told us, and now Seth was very uptight because it was no longer clear. It had become so fuzzy and faint, that he couldn't remember what it was. He was very frustrated as he was telling his Aunt Mary about it. Mary listened and then looked at Seth and said, "Don't stress about God's plan for your life, Seth. You just have to know that you want to be His instrument and pray, 'God, I am yours. I am your instrument, show me how you want to use me today.' It's God's work." Mary has such a beautiful and strong faith. These were comforting words, and exemplify how blessed we were to continually be surrounded by family and friends with such remarkable faith and trust in God.

Tuesday, March 21, 2017-

Dr. Ho walked into Seth's room this morning and exclaimed, "Seth, you are amazing!" He pointed at him saying, "Your MRI says you should have severe brain damage." Then Dr. Ho proceeded to point upward as he said, "Somebody up there makes all the decisions and does everything for us." Even Dr. Ho recognized that Seth's recovery was a miracle. This thought was confirmed many times on this particular day. Seth's nurse, Dez, said, "I have seen many miraculous things here at Mary Free Bed, but Seth is an anomaly. The rate he is changing is not normal."

As if that was not enough confirmation, we got to speech therapy to receive even more. Laurie had Seth trial eating mixed consistencies, like cereal with milk. He handled it perfectly. Laurie took all restrictions off Seth's food. He could even use straws if he wanted. Laurie, too, was amazed by Seth's progress and the speed of it saying, "Every twenty-four hours Seth changes! That doesn't usually happen." I remember that morning feeling like my heart was going to explode hearing and realizing what an amazing miracle it really was. I couldn't wait to call Chris and tell him what they were all saying.

Seth had only two and a half hours of therapy because he was going to McDonalds for lunch. The first time Seth left Mary Free Bed to go to the doctor at Spectrum, he was transported by ambulance in a wheelchair. This time, only 8 days later, Seth went in a van with no wheelchair. He walked with assistance to the van, got in the van, and sat on a regular seat in the van. He then got out of the van and walked into McDonalds with only his physical therapist, Kelli, holding his gait belt. There was no wheelchair used at all on this outing!! Seth and I and his physical therapists, Kelli and Kris, and recreational therapists, Elle and Brie, all sat and ate together at McDonalds. They were incredible people. Besides being fantastic at what they did, what was the most amazing and impressive was the love and dignity with which they treated their patients. They treated Seth with love, patience and kindness no matter how he looked or acted, regardless of what he could or couldn't do. None of that mattered to them. We were honestly blown away by the entire staff at Mary Free Bed. It is truly a special place, and we were extremely blessed to have Seth there. We are so grateful and can never adequately thank them enough.

During lunch, Seth entertained all the therapists joking about how he would be able to use the "coma card" to get whatever he wanted. Anyone would feel sorry for him when he told them he had been in a coma, right? He had them laughing in true Seth fashion! However, they implied he would never be able to use the coma card on Chris or me. Seth agreed, realizing he had already put us through enough. In the depth of his heart, Seth was so thankful for Chris and me and his siblings and how we had been right there with him every second and every step of the way.

Seth loved eating every bite of that Big Mac and fries, and drinking his pop with a straw, but to be honest he was quite exhausted afterward. Though he could eat whatever he wanted, he still had to concentrate and think about eating slowly and carefully. Little things that people do every day had become huge tasks and great accomplishments for Seth. He realized more than ever what great gifts such things really were and wondered if such normal things would ever really be or feel normal to him again.

While we had heard so many positive comments about Seth's progress, we were still riding that rollercoaster of ups and downs. Despite all the praise of Seth's progress, his social worker was giving us information on filing for disability and long term assisted living homes for Seth, as if he may never come home. It was confusing and upsetting for us. We hoped that maybe the social worker hadn't been caught up to speed on all of Seth's progress and was still basing his information on the MRI results. It was another reminder to us of how bad Seth's injury actually was. We didn't know what he was thinking. While this concerned and frightened us, we tried to focus on all the positive comments and the incredible miracles we were witnessing, giving glory and praise to God.

Kathy Barth updated her status.

March 21 ·

Latest update on Seth Alfaro - 3/21

I couldn't wait to share...

Seth's doctor came in this morning and told Seth he is "truly amazing." He told Seth that his MRI says he should be severely brain damaged. (Thank you for your healing touch, Jesus!)

His comments are a total confirmation of a miracle!!!

Seth's nurse said she has seen many miraculous things here, but Seth is an anomaly. The rate he is changing is NOT normal.

His speech therapist took all restrictions off his food. She said every 24 hours he changes! She said that doesn't usually happen!

THREE confirmations in one day that we are witnessing a miracle (or several miracles) right in front of our eyes! PRAISE GOD!!!!

Don't ever let people tell you that miracles don't happen today, because they DO! You are living witnesses to the fact. Keep praying and spread the word so that others' faiths may grow like all of ours have.

Seth is alive and walking (taking steps on his own), talking (his voice truly returned Sunday morning, stronger and lower -- more like his normal voice), eating, drinking, sharing his amazing experiences and faith, laughing, loving. He is himself...only better! And he's getting stronger every day. All glory and praise to our mighty God who works miracles, regardless of what tests show!

Please keep the prayers coming! God isn't done with Seth yet. Praise God, He isn't done with us either! We are BEYOND grateful and can't wait to see the plans God has in store for Seth. Thank you! Thank God!!!! #allforhisglory#sethstrong #beyondourhopesanddreams

Seth's time at Mary Free Bed was all during lent. It was fitting in that we were all asked to sacrifice in a much bigger way than we could have planned for ourselves, especially Seth. But it was also fitting in that we were continually inspired and challenged to grow by Seth's experiences. I remember one night Sarah asking Dave if he wanted to go to a lenten event at church, and Dave's answer was, "I want to go see Seth. He's so inspiring." Our hearts were being touched and changed on a daily basis. Today Seth told us, *"If there's anything you want to do or change about yourself, do it now! Change it NOW. You may not have another chance. If you want to go to heaven, live like it now. This life seems so attractive, but it's not, especially when you've seen the other side, the spiritual world, and experienced God's love. Heaven and hell are so close. They are right here, right now. We just can't see it. When I pray it's different now, because I know God is right here."* He stressed again, *"He is right here!"* When Seth said these things, I was dumbfounded. These statements were coming out of the Seth I raised. The kid who had always been so strongly attracted to everything this life had to offer, probably the most of all our kids. These statements are incredible of themselves but knowing Seth and hearing them come from his lips with such humility, sincerity, and conviction made them even that much more powerful.

It was "transformation Tuesday" on instagram, so that night Seth posted a transformation picture of himself in the ICU side by side with a current picture of himself at Mary Free Bed. The difference was captivating, like he had gone from death to life again. Seth was looking so good. His caption read: *"I owe my life to God and my gratitude to everyone who prayed for me. It's crazy how your whole life can change in an instant. So live today like it's your last and make it good because heaven and hell are real, trust me. So choose today what you are living for because once you die it's too late."* Seth didn't sugar coat it. It was and is a powerful message to live by.

Wednesday, March 22, 2017-

The day started like usual with OT dress. Day by day, Seth was getting more independent with dressing and hygiene. After breakfast, his occupational therapist, Kate, took Seth downstairs to the Biggby coffee shop that is in the front lobby of the hospital. Seth was excited. He used to get Biggby coffee almost every morning. He got the same thing, his favorite, every time he went. Kate pushed Seth's wheelchair up to the counter for Seth to order. At that moment it dawned on Seth that he had no idea what he liked or what he always used to order. That memory was completely gone. It was shocking and very discouraging for Seth to realize that no matter how hard he tried, he couldn't remember something that was such a normal part of his typical morning. It was a strange experience for Seth. He had unexpectedly been hit in the face with his new reality. He no longer knew what was normal for him.

When Seth first arrived at Mary Free Bed, Dr. Ho thought Seth would be there at least ten weeks, with no idea what his outcome would be. Each week on Wednesdays, Dr. Ho and Seth's therapists had a conference meeting to discuss and evaluate Seth's progress and continued therapy plan. Most weeks after the conference, the social worker would give us an update and a prospective discharge date. After today's conference, only three weeks after Seth had arrived at Mary Free Bed, Dr. Ho came in to give us the update himself. We were astounded as Dr. Ho stood there saying, "Seth has completely blown away all of the predictions!" Then he gave us the best news ever, the news we had been waiting for. They were planning to discharge Seth the following week on Thursday, March 30th! Unbelievable!!! The week before they had told us Seth would probably be at Mary Free Bed five to seven more weeks, and suddenly it has been changed to only one! We wanted to shout it from the rooftops. Seth was coming home. He was really coming home! We had just been given information on long term assisted living for Seth, and suddenly he was coming home. We couldn't believe it. We were ecstatic! Dr. Ho went on to explain that Seth would still need outpatient therapy, but that they believed he would be able to walk around our home safely on his own by the time he went home. They didn't expect him to need a wheelchair at all!!

Seth's friends, Nate, Jake, and Hunter, who had been with him the night of his accident, came to visit him again. It was the first time that they were able to have a full conversation with Seth. To our surprise they had video and pictures of Seth laying lifeless and bloodied on the ground right after he fell. Seth was intrigued by them and wanted to have the images for himself. I, on the other hand, did not. The thought of seeing Seth like that made me feel sick inside. I couldn't believe they took pictures of him that way. Eventually, I did look at them. It drove home even more the miracle and gift we were living in the middle of.

The four young guys talked and laughed a lot that night. They talked about God and their faith. They also talked about fun things they wanted to do together with Seth in the summer. Two of the guys were in pilot school, so they talked about taking Seth flying, skateboarding, and other such activities. I could tell that thinking about those things was making Seth quite nervous with all he had been through and was still going through. I don't think anyone but family understood the extent of what Seth had lost and needed to relearn. None of us, not even Chris and I, will ever be able to fully comprehend what this has been like for Seth. But nonetheless, Seth looked forward to the possibility of doing those things again someday.

While it was my prayer that Seth could enjoy a "normal" life again someday, the thought of him doing some of those things terrified me. He wasn't even steady enough to fully walk on his own yet. Personally, I hoped he would give up his "adventuring," climbing on roofs, moving trains, billboards, etc. He was twenty-one years old, and I didn't want to become an overbearing mother, but at that moment I couldn't handle the thought of him doing anything even remotely dangerous again. I couldn't even imagine him walking without someone holding onto him. So as beautiful as it was to listen to the guys talk about the future with so much hopeful anticipation and excitement, it was extremely difficult for me. My heart just couldn't take it. We were still in the middle of it. I began to realize as I listened to the boys talking, that it was not only going to take time for Seth to heal, but it was also going to take time for me to heal from this whole ordeal as well. That night, I held onto and took solace in the promise Seth had already made to Chris and me that he would never climb on roofs again!

Seth continued to have several hours of therapy each day, as well as several visitors each evening. By Friday, Seth was walking to all of his therapy sessions with someone holding his gait belt instead of using the wheelchair. Therapists had expected Seth to plateau at some point, like most patients do, but he never did. He continued to progress at an abnormally fast pace. They had warned us in the beginning about how patients typically plateau. They wanted us to be prepared and not get discouraged when it happened, but it never happened! This was just another sign of the incredible miracle that was unfolding. It was unmistakably obvious that God was in control of Seth's recovery, and we were rejoicing and grateful beyond words.

Latest update on Seth - 3/24

Dr. Ho came in to see Seth today. He is still totally blown away by Seth's progress. While talking to Seth's parents, he was amazed when they told him that Seth is totally back--with his personality and sense of humor completely intact. Of course he knows Seth is doing great, but not knowing Seth prior to the accident, he had no way of knowing exactly how well Seth is really doing and how great Seth's miracle actually is. Every time we talk to the doctor, we learn more about how serious Seth's injury was and how all of his amazing progress is nothing less than a true miracle. Seth's MRI showed brain shearing throughout his brain. Brain shearing is the worst type of brain injury you can sustain. It basically means the brain was shredded. And, in Seth's case, this shredding occurred in multiple places throughout his brain. By all accounts, he "should" have major brain damage. Instead, he's making arrangements to go home in less than a week--with some weakness on his left side and some short term memory issues, but otherwise healthy and amazingly

himself and healed. THIS IS BEYOND EXCELLENT MEDICAL
CARE. IT'S A MIRACLE!

I know we've said it before, but the truth just keeps hitting us over the
head. We are witnessing a miracle and we want to thank you for your
part in it. We are humbled, and awed, and grateful beyond words. Thank
you!!!!

We thank Blessed Pier Giorgio Frassati and Venerable Solanus Casey for
their intercession. We thank our Blessed Mother for her prayers. We
thank our Heavenly Father for His healing power.

Thank you, Lord, for hearing and answering our urgent pleas for help
and healing. We are forever grateful. #allforhisglory
#sethstrong#beyondourhopesanddreams

Saturday, March 25, 2017-

Even though it was the weekend, Seth still had 2
hours of therapy. It was admirable how committed his
therapists were to helping him recover and be ready to go
home. He received countless hours of therapy above the
norm. They seemed excited to work with Seth. It was
remarkable for them and all of us to witness Seth, who
once was considered a "hopeless case," recovering so
miraculously. They all seemed to really love and enjoy
Seth. Two of his PTs, Kelli and Kris, often joked around
with Seth calling him the "big deal." I'm unsure of how
that came about, but Seth didn't argue it. He was
perfectly content with being called the big deal and
added plenty of comments about it himself.

Since Seth was talking and had passed all the
levels of swallowing and eating safely, his speech
therapy sessions became much more focused on attention
and memory. With each passing day, it was getting much

more difficult too. I remember times when Laurie would ask Seth questions that Andrea and I couldn't answer. We would just look at eachother, smile sheepishly, and shrug our shoulders. We thought Seth was doing a great job.

Seth had a great day in physical therapy. He took a long walk to Lacks Cancer Center, which is connected to Mary Free Bed, walked up and down a full flight of stairs, rode the elevator up to the fifth floor, and then walked back to Mary Free Bed without anyone holding on to him!!! Wow! That was truly amazing! It was crazy considering just three weeks ago he couldn't even stand or move his left leg at all.

Even though Seth's memory of his experience with God was fading, he still continued to reveal new things to us. This Saturday he told us that *when he was in the coma he could see a thin veil, like a thin, white plastic that he could move aside. He said that's how he knows that God is right here. He said he couldn't see through it though. He had to move it aside.* He said, *"I've seen how thin that veil is between the physical and spiritual realm and how easily it moves. Heaven and hell are right here."* It was amazing to listen to these things. They weren't the kinds of things that Seth knew or would have talked about before. And there was still an incomprehensible peacefulness about him.

Seth's memories and thoughts still felt jumbled and confused sometimes. But even though Seth still struggled daily with different physical and mental limitations, he accepted it all with gratitude. In fact, this particular day he awed us when he said, *"It's a good thing I jumped first, or I wouldn't have had this experience. More and more I feel like I am growing in appreciation for the whole experience. It has dramatically changed me, maybe saved my soul. It's a blessing in disguise. I've said this, but today and yesterday, I am starting to really see and feel it. I am a changed man. I would never want to go back to the way things were."*

How is a mother supposed to respond to that? I felt blessed beyond all measure. God had answered my prayers and given me my son back in a way far better than anything I could have ever hoped for. I was afraid that Seth may come out of this angry and bitter toward God. It was exactly the opposite. I had my son back so pure, so loving, so filled with God's presence. I was realizing that though Seth still had limitations, God had actually answered the greatest and deepest prayer of my heart for Seth, and all of my children. That is that they know and love God with all their hearts, surrendering their lives completely to Him. That was exactly what I saw in Seth. I don't think there is anything more beautiful that a mother could ask for. I was humbled once again, as I had been many times throughout this journey. While I was still doubting God and worrying about every step, he was blessing me and my son in ways far beyond my limited human comprehension. Our God truly is good!!

It is very difficult to explain all that we had been witnessing and experiencing in and through Seth. Conversations with him were deeply inspiring. So much of the time my heart and spirit were filled with awe and burned within me. Here is another facebook post from Kathy after she had the opportunity to visit with Seth. Reading the actual words she wrote at the time, exemplifies and captures some of the excitement, awe, and gratitude that we felt as we were going through it.

Kathy Barth
March 26 ·
Latest update on Seth - 3/25 (late) or 3/26 (early)
My heart is overflowing! I was blessed with the opportunity to talk to Seth tonight one on one about some of the amazing spiritual experiences he has had since his fall, especially while in his coma, and the impact this "tragedy" has had on his life. What a blessing to listen to him talk about what happened to him as a gift for which he is truly grateful. I know in human terms, that just doesn't make sense. But, when you listen to Seth and you're able to see this all--as he has been able to do--through an eternal and "Godly" lens, then everything takes on a whole different perspective and meaning and you see his fall and healing (both physical and spiritual) not as a tragedy, but as the blessing it has been. This hasn't just been a renewal for Seth, I think it has been a reawakening and renewal for many of us, me included.
Seth can't wait to share his story and true "conversion" with all of you. He really can't wait to get started doing whatever it is God is calling him to do with what he is calling his "second chance" at being the man that God made him and called him to be. You can't help but get excited when you talk to him. I mean, really excited!!! He wants so badly to help and

touch others by sharing all that God has done in his life...I see some new songs and, God willing, lots of talks in his future. He wants to write praise and worship songs to the Lord, songs that will bring people closer to God. He said it's one way he can give back to all of you who've prayed so hard for him and to the Lord for saving and healing him.

Physically, he walked all over the place today, including up and down stairs, without anyone helping him. He can get up and down and sit or stand without assistance. There is no comparison to where he was even a week ago when I first got here this trip. I can't believe his improvement in the last week. God definitely has his recovery on the "fast track."

I really thought that once I got here and could see Seth every day, these updates would get easier to write. But, the opposite has been true. After spending time with him, it's just truly hard to put everything into words. The words that come to mind are words of overwhelming praise and thanksgiving, awe and wonder, and tremendous grace. I am humbled and awestruck by the amazing love and power of our God.

Seth kept telling me, "We all think God's so far away...off somewhere praying. But, He's not! He's right here beside us. If you could only see like He let me see. He's right here. And all it takes is one touch from His hand to heal us. The veil is so thin."

He's right here with us...

Thank you, dear prayer warriors, for your constant prayers, your faith, your love, your sacrifices, your support. May you always know and feel the presence of our amazing God and Savior who is truly "right here with us." To Him be the glory forever. Please keep praying. I can't wait to see where this journey takes Seth and all of us. #allforhisglory #sethstrong#beyondourhopesanddreams

Sunday, March 26, 2017-

Due to Seth's accident, our fourteen-year-old son, Caleb's Confirmation was postponed until this Sunday. At the time that we rescheduled it, we didn't know how Seth would be, but this was the last date we could choose. Once again, God's timing was perfect. We were actually given an off grounds pass with permission to bring Seth to the Confirmation Mass with us.

Seth's OT, Kate, got him showered and ready for the occasion. We took Seth in our car and brought him into the church in a wheelchair. We left the wheelchair in the back of the Cathedral though. Seth sat on a cushion in the pew with us. I can't describe the feeling for me, as a mother, to be in church together for this occasion, when just a few weeks ago we weren't sure if we would ever get Seth back.

Seth was so excited to be in church. He hadn't been to Mass since before his accident. He was so elated to think that God was right there, and that he would be able to receive the body and blood of Christ again. Seth's pure, renewed faith was so evident. He was overjoyed. It's hard to explain, but God had become so personal to Seth that it was like he had gone to church to see his best friend. Seth's spirit was so on fire that as we sat in the pew, he leaned over to me and said, *"I was so close to death. I was about to die, but He saved me. He allowed me to live, but He died. He chose to die. And when He died, He was thinking about you and me. He gave me this incredible miracle, but He gives each of us an incredible miracle every time we go to Mass... Himself, in the Eucharist."*

The Confirmation Masses with the bishop at the Cathedral were typically quite packed. So we sat toward the back of the church. When Communion time came,

Seth walked all the way up to the front of the church with Chris only lightly holding his gait belt, which he had worn under his sweater. He walked slowly, so when the rest of the family and I got back to the pew and knelt down after receiving Communion, we could see Seth walking back down the aisle after receiving Jesus. There are no words for the emotion and gratitude we experienced at that moment. It was a gift beyond words.

Since Mass was during nap time and Michael was Caleb's Confirmation sponsor and had to sit up front with him, Meg wasn't able to be at the Mass. But afterward, we all met at the Pizza Hut near our home. Chris and I, Michael, Meg, Christopher, David, Andrea, Seth, Ethan, Caleb, Mary, and Peter were all there together around one large table. It was a glorious celebration, and to make it even better, Seth got to have pizza for the first time since his accident! It was the one food he had wanted and had been waiting for the most, when he wasn't able to eat. It had been an incredible day, but by the end of dinner, Seth was completely exhausted. I think if he could have laid his head down on the table at the restaurant he would have. We took him back to Mary Free Bed, and he was asleep for the night before 8pm.

Seth described the day as both amazing and terrifying all at the same time. He was so touched to be in Mass and so delighted to receive the Eucharist, but nothing felt normal to him. He was disoriented on roads he had driven on hundreds of times. He loved Grand

Rapids and knew downtown forward and backward. Now it was all very weird to him. He didn't understand it, and he couldn't explain it. He said it wasn't overwhelming, but it also wasn't normal. Everything felt different and uncomfortable to him. In a way, he was anxious to get back to Mary Free Bed. It was disconcerting for him to realize that Mary Free Bed hospital was the only place that felt comfortable and normal to him. Deep down, it scared him that he might never feel "normal" again. He clung to Brian's words that he would look and act normal long before he felt normal. Those words brought him hope because while Seth was looking and acting more and more normal, he most certainly didn't feel it.

Monday, Tuesday, and Wednesday, March 27, 28, and 29, 2017-

The next three days were very busy as therapists worked tirelessly with Seth to have him ready to go home on Thursday. We continued to watch Seth's progress each day. In physical therapy, it was so cool to see Seth casually walking down the halls of Mary Free Bed conversing with his PT, Starr. This may not seem like a big deal, but it was! It was not only huge that he was walking, but also that he was carrying on a conversation at the same time. Just a couple weeks prior, it took every ounce of Seth's concentration just to move a leg or formulate a single word. Yes, walking and conversing so casually at the same time was absolutely amazing! It was another one of those things that we take for granted all the time.

By Tuesday, Seth had aced his balance test, scoring fifty-six out of fifty-six, a perfect score! He was pumped! His athletic drive seemed to be coming out of him. He was determined to pass it after having scored only thirty-six the week before. He also passed his walking test, walking over thirteen hundred feet in six minutes. This was an improvement over the week before when he only made it eight hundred feet in six minutes.

After passing these tests, Seth was switched to independent, meaning that he no longer had to use the gait belt. No one had to hold onto him anymore! The best part was the privacy and dignity he had longed for. He had already gotten to shower himself in a shower chair that morning. It was a little tough. He held the shower head in his left hand while he washed himself with his right. Being that he still didn't have great control of his left hand, he said he sprayed himself in the face quite a few times! Thankfully, Seth was able to find the humor in it. He referred to his left hand as "leftie." Over time he made many jokes about leftie! Spraying himself in the face or not, Seth was exceedingly grateful and happy to finally get some of his independence back.

The most exciting part of this for Seth was the fact that he could finally go to the bathroom on his own. However, in true Seth form, when he used the bathroom, he would joke about how he was lonely in there. He especially loved to tease Andrea, calling for her when he was in the bathroom, saying how much he missed her! We definitely had our goofy Seth back!

Two of Seth's PTs, Kelli and Kris, celebrated Seth's independent status and progress by playing the Jay Bruce Tribute called "The Deal" in honor of Seth being "the Big Deal!" Seth had told Kelli weeks ago that he wanted to run, and he had not let go of that desire. She decided to let him try as long as he used the gait belt. They still needed to be very careful that he did not fall and hit his head. So with very little assistance, on Wednesday morning, the day before he left Mary Free Bed, Seth jogged down the hallway! I think my heart could have exploded with joy and gratitude at that moment.

The celebration continued into Wednesday afternoon as his therapists planned a pizza party for Seth during lunchtime. They wanted to recognize and celebrate all of his accomplishments before he left. They talked about how Seth literally changed every twenty-four hours. They said they didn't even know how to plan for him. They would see him one day and write a plan for him, but then by the next day, he would have already passed it. There was a lot of laughing and joy at Seth's pizza party. It was painful for Chris to have to miss this special lunch, but he had to work in order that he could be off the following day to bring Seth home. Michael and I were blessed to enjoy the party with Seth and the therapists, who I had come to deeply respect, admire, and appreciate. Seth's therapists and nurses and the staff of Mary Free Bed will always hold a special place in my heart.

Throughout those last couple days, everyone signed a "graduation tee shirt" for Seth. For four weeks we had seen those tee shirts hanging outside patients' rooms for the staff to sign as someone was getting ready to be discharged. We always looked at them with excitement and anticipation, hoping one would someday hang outside Seth's room. Finally, it hung there, and it brought us great joy to see it! The therapists and nurses each wrote such encouraging and joyful words on it.

There seemed to be a buzz of excitement around Mary Free Bed about Seth. It was an undeniable fact that Seth was a miracle, and everyone seemed to know it. Simply walking through the halls, I heard random staff members we didn't even know talking about Seth and what a miracle he was. I have never heard so many medical professionals actually using the word, MIRACLE! There was no doubt that God was good, as Seth had written. We knew we were extremely blessed to be bringing our son home alive and well the next day.

Thursday, March 30, 2017-

Six and a half weeks before this day, Seth walked out the front door of our home with a big smile on his face and a heart full of ambition and dreams. By 7pm

257

that same day, we didn't know if we would ever see his smiling face walk through that door again. After six long weeks filled with moments of both triumph and despair, we were finally bringing Seth home with not only that same beautiful smile, but also a new hope and joy that radiated through it. God was good right in the middle of our suffering, blessing us in ways far exceeding anything we could have ever anticipated or imagined. It was more than my mind and heart could even fathom. This was a long-awaited day by every single member of our family. Our family would be whole and home together again. We got the miracle that hundreds, possibly even thousands of people around the world, had prayed so hard for. We got our Seth back!

CHAPTER TWELVE
- HOME AT LAST -
God is Good... in the Peaks and Valleys

For many, the story ends with Seth coming home. It would be nice if I could wrap up the miracle with a nice, neat, pretty bow and end the book here, but that would not be reality. For Seth and our family, it most definitely was not the end. Sometimes I ask myself why I am sharing the nitty gritty details, the continuing peaks and valleys in this story. Well, life is messy. What we felt and experienced was messy. It was both beautiful and broken all rolled into one. We had Seth back! He had a miraculous recovery! So why were we still hurting? In many ways we felt like we shouldn't be, but we were broken and there was much healing still needed in Seth as well as the rest of us. My hope is that sharing the rest of the story will perhaps help other families who are suffering. Every family experiences peaks and valleys, and God remains good in all of them.

We were so excited to finally be bringing Seth home, but we didn't know what to expect. We had no idea of the many peaks and valleys we would still encounter. We didn't even know what to expect for that day, after Seth had been in the hospital for six and a half weeks. I thought just getting Seth packed and home would probably wear him out. Michael and Andrea wondered if they should try to get out of work, so they could be there when Seth came home. I kind of anticipated that he would be completely spent and come home and take a nap. So I told them it would be fine for them to work and just come for dinner. Ethan also was planning to stay at school, and Peter had a field trip that day too. So I thought it would work fine for us to have a family dinner with everyone and celebrate Seth's homecoming later in the day when everyone finished work and school. So that was the plan.

First thing in the morning, Dr. Ho came in to see Seth before discharging him. Dr. Ho asked Seth what his plans were for the future. Seth was a bit taken back by that question. Seth looked at him and said, "I don't know. I was just trying to get through this first." Dr. Ho very definitively said, "Make plans!" He said it so matter of fact as if to say, "You can do whatever you want. You have a great life in front of you. Go live life to the full!" This blew me away. It was so unbelievable that it had all turned out this way. It could have been so much different. And Dr. Ho had reminded us often that according to medical science, it should have turned out way differently. Numerous times over the course of Seth's time at Mary Free Bed, Dr. Ho had walked into Seth's room exclaiming, "You are incredible! Your MRI says you should be dead or severely brain damaged." Similarly, he also repeated, "Somebody up there is making all the decisions and doing everything for us!"

Today was no exception to that, except that he surprised and elated us when he excitedly told Seth to make plans for his future. God is good! I can't say it enough.

Not only was Seth coming home, but he was doing so walking on his own, with no wheelchair, no walker, no equipment at all except to use a shower chair to protect him from falling in the shower. He also still had no pain, not even a single headache. He was even coming home without any medications. It was all so amazing.

At home, we moved Seth's room from our basement into our family room so he wouldn't have to go up and down stairs too much. His therapists still wanted him to hold a rail and have someone near him for a little longer while on the stairs.

That morning, we got word that the faculty, staff and students at St. Thomas School planned to line the streets in front of the school, which was around the corner from our house, to welcome Seth as we drove him home. In the meantime, a local news reporter, Casey Jones, contacted us about possibly covering the story. We didn't really know what was going on, just that we were supposed to drive past the school on our way home.

Seth recorded himself on his phone as he walked out of Mary Free Bed. He felt free! He put his arms out and slowly spun around a little. He realized quickly that his balance wasn't quite what it used to be, and things weren't exactly normal yet. But nonetheless, he was extremely excited to be free and heading home.

It was a gloomy, rainy day, but nothing was going to dim our joy. There are no words to describe our feelings as we left Mary Free Bed and headed home with Seth. My heart was overflowing with joy and gratitude. I literally felt like it was going to burst as we drove past St. Thomas school. It is hard to convey the overwhelming love that I felt from our parish and school community. There were adults and children lining the street in the pouring rain. They were holding soaking wet, dripping #sethstrong signs, shouting and cheering with excitement and joy. Seth rolled down the window and waved at all of them as we passed by. What a celebration! I had not anticipated such an outpouring of love. Casey Jones, the local tv news reporter, was also there capturing the joy and excitement of answered prayers and Seth's long-awaited return home!

Caleb, Mary, Aunt Sarah and some of Seth's cousins were also in the crowd cheering. They ran from there down the street to our house to meet us. Friends had also decorated our front porch with signs and balloons. To our surprise and utter amazement, Seth got out of the car and just naturally, without thinking about it, bounded up the steps of the sidewalk in front of our house just like he had done his whole life. He caught us all, as well as himself, off guard when he did that. He did it naturally and effortlessly without any assistance at all. He had only just started walking on his own, and here he was hopping up the steps like it was nothing. Amazing! Caleb and Mary ran over and greeted him with big hugs.

When Seth entered the house, he slowly went through every room taking in every sight and smell. Seth's sense of smell is closely tied to his memories. I remember him even picking up the throw pillows on the couch to smell them. I had thought Seth would crash, but he didn't. I think he was running on adrenaline because he was so happy to finally be home. In fact, he had so much energy and was so touched by the welcome that the St. Thomas students had given him that he wanted to go to the school and thank them. I had assumed that would happen at a later date, but Seth wanted to do it right then, and he even wanted to walk there. It was two and a half blocks to the school; it was a walk that Seth had taken every day to and from school and every Sunday to Mass throughout his life. What a joy it was to take that walk with him once again. We relished every little thing that we had the opportunity to do with Seth again. It was a true cause for rejoicing after wondering for so long if we would ever again have these moments with him.

At the school, Seth saw many of his old teachers. He hugged them and thanked them for all of their prayers for him. He stopped in many of the classrooms and thanked the students also for their prayers. It was so cool for the kids to see Seth, this guy who they had been praying for continuously over the last six weeks. Teachers handed us stacks of cards that the children had made for Seth. It was all such a blessing. We cannot adequately express our love for the people of St. Thomas parish and school or our gratitude for their love and support for us, through this and throughout the years since we first joined the parish when Seth was only one year old.

After our visit at the school, we stopped in the church to say a prayer. Chris' mom had been struggling with severe sciatica pain at that time. It was so severe that she couldn't even walk. The doctors didn't know what else they could do for her. She had recently called Chris crying, not knowing how much longer she could take it. She asked Chris to please ask Seth to pray for her.

When we were in the church before the Blessed Sacrament, Seth knelt down and prayed very intentionally for his grandma. Before we left the church, Seth told Chris, "Grandma will be fine. Tell Grandma that God's healed her." That was a bold statement. Chris didn't say anything, but in his head he thought, "Really? Could it be true?" But then the doubts came, and he wrestled with his thoughts, thinking, "No, Seth's just on this spiritual high right now. He's naive. He doesn't know how the real-world works." Chris knew deep within him that Seth could possibly be right, and he hoped so, but he certainly was not going to tell his mom that and give her false hope.

It had been a beautiful and very full day, but very sadly, only part of our family got to enjoy it.

Unfortunately, by the time Ethan and Peter got home from school and Andrea, Michael, Meg and their boys got to our house in the late afternoon/evening, Seth was completely exhausted and didn't say much at all. They were all extremely disappointed and actually very upset. It hurt to have missed the beauty of that special moment of Seth's homecoming. They missed it all... his joy, expressions, thoughts... It was a moment we had all prayed so hard for and longed for, much of the time with no assurance that Seth would ever come home again. It was a moment we could never get back, and that was very difficult for them to accept. It was very anticlimactic for them and not the ending they anticipated and needed emotionally after having been at the hospital with Seth for six and a half weeks straight. They had sat at Seth's side for weeks, holding his hand, crying, hurting, vulnerable and scared. This was a celebration they needed to bring the journey to a joyful culmination in which their hearts could begin to heal.

No one really understood all they had been through. Michael and Andrea later commented about how, throughout the whole thing, people didn't ask them how they were. Everyone always asked how Seth was and how Chris and I were. Many didn't realize the immense suffering the siblings had been through, not even me in many ways. I had been too wrapped up in Seth and my own emotions. I felt so bad. Even on such a joyous occasion, we were still riding that emotional rollercoaster of peaks and valleys. Our emotions were all still so raw and bleeding.

In many ways I was responsible for their pain that day. It wasn't intentional, but still it was my plan that caused them to miss out on the excitement and joy of that day. That night, my heart was filled with joy and aching all at the same time. It was my first glimpse of the scars left from this tragedy that would need healing in our family. It was beginning to become evident that we were all going to need some time to process and heal from the events of the past month and a half.

Over the next couple of days, Seth kept asking Chris if he had talked to Grandma yet to tell her that God was healing her. Chris kept putting him off and making excuses saying he hadn't had a chance yet. He really did not want to call his mom and tell her what Seth had said. He was afraid he would be giving her false hope. Seth was pretty insistent though. So a couple days later Chris finally called his mom. When he asked her how she was feeling, she said, "Actually I haven't had any pain for the past few days! It's completely gone!" Chris was completely humbled at that moment. The words from scripture (Mt. 6:30), "... O ye of little faith" went through his head as he thought to himself, "How many miracles is it going to take for me to believe?" Seth had the faith of a child who totally trusted in his Father's goodness. That is the kind of faith we are all called to have.

Being home was strange for Seth. The reality of his life now hit him once he was home. He was home, but everything was extremely different than how it had been when he left the house 6 weeks ago. Seth began to make personal notes on his phone about how he was feeling. This is what he wrote: *"Everything is work. If I want to shave, it's work. If I want to go to the kitchen to grab something, it's work. Even if I want to think about something, it's work. Even the thought of something and remembering something is work. Everything makes me tired and it's so strange to me, but I guess that's a part of recovery."*

Along with that, nothing felt normal to Seth. He couldn't explain it. He remembered the words Brian had spoken to him, "You will look and act normal long before you feel normal." He now understood those words more than ever, and he desperately craved for things to feel like they used to. He hated the way he felt. Even walking outside where he had walked a million times before felt different. Everything was bigger, clearer... He didn't know, just somehow everything was a little off, actually
a lot off. He clung to Brian's words with the hope that one day things would feel normal to him again. This is what Seth had written about it: *"I see things here at home and it looks and feels different, but I know it's the same. It's a weird feeling, completely crazy, but I know it's going to feel normal again. Everything outside... it's just everything's bigger. There's more space.*

I walk room to room, and in each room I can really feel the difference. Words can't explain how I feel. I look at things that I've seen 1000 times, but I see it so different, in a good way and in a weird kind of feeling. But I know it's what it was and I know it's going to get back to that same feeling of what it was. I just have to have faith in God and trust him." None of us knew why everything felt different to Seth. We all took comfort in what Brian had told Seth, trying to encourage him and holding on to hope that things would eventually feel normal for Seth again.

Being able to attend mass together at St. Thomas again was a great blessing. People were so excited to see Seth there. Seth felt a little uncomfortable, like everyone was watching him, but he handled it with grace. He was deeply grateful for all of their prayers for him. So many of them had been praying for Seth, even those who didn't know him. Seth being there was an answer to their prayers. Many of them had followed the updates every day on Facebook and had poured their hearts and souls into praying for him, knowing that the outcome looked bleak. Seth was a walking miracle, a reminder to everyone that miracles still happen. His presence had become a beacon of light and hope. To all of us, he was a living witness to the power of prayer and the goodness of God! When we were in mass together, I was filled with immense joy, and I was overwhelmingly grateful not only for Seth's life but also for the incredible love and faithfulness of our parish community.

Seth began outpatient therapy right away the week after he came home. Even though it was still at Mary Free Bed, his therapists were all different from the ones he had as an inpatient. Being new in the outpatient department, his first day consisted of four hours of evaluations, meeting with the physical therapist, occupational therapist, speech therapist, psychologist, and nurse. They decided he would have therapy two days a week for four hours each time. It was scheduled for Mondays and Wednesdays from 1-5pm.

Wednesday, April 5th, was a day that Seth had been waiting anxiously for. It was the day he was finally going to have his feeding tube removed. Even though Seth had been eating regular foods for quite a while at this point, the feeding tube could not be removed any sooner than six weeks after being put in. Seth hated that food tube. It was very uncomfortable. It always had to be taped to his abdomen so that it would stay tucked up under his shirt. It stuck out and got caught when he tried to roll over in bed. It made it impossible for him to sleep on his stomach, and it got in the way and was embarrassing to him if he wanted to hug someone tight. It also hurt when pressure was put on it. Since it was no longer being used, it had to be flushed out every night with water to keep it clean. Seth's nurse taught me how to do it before we left the hospital.

Seth wanted it out so badly that he had begged Dr. Ho to take it out before he left Mary Free Bed. To Seth's dismay, Dr. Ho's answer was "no." In one last desperate attempt, Seth sweet talked one of his nurses into asking Dr. Ho about it again. She agreed to advocate for Seth even though she knew the answer would be no. It was a week too soon, and apparently removing a feeding tube too early, can be extremely dangerous, even fatal. So Seth had to resign himself to waiting about a week longer until April 5th.

That morning, Seth was extremely excited! Here are Seth's personal notes from that day: *"Today's the day. The day I'm getting my food tube out finally. I've been able to eat regular food. I'm back to the solid McDonald's diet, but they're required to wait six weeks from the time that they put it in to the time that they take it out, because they found if they take it out before then there's complications and problems.*

I'm just so excited to get it out finally. And I'm just excited to lay on my bed, stomach down or lay on my back and put my laptop on my stomach when I'm watching something. And if someone's really excited because they haven't seen me in a while, they can come and squeeze me real tight without putting a lot of pressure on it. Or even tossing and turning at night, I won't have to be careful so my tube doesn't get caught on anything or pull my skin. It just hurts, so I'm excited."

I took Seth to Dr. Ho's office to get the feeding tube removed. We didn't know exactly how he would remove it or what to expect. It turned out that there was no fancy medical procedure. Dr. Ho just simply had to pull it out. Only it wasn't that simple. The end of the tube which was inside Seth's stomach was about the diameter of a quarter while the tube itself and the opening through Seth's abdomen was only about the size of a straw. As Dr. Ho yanked, there was so much pressure and pain that it literally took Seth's breath away. With my heart in my throat, I waited for Seth to take a breath. It took a bit for him to catch his breath and then calm his breathing down afterward. He was so thankful though to have that over with and the feeding tube finally out!

Within a week of Seth being home, Casey Jones, the TV8 reporter, was back at our home to interview us. He spent two and a half hours one night interviewing Chris and I first and then Seth's siblings as a group. I was so nervous. I have never been comfortable talking in front of people, much less a camera. I had to try to forget about the camera and try to think of it as just a conversation with Casey about Seth's accident and all that God had done for him and our family. At first it was pretty uncomfortable and nerve wracking, but it got easier as it went on. Anyone who knows me well, knows that I love talking one on one with people, especially about my faith and my family. The whole purpose for Casey doing this story was to proclaim the glory of God and the power of prayer. How amazing is that on a secular TV station!

It was interesting for Seth to sit there and listen to Chris and me and all his siblings talk about him for hours. In some ways it was very upbuilding. It made him feel so good to hear each of us talking about how much we loved him and how scared we were of losing him. It was for him another realization of just how loved he was. However, in other ways, it made Seth feel a little uneasy, almost left out. It was like we had all gone through something without him, something that he was asleep for most of. I remember while he was in the ICU feeling, at times, like we were going through a family tragedy without him, even though he was the one laying there in a coma fighting for his life. It was a strange feeling. I just remember missing him so much and wanting to talk to him so badly about all of it.

Being able to share our experience with Seth while doing the interview with Casey was really nice for our family, but definitely a bit unsettling for Seth. It was difficult for him to hear over and over how much we had all gone through and sacrificed for him. Sometimes it made Seth feel really bad, as if we had given so much, and all he did was take. We knew, though, that wasn't true. None of us felt that way. We knew that had the tables been turned, Seth would have given everything for us too. In fact, we all knew that Seth had been through much greater suffering and that everything he did took incredible work, love, and sacrifice on his part. Still, it was hard for Seth to accept. We shared an experience that he will never fully understand. Likewise, his experience going through it all is something we will never fully understand. That's just how it is and has to be. We each walked the road God set before us, and Chris and I couldn't be prouder of how each of our children went through it with their own unique peaks and valleys. We have been truly blessed by each one of them. God is good!

Casey came back a second day to interview Seth. I was really worried about how it was going to go, because Seth was having a particularly tough day that day. He hated the weird feeling he had and was sick of it. He just wanted to feel the way he always used to. On this day he was done dealing with it and felt like he just couldn't do it anymore. He had lost his excitement for doing the interview. He wasn't feeling good or positive about any of it at this point. His memories of the spiritual were fading more and more, and he just didn't want to do it.

I didn't blame Seth for being discouraged. It was certainly understandable, but something about this felt like spiritual warfare. Afterall, the evil one does not want a message like Seth's to get out. We reached out to our extended family members and friends, asking them all to please pray for Seth as he did this interview.

Knowing how he felt that day, I was very nervous. It was hard for me to relax during his interview. Part of me wanted to jump in and help him remember things, but I held myself back. Honestly, there were so many amazing things that Seth had told us about his spiritual experience and so many miraculous things that happened along the way, that even if I tried to remind him, I fumbled over my words and forgot most of it. I should have known that I wasn't supposed to say anything and trust that God would work through Seth.

Seth did a beautiful job with the interview. It was amazing to watch the grace of God abound in him as his peace and gratitude returned even in the midst of a very tough day. God was obviously good even in the valley. Seth's answers were heartfelt and sincere. Casey noticed that his gratitude for those who helped him and his love for God emanated from every word he spoke. He was so vulnerable and genuine as he spoke, *"Seth before the accident was always looking out for himself, was shallow. You couldn't have a heart to heart and really talk about the faith. Now, I want to talk about the faith. I want to become closer to God."* He shared how his priorities had changed, explaining that *his self-worth used to be based on how many likes he got on social media, but that now it was in being a son of God.*

Seth was very grateful that I had written down all the things he had told us when he came out of the coma and could finally talk. Sharing those things with him helped him to remember. Seth tried to explain to Casey what it was like for him when we read his own quotes back to him. He said, *"It's crazy even for me, even hearing that back. Like, wow, I said that to them. But in*

274

some ways, it's kind of weird because they'll say it and it almost brings it back. It's a memory. It happened. I can't explain it. It's amazing." Although Seth's specific memories about the spiritual were fading, his faith and the ways in which the experience had changed him were dramatically clear.

At one point in the interview, Casey asked Seth if he would ever like to change what happened the night of the accident. With no pause whatsoever, Seth answered immediately, *"No. Because the way that God's blessed me, through this whole thing, experiences, and just the person that I am now, I don't think I would've changed like that and this quickly. It is hard going through some of this stuff, it is. There's no other way to put it. But it's God's will, and that's what I try to remind myself. I'd rather be doing His will than my own."* God's grace was so abundant and visible in Seth, considering this was his response on what had been a tough day for Seth, a day in which he felt like giving up. Wow!

Seth continually blew us away. This was the prayer he wrote in his personal notes that evening after the interview:

"Hold me, direct me,

Help people see you straight through me,

You found me,

You saved me,

All the ways I didn't see,

You brought me to the man I'm meant to be."

What a day it had been. It went from discouragement and despair to hope and once again complete trust, at least for Seth. I, on the other hand, still felt a little uneasy inside even though the interview had gone very well. There was so much to the story, that we couldn't possibly put into words all that Seth had said and shared with us since he had awakened from the coma. I couldn't help feeling like so much got missed, and I hoped that the right things had been shared. "...O ye of little faith!" (Mt.6:30)

The news story was set to air a week later on Good Friday, just two days before Easter. Casey was able to get
a half hour spot, and the TV Station agreed to take out all the paid commercials so there would be more time for the story. This is virtually unheard of with news stories, especially considering it was a story giving glory to God! It was another miraculous sign of God's hand and providence in all of it.

Good Friday is a special day for us as Catholics, commemorating the passion and death of Jesus. It is also a day that my sister, Kathy and I started what has become a very special tradition. For years, each year on Good Friday, Kathy and I and our husbands and children met at the cemetery to pray the Stations of the Cross. We always gathered at the cemetery where Chris' and my four babies were buried. The kids would run through the

276

cemetery finding new graves from within the past year, and then we would stop and pray a station there. After each station, we prayed for the repose of the soul of the newly deceased person buried there and left a flower by their grave. We would do that for each station, ending up at the giant crucifix at the top of the hill for the twelfth Station - Jesus Dies on the Cross. Then we always ended by celebrating the Resurrection at the graves of our four babies, because as baptized infants, we knew they went straight to heaven. Our living children would place flowers at the graves of their siblings. Kathy and Keith had also experienced loss. Their first and oldest son had died unexpectedly at only fourteen months old. Although he was buried in Wisconsin, we celebrated his life and resurrection with Christ as well.

This has become a very treasured tradition for us, and since our Mom's passing in 2009, our Dad and our other siblings, Dave and Sarah, Mike and Mary, and their children have joined us as well. Our mom is buried at the same cemetery on the hill overlooking our babies' graves. Each year since 2009, we have also prayed at her grave and then lined it with her favorite flower, yellow roses.

This particular year, 2017, was extremely emotional for all of us. We were all acutely aware of the fact that we could have very well been going to Seth's grave that Good Friday. Instead, only two weeks out of the hospital, Seth was there with us, alive and well, walking all through the cemetery, praying the Stations of the Cross with us. Things could have been so different, and believe me, we all knew it. It was a constant battle to fight back the tears. No words could express the joy and gratitude we felt to still have Seth there with us.

That night we gathered with our whole family and some of our extended family, as well as Tyler and his mom, to watch the news story. We were both excited and nervous at the same time, since we weren't sure how it had been put together and would turn out. Casey literally had hours of footage to sift through and somehow put together into a cohesive and succinct story, while also making sure it gave a clear and strong message of God's love and power. I couldn't have done it. Just the thought of it overwhelmed me.

Casey did an amazing job of portraying who Seth was, what he had been through, how miraculous his recovery was, the power of prayer, the immense love of God, and the change it produced in Seth. It was powerful. And it was so well received that TV8 played it over again on Easter Sunday.

After watching the news story, I realized that Seth had said exactly what needed to be said. It was honestly perfect, and God used his words to touch the lives of so many people. Sometimes I wonder when I will ever learn to stop worrying and trust God. It was beautiful to see how the Lord helped Seth remember the parts of the experience that He wanted him to. It was just as Fr. Jim had said, "Surrender it to Him and trust that He will give it back to you when you need it." God is good. He can turn our valleys into peaks if we let go and trust Him.

An interesting thing happened after the news story aired. A man we didn't know reached out to my sister, Kathy through facebook. He heard about "Aunt Kathy" and found her facebook after he saw the news story. The news TV8 story was an answer to his prayers. He told Kathy that he had been praying for an unnamed young man since February 13th. He had been worried sick about this young guy but had no way of knowing if he was dead or alive. You see, he was the owner of the building that Seth had fallen through. Since February 13th, he had carried a deep hurt knowing someone had been seriously injured at his business. However, because of privacy laws, the police could not give him Seth's name. He had been praying for this young guy but never knew how he was until he happened to see the news story on TV. He contacted Kathy, relieved and grateful to see on the news that Seth was not only okay, but better yet, had been touched by God through the ordeal.

Over the next week or so, Seth continued to improve in many ways. In therapy he began doing more normal exercises like push-ups and swimming. Seth had been a lifeguard in highschool, so it was amazing to see him swim underwater, freestyle, and other strokes like he used to. It was also a huge comfort to me to know he would be safe in the water with summer coming right around the corner.

Seth's drive and determination kicked into high gear challenging himself each day. It was cool to watch him progress from barely being able to do a push up to doing up to twenty in a row in about a week's time. Besides being a former lifeguard, Seth was also a certified personal trainer. So pushing himself this way was normal for him before. At this point, being normal again was what Seth desired. He was pumped with every new accomplishment.

Seth also began having days with a little more energy. This was exciting to Seth. It had been terribly hard and upsetting for him to be tired and worn out so much of the time. So every bit of strength and energy he got back was encouraging and exciting. One night Seth and Tyler went to Steak & Shake at 11pm, and Seth hadn't even napped at all that day. These types of things may seem insignificant, but they were actually monumental for Seth. Having a brain injury, being through everything he had been through, and having everything look and feel so different, every little step toward being and feeling like his old self was incredibly significant for Seth. Every little step forward was a victory for him and a joy for us to see him returning to his normal life.

Seth had both good and bad days, days in which he felt positive and accomplished and days in which he felt negative and defeated. One of the first things Seth wanted to do when he got home from the hospital was go to the mall to get a new pair of black jeans like the ones the doctors had to cut off him the night of his accident. Andrea and Seth both loved shopping, so she took Seth to the mall. Seth learned very quickly that the mall was no longer what it used to be for him. He was exhausted simply walking through the mall, and everything felt weird and overwhelming to him. There continued to be constant ups and downs, but God is good in both the peaks and the valleys.

CHAPTER THIRTEEN
- A NEW NORMAL -
God is Good... in the Unknown

As Seth was trying to return to normal life, he was also trying to process his spiritual experience and what it meant for his life moving forward. It was hard because the further he got from it, the less he felt God's presence with him. In some ways he sort of felt abandoned by God. It was hard for him to accept that while on this earth he would not experience God in the same way that he had in the coma.

Seth decided to start meeting with Fr. Jim for spiritual direction about every other week. Each time he met with Fr. Jim, it would rejuvenate his spirit. After the first meeting, Seth came home saying, *"I don't care as much about walking and all the stuff here. My goal is to get to Heaven. What God has waiting for us is so much better than anything here."*

Seth also began going to a Catholic young adult group, which was very good for him. He said that the more he was in groups like that and environments where he could talk about and share his experience, the more real it became to him and the more he was able to feel it again.

By Sunday, April 23, 2017, three and a half weeks after returning home, everything finally looked and felt normal to Seth again! This was what Seth had been waiting for. We never knew exactly why everything had felt so different to him. The thought, as explained by one of his outpatient therapists, was that it had to do with how his brain was processing things. When we walk into a room or any space, our brains automatically filter out what we don't need and focus on what is of importance to us in that moment. For Seth, his brain wasn't filtering anything out. It was seeing and trying to process everything all at once. They also thought it may have had something to do with the processing speed too. So if Seth was in a new place he had never been before, things felt normal because he had nothing to compare it to. However, when he was in a familiar place, his brain was processing everything differently and much more slowly than he was used to, so everything felt different. It made sense, but it had been very hard for Seth to live with, and he was extremely happy to have that part of the recovery behind him. It was another hurdle jumped, another aspect healed!

Seth's outpatient therapists noted that Seth continued to heal at "about ninety miles per hour." Outpatient therapy continued into May, and as one thing healed, it seemed that another hurdle would present itself. There was just so much more to a brain injury than we had ever realized. It is so different from any other type of injury, because the brain not only affects every part of the body, but it affects a person mentally and emotionally as well. The brain literally controls everything, even the way you feel and experience things. And the hard part was that not everything Seth experienced could be explained. For instance, Seth would smile and laugh when he was upset, and he had no idea why. Some things, like that and the weird feeling he had, just took time and lots of patience.

The new problem Seth began experiencing at this point was random tremors. For no apparent reason, his left arm would twitch and shake. It started with just his left arm at random times. Then his head began twitching at other times. His outpatient recreational therapist thought it almost seemed like seizures of some sort, but the doctors never mentioned that and Seth never had any seizures at all while he was monitored in the ICU. In the back of my head, the thought that Seth may be having seizures scared me. I didn't even want to entertain the idea of that possibility.

In May, Seth also started having what we called "weird episodes" for lack of a better name. They seemed sort of like panic attacks, but Seth didn't actually feel anxious about anything. These odd things began happening cyclically about every four to five weeks. That too, was a mystery.

On top of these new physical difficulties, Seth was still dealing with the old ones. Life was definitely not normal for him yet by any means. While getting better, everything still took a lot of effort. Take eating for example. Seth couldn't just eat carefree like he used to. In fact, he was scared to eat if he was alone. It had been so strongly emphasized for so long that he needed to be careful, or he could choke. His confidence in himself and his abilities suffered greatly. He no longer felt confident in what he could or couldn't do. In the past, Seth had no fear and total confidence when it came to his physical abilities. Athletically he could watch just about anything on YouTube and then go out and do it naturally and successfully, with very little effort. But at this point, Seth was very unsure of his abilities, and he was not used to that. His first attempt at skateboarding after the accident was him standing on the skateboard while his friend, Tyler, held his hands and walked with him. That is definitely not how that would have been before. Understandably, Seth approached everything very differently than before. None of this was his normal, and that was hard for him to accept.

On Mother's Day, we had a picnic at the park with the family. We played frisbee and croquet, figuring they wouldn't be too difficult for Seth. While we were all so happy and grateful to be there together, for Seth it was depressing. Even those activities were a challenge, and he approached them with tremendous uncertainty. While we were celebrating having him back, he was grieving all that he had lost. To him, so much of himself was not back. He said it was hard waking up every day not knowing who he was or what his capabilities were. He just didn't feel like himself. He no longer knew what normal was for him.

While Mother's Day was a joyful and fun day of celebration with Seth home and our whole family together, it was also a sorrowful day, realizing Seth's continual pain and grief. It was eye opening for me in a couple ways. It reminded me that while he was physically getting stronger every day, he still had quite a way to go. And it also gave me a glimpse into the emotional battle he was beginning to encounter. There were many hardships that Seth had to deal with that others weren't aware of. These were more ways that Brian's words, "You will look and act normal, long before you feel normal," continued to ring true for Seth.

He worked very hard to try to get back to what he used to be physically. He would go out running late at night so no one would see him, since his coordination was still lacking. He felt awkward and feared that he looked awkward too. Running even a block was a challenge. Usually before the end of the block, he was gasping for air. He didn't tell us that. He just pushed through it. Seth may have lost a lot, but he definitely didn't lose his determination and hard work ethic. He was determined to get back to what he once was.

Seth continued to grapple with the spiritual as well. He continued to meet with Fr. Jim and frequented the sacraments, going to Mass and the sacrament of reconciliation often. But his absence of feeling God was disheartening for him. It was another loss, and the feeling of abandonment was overwhelming him.

Along with this, Seth was also beginning to experience spiritual warfare. Seth had met up with a friend who was no longer living out his Catholic faith. While they were together, Seth felt a very heavy spiritual attack. He felt overwhelming despair and extremely alone and abandoned. Seth was very bothered by this and didn't understand what it was. But as God's timing is always perfect, Seth's next meeting with Fr. Jim was scheduled that same week.

Seth told Fr. Jim what had happened. Fr. Jim explained that Seth may have been feeling the attack that his friend's soul was under. Fr. Jim was not surprised by it at all. He explained to Seth that when God allows someone to experience the spiritual realm, they often also experience some of the evil side as well.

Over the next few days, Seth experienced more spiritual attack. One night while lying on his bed in our family room, Seth felt satan right over him. It was a very frightening sensation. He had a very strong sense of satan's presence right over him. Chris and I prayed over Seth, rebuking satan in the name of Jesus and calling on the Holy Spirit. Unable to shake the feeling he had and the fear it produced in him, Seth later went to Michael and Meg's house to talk to them about it. Having been a part of NET (National Evangelization Team) Ministries, they had some experience dealing with that kind of thing.

They talked for a while and eventually ended up praying with and over Seth too. It was such an extraordinary blessing for Seth to have not only Fr. Jim, but also family members he could talk to and pray with about this.

We tried to help nourish Seth's spirit and keep his incredible spiritual experience alive the best we could. We had a beautiful visit with a young woman who had an unbelievable amount of suffering in her own life. Her story was heartbreaking, and unlike Seth, she had not been healed. She lived with tremendous pain and a very poor prognosis. However, her faith and complete surrender to Christ was absolutely amazing. While Chris and I were uplifted and inspired by meeting her, Seth was left uneasy, almost as if he was feeling guilty or afraid of what more God might ask of him. We weren't sure. He wasn't sure. He was just struggling, and he felt like no matter how much he prayed, he just kept getting further from Christ. He was getting further and further from the spiritual realm, and that was hard to deal with. He no longer experienced the same overwhelming peace and grace, which had gotten him through everything thus far.

It seemed to me that there was a part of Seth that wished he could just go back to the way things were, his "normal" life. It would have been easier, so I kind of understood that, but at the same time, I didn't. I just couldn't dismiss the incredible spiritual gift he had been given. I saw an undeniable change in Seth and the grace of God so strong in him, and I felt like he had a higher purpose for his life now.

Someone from church had told me that when she looked at Seth, she felt like she was looking at Christ. Chris and I thought that was beautiful, not because we thought Seth was Christ or was perfect or anything like that, but rather because he had been with Christ and experienced Him in a profound way, unlike any we had ever known. Chris felt very strongly when he was praying in Mass that Seth was called to be a mirror of Christ. All of this, however, put a lot of pressure on Seth. I know now that I, myself, put a lot of pressure on him too without even realizing it at the time.

There was just so much we didn't know and didn't understand. We had seen God so vibrantly in Seth, but the reality was that he was called back to the physical realm and with that came all the natural, human temptations, sins, doubts and struggles that we all have. So while we were all still looking at Seth with such high esteem, he was seeing all of his weaknesses and failures. On top of that, he felt abandoned by God since he could no longer feel God with him in the same way. Add to that the fact that he was dealing with a brain injury, which changed many of the parts of himself that he had loved the most and had put his identity in. He was in an exceedingly difficult position. His life had come to a screeching halt and been changed in a single instant the moment he fell through that roof on February 13th.

Nothing was normal to him anymore, and he didn't know if it ever would be. He had to continually trust that God was good even in the unknown.

Seth had also become more aware of and self-conscious about his deficits. From the moment he had woken up, every move he made had been analyzed by us, as well as every doctor, nurse, and therapist. And things got even more nit-picky and specific in outpatient therapy. Some of the things they asked him to do were quite difficult. I often sat there thinking, "Gosh, if I ever had to go through this, I'd be in trouble!" At home we would even try some of the things he had to do and couldn't do them successfully. Mary-Kate specifically kept trying one of the practice exercises he had to do and failed it over and over again. Along with the difficulty of the tasks, it was becoming increasingly disturbing with each passing day for Seth to have people looking at him, watching him, analyzing him physically, mentally, emotionally, and spiritually. Sometimes he felt like they were all looking at him like some kind of freak show, "the guy with the brain injury." We tried to reassure him that many people were actually looking at him in amazement rather than criticism, but that was hard for him to see because he looked at himself quite critically.

Even with all of this going on in Seth's mind and heart, he never relaxed in his recovery. He continually pushed himself to get better and better. It paid off, because by May 24th, within two months of leaving the hospital, Seth had his last day of outpatient therapy. When Seth first came home from Mary Free Bed inpatient, his goal was to be completely done with all therapy by June. Seth loved summer and wanted the opportunity to enjoy it fully. Once again, by the grace of God, Seth had met his goal! And not only that, he had also nailed all of his tests and evaluations that were necessary for him to be allowed to drive again. They said he did better on parts of it than practically anyone they had ever evaluated! However, that being said, we still weren't sure if he would be allowed to drive yet or not. Typically, people have to wait six months to drive after a traumatic brain injury. The therapists were going to pass Seth's scores on to Dr. Ho. Ultimately, it would be up to him. Still, this was huge for Seth to have completed all the evaluations so successfully and to also be finishing therapy.

The last day of therapy was a very emotional day for Seth. He wanted to celebrate it. To him it was another huge victory, but his therapists treated it like any other day, using every last second to do therapy. His final session was speech therapy, which by this point felt like schoolwork for Seth. Anyone who knows Seth well, knows that he never liked schoolwork. So this particular day Seth became very frustrated and impatient with it. He was tired of having everything he did picked apart or looked at through a microscope and critiqued. On this last day, he figured, "What's the point? I'm done. Why are we still doing this?"

While in therapy, he sort of lost his patience with the therapist. This had never happened before. The therapist didn't think much of it. She said, "Nobody likes coming to therapy." But it was an odd feeling for Seth and me. Right after the accident, Seth was full of peace. He was gentle, super polite, kind, and considerate of others. But the further Seth got from the spiritual experience, the more he became himself again. This is completely normal and should have been expected. After all, he was only human just like the rest of us. However, it was hard for Seth and for all of us. I mean, don't we all love and desire to be our best self? That was what we had been privileged to see in Seth, and it was hard to let that go... that innocence and purity from having just been in the presence of God had been truly beautiful to experience.

Seth felt bad and confused by his reaction. I did too, but the reality was that Seth was human. Before he left therapy, he apologized to his therapist for having been frustrated and impatient. I tried to reassure Seth that the experience with God wasn't going to make him perfect, and that we shouldn't expect him to be perfect and neither should he. I told him, however, that it was still very obvious that the spiritual experience had really changed him. It was evident in how he recognized his mistake and had the humility to apologize right away. It takes a big person to do that and it showed a lot of growth in Seth. Chris remembers Seth saying, "I feel bad. I feel like all I do is apologize now." While Seth felt bad about that, Chris was extremely proud of Seth. He thought to himself, "How beautiful is that! It takes tremendous humility and strength to apologize." We saw such beauty in Seth that he didn't always see. It was all a lot to process and seemed to still be a constant rollercoaster ride of ups and downs. While we were rejoicing over the completion of his therapy, we were also dealing with the emotional and spiritual aspects of Seth's accident.

Spiritually, it had become very confusing for Seth. He told me one day, "It feels like it's all downhill from here. I will never feel like I did in the presence of God. I will never feel as close or be as close to Him again until I die. So it just feels like there's only down to go, and that I might just get further and further away from Him." I tried to tell Seth that his relationship with God was not based on a feeling, but I have to imagine that it must be really hard to understand and accept once you've actually felt what it's like to be in the presence of God! None of us could fully understand what that was like for him.

Seth, like most of us, has always been very driven by feelings, and whenever he had talked about his spiritual experience, it was obvious that what made the biggest impression on him was how it felt. Truthfully, it was very difficult for me to help Seth figure all of this out. I didn't know how to direct him. None of us had ever been through a near death experience before. It broke my heart to see his suffering through this, yet I didn't know what to do. I would become very uptight and couldn't figure out what God was doing with him. I always wondered why God didn't allow Seth to hold onto those memories and feelings even just a little.

I would at times become very anxious trying to figure out and control it rather than trusting God and letting Him be in control. When I would pray and seek God's direction, the answer was simple. He kept telling me to simply seek Him, and that if I continually grow closer in relationship with Him, He would lead us. Sounds simple, but I struggled to surrender because I like to have things figured out. I most certainly did not have this figured out. We had to trust God as we continued to ride that emotional rollercoaster of ups and downs. We had to hold onto the truth that God is good even in the unknown.

Not only did I have to let go and trust God, but I also had to let go and trust Seth to be out on his own again, because on May 30th he received a call from Dr. Ho's office, removing all of his driving restrictions!!! God is good! I remember Seth sitting on the edge of his bed after he got off the call. He looked as if he could cry. His goal was to be completely done with therapy and able to drive by June. He got both! He would have his summer. He was overcome with gratitude. He recalled how many times he had wanted something and received it. He said, "At first all I wanted was to be able to talk, then it was a drink of water, then to walk..." The list went on, and in that moment, Seth knew how incredibly blessed he was. He began to recognize that the more he got back, the more he wanted. He didn't like that pattern. He wanted to make sure he didn't ever take these gifts for granted.

One of the Catholic schools in our diocese had asked Seth and Chris and I if we would come talk to their eighth-grade class before graduating and heading off to high school. They thought it would be great for the students to see and talk to Seth after having prayed so much for him. We agreed to do it, and it was set for the end of May.

I was pretty nervous about it because I didn't like to talk in front of people. Chris would have been fine with it. He has no problem talking to groups. Unfortunately though, he wasn't able to take the time off work. I figured it would be okay though, because I was just there to support Seth. He was the one they wanted to hear from. However, as the day approached, I got more and more uptight. I worried that Seth wasn't prepared and wouldn't remember things when they asked him questions. His short-term memory had been significantly affected by the brain injury and the spiritual experience was becoming increasingly dull in his mind with each passing day.

The morning we were supposed to go, I began reading from the journal I had kept at Mary Free Bed, hoping that would help jog Seth's memory. As I was reading, Seth said something like, "Those are some really inspirational things someone wrote." I responded saying, "These are all things you said." Seth became very upset and said, "I don't remember any of that." At that point, I was panicking. I wondered how we were possibly going to do this. I questioned, "How can he go talk to a group of kids when he doesn't remember any of it?" I sincerely hoped that Fr. Jim was right, that God would give the memory back when Seth needed it and give him the words to say to these kids. We had to go, putting total trust in God.

When we got there, Seth was very personable and comfortable with the students. He has a great way of relating to them. We began by showing the TV8 news story. This gave them some of the details of his accident and recovery, and then after they were able to ask questions. As I listened to Seth answer their questions, I was completely awed and humbled... again. When was I ever going to learn to stop worrying and trust God? He gave Seth all the memories and all the words he needed.

In fact, Seth's memories were even more vivid, and he began describing things in more detail than he had before. Remember how he had said that *in an instant he saw all the times he could have chosen God and whether he did or didn't and how he felt the weight of his own sin*? Well, this time he began describing that in more detail. He described **standing in judgment line.** He told them, *"It was a longer line than the human can even imagine, that it didn't even make sense how long the line was, like thousands waiting for judgment."* He went on to say, *"Souls were being judged so quickly, like the snapping of a finger. The judgment line moved so fast. God didn't need time to deliberate. He already knew by how people had lived their lives."* I was shocked. Seth had never described that before. Later when I asked Seth about it, he said that he remembered it all so clearly while he was talking to the students. It was amazing and miraculous to see how Fr. Jim's words rang true and how the Holy Spirit worked in and through Seth.

While we were there with the eighth graders, Seth also described **Jesus' hair as being wet and bloodied when he was crying over the injured ball player.** He had never described what he looked like before. When Seth described Jesus this way, it made me think of how Jesus had sweat blood in the garden of Gethsemane. A few days later while I was doing laundry, I was thinking of Seth's description of Jesus crying and praying for the injured player. Seth had told us many times that *Jesus cries over us in the same way when we are suffering.* He would say, *"Jesus doesn't want us to hurt. He cries with us for our pain."*

As I was mulling this over in my head, I suddenly recalled a homily I had just recently listened to online. In the homily, Fr. Mike Schmitz said, "If we asked Jesus what He was thinking about in the garden of Gethsemane, He would answer, 'You.' He sweats blood for us. That's how much he loves us!" In that moment, I was blown away as I realized that Seth actually saw that! He saw exactly what Fr. Mike Schmitz described. Wow! Unbelievable. It was all so unfathomable, yet God continually gave us confirmation for the things Seth was saying.

The time we spent with the students at St. Paul was very blessed and eye opening. It was amazing and humbling to continually witness God at work. He is so good even in the unknown, and yet I constantly doubt and try to take control of things.

Looking back, I can see how God had been in control since day one. God had shown me countless times that Seth's accident was so much bigger than just Seth or me. Yes, God had used it to change the course of Seth's life, but there was so much more to it. It was clear to see that God wanted to use it to change the lives of numerous people, and He already had been all along. I could hardly talk to a person without them being in tears. Hearts were being touched, and it appeared now that hearts could continue to be touched through Seth sharing his experience. God had done that day exactly what Fr. Jim had said. He allowed Seth to remember what he needed, when he needed it, and no sooner. Seth was being asked to walk a profound road of total surrender and trust in God. I was so proud of Seth and so amazed by his faith and willingness to go when he couldn't even remember anything that morning and what he was going to say was completely unknown.

As Seth continued to heal and began driving and hanging out with friends more, his desire to get back to what he once was went beyond just his physical abilities. Seth was still struggling spiritually and emotionally as well. Fr. Jim had told him in the hospital that he had been given a rare opportunity to reinvent himself. Seth wrestled between the changed man he had become in Christ, and the confident, cool, full-of-life twenty-one-year-old he used to be. He didn't necessarily want to reinvent himself. He just wanted to be himself again, minus the sins he was caught up in of course.

I truthfully can't imagine going through all that Seth did. I would not want to be in the position that he was at this point. It was confusing. He had muddy waters to navigate through. It's hard to explain, but as I've said many times before, a brain injury makes everything so different. It's not the same as healing from another type of injury. Even for me, it was weird. I would look at pictures of Seth before the accident and pictures of him after, and it was almost as if they were of two different people. I don't really know why. It took years before I could look at pictures of Seth, from whatever time, and just see Seth.

If it was hard for me, I can't imagine what it must have been like for Seth. His whole life literally changed in an instant. Typically, people change over time by their own choice. For Seth, it was like he woke up a different person and not because he had willed it to be that way. The accident had taken so much from Seth. And at the same time, it had given him so much that he was grateful for. It was confusing, and an awful lot to deal with. So that first summer after his accident, Seth embarked on a quest to find himself.

Seth wanted so badly to just be a normal twenty-one-year-old guy again. He and some of his friends even started talking about moving to Hawaii together. I have to be honest, this caught me off guard and kind of hurt. After all we had been through with Seth, this was emotionally difficult for me. The idea of letting him go was painful, and in some ways, his wanting to go almost felt like a rejection. Chris and I and our other children had given up just about everything to be with Seth night and day through the whole ordeal. All our energy and practically every thought had been Seth for the past three and a half months. We had been so afraid of losing him and so thankful to have gotten him back, but suddenly I was faced with possibly losing him to Hawaii and his friends. I wasn't prepared for that.

I knew Seth needed to be an independent young adult again, but it scared me. I also didn't want to feel hurt by it, but I did. Having trouble sorting through my emotions, one night I took a walk over to my brother and sister-in-law, Dave and Sarah's house, which was just around the corner from ours. Dave always seems to have a positive attitude about things. He helped change my perspective that night. He said something like, "Praise God that Seth is acting like a normal twenty-one-year-old!!! That's exactly what we have been praying for all this time! We didn't know if he was ever going to be able to live a normal life again."

I knew Dave was right and that I needed to let go, but I told him that it hurt after all we had done and been through to think that he would just want to leave and live so far away. Dave responded, "Of course it hurts!!! That's parenthood!" That statement definitely resonated in my heart, as I am sure it would for anyone who is a parent. Still, I continued to question it all, wondering how Seth could be with God and then just try to go back to his normal life. I mean, he was praying more and following Christ, but I sort of felt like he would still be on fire with that same peace and joy he had in the hospital. Dave said, "We all receive the same miracle every time we receive the Eucharist at Mass, and yet we all just go back to our same old selves. We all do it all the time." Dave was exactly right. God had even shown us that the first time Seth received the Eucharist at Mary Free Bed. *God showed himself to Seth in the Eucharist in the exact same way He had shown Himself to Seth in his coma.* It was the same miracle… Jesus! I was humbled and ashamed, again.

Processing the out-of-body experiences that Seth had was difficult not just for Seth, but for me too. It wasn't understanding the spiritual that was difficult, but more understanding the transition from the spiritual back to the physical and knowing how to support and guide Seth through it. With each new day, it became more and more apparent that the peace and joy Seth had in the hospital were not normal. They were truly miraculous and supernatural gifts from God. Like Fr. Jim had told us though, Seth had to return to the human physical world.

Talking to my brother, Dave, I began to realize that because of the miracle Seth received, I had been holding him to a higher standard than myself or anyone else. I kept expecting Seth to be completely changed spiritually and have complete trust in God, while I, on the other hand, was not. I started to understand that God wasn't just calling Seth to a new and greater holiness. He was calling me too. He IS calling each of us. We, too, can encounter peace if we surrender completely to Him in all the circumstances of our lives, even the unknown and that which we do not understand. We, too, can receive the same miracle, that of Jesus, each day in the Eucharist. God wasn't just calling Seth to seek Him. He was calling me too. He continues daily to invite and call each of us to seek Him and grow in an intimate relationship with Him. He doesn't just want us to seek

Him when we need something. He said, *"I am here always."*

It became evident that some of his siblings had been holding Seth to higher standards too. The younger kids would say, "Seth fell a sinner and woke up a saint." I can't lie, that is truly how it appeared. We got to see the beauty of Seth's purified soul, at least as much as is probably possible here on earth. It was beautiful beyond words, but it put a lot of pressure on Seth to be perfect. Not only did we put pressure on him, but he put that same pressure on himself too, when in reality he once again had all the same temptations to sin that he used to. After all, he had returned to the physical realm and couldn't live in both, as Fr. Jim had explained.

While it was hard for us to understand and accept, it was a hundred times more difficult for Seth to understand and accept. And on top of that, when he would fight with his brother or sin in some way, he remembered the pain and fear he had felt standing in judgment line. He told us *the weight of his own sins leveled him.* He would say to me, "Why do I act like this? I don't want to. I don't ever want to feel that feeling I had again." Why did he act like that? The answer was simple, Seth was only human, just like the rest of us. Yet at the time, nothing was that simple for him or any of us to understand.

I was learning in a deeper way each day that God was calling me to seek Him and trust Him completely whether I understood things or not. I needed to continue to just ponder each step in my heart, quit worrying about the future, trust God and praise Him for Seth's life, wherever it took him.

It turned out that Seth never ended up moving to Hawaii with his friends. It was just one of many ideas in what, I later realized, was the beginning of a very long process of trying to find himself and figure out what direction his life was heading in and what God was calling him to. While there was still much unknown, God was good and continually leading him.

Despite the continual physical, emotional, and spiritual challenges, Seth was extremely happy to have his independence back, living life to the full again...at least as much as possible. Although he was gone a lot with friends, he napped… a lot, at their houses, in cars, or wherever they happened to be. With his friends, he quickly became the target of constant jokes about how much he slept. Brain injuries take lots of sleep to heal. Seth had been told it could take years to get his normal energy level back. That was definitely true for Seth. Even so, he perpetually pushed himself. He never knew at what point his recovery may come to an end, but he knew that God is good even in the unknown.

Seth worked relentlessly trying to build up his endurance and stamina by running each day and hiking up large sand dunes along lake Michigan. He constantly had to stop to catch his breath, but he was determined not to quit. From the moment Seth had woken up from the coma, he had been on the fast track to heal and recover. That is the way he had always been, so it was great to see that same determination in him. Seth took life by storm that summer, excited to be living again!

CHAPTER FOURTEEN
- NEW CHALLENGES -
God is Good... in the Unexpected

In May, Dr. Ho had referred Seth to an ENT (Ear, Nose, and Throat) doctor, because his breathing was very loud, and he would get super winded whenever he did any type of physical activity. It took about a month for him to get into the ENT. Seth finally had his appointment with Dr. Sprik on June 8th. During the exam, Dr. Sprik put a scope down Seth's throat and discovered that his airway was half the size it should have been. He had scar tissue all the way around it in the area where he had the tracheostomy.

As Dr. Sprik continued the exam and put the scope down further, it completely closed off Seth's airway. The doctor was asking Seth to make sounds, but Seth literally couldn't breathe. Dr. Sprik had to quickly remove the scope and wasn't able to complete the exam that way. It was no wonder that Seth's breathing had been so loud, and he was getting worn out and winded so easily. He had basically been trying to breathe through a straw.

Since Dr. Sprik was unable to see with the scope how far down the scar tissue went and how extensive it was, he had to order a CT scan. That would help him determine how to correct the problem. Dr. Sprik talked about a procedure in which they could try to dilate Seth's airway. It sounded like a pretty simple procedure. Seth was hopeful and very excited about the possibility that he may be able to breathe normally again and not have to struggle so much with physical activity and exercise. Seth had the CT scan four days later, but we had to wait over a week for the results. Seth was anxious to get on with this and get it done. He couldn't wait to be able to walk, run, talk, and sing with full breath support.

To our surprise, Dr. Sprik called us at 9:15pm on Wednesday night, June 21st. He had the results of Seth's CT scan. Usually when a doctor calls you from home at night, it's not good news... Dr. Sprik told us the scar tissue (stenosis) in Seth's trachea was very significant, much more so than he had originally thought. He told us that Seth would probably need a very serious and invasive surgery called a tracheal resection. He told us that the surgery would require a very large incision across the front of Seth's neck, and the removal of the entire section of his trachea that was affected by the scar tissue. Then they would piece back together the remaining sections of the trachea. This would also involve time in the ICU on a ventilator while the trachea healed. We were stunned by the news. We had not anticipated anything like this, and the thought of having Seth back on a ventilator in the ICU made me literally feel sick.

Dr. Sprik went on to say that he had no experience with this type of surgery. He thought he would probably have to refer us to another surgeon in another city. He wasn't sure where exactly. He was going to consult with one of his colleagues first to see if she might be comfortable with doing it.

Dr. Sprik also explained that there was no way Seth could go on as he had been because the CT scan revealed that his airflow was only one sixteenth of what it should have been. He told us that Seth should not run or do any type of physical activity that would affect his breathing until this problem was corrected. It could be extremely dangerous. He even went on to say that if the problem couldn't be resolved with surgery, Seth may have to live with a tracheostomy for the rest of his life.

I ended the call in shock and completely distraught. My heart was pounding, and I was trembling as I tried to convey to Chris what the doctor had just said. We were devastated and didn't know how to tell Seth. We called Seth, who was out with friends at the time, and asked him to come home, telling him that we needed to talk to him about something important.

When we first told Seth, we didn't mention the fact that having a permanent tracheostomy was a possibility. I couldn't even accept that myself. I knew there was no way that having a permanent tracheostomy was going to be an acceptable option for this young guy who was so eager to get back to normal life. I couldn't handle the thought of that possibility and didn't even want to admit that Dr. Sprik had said it. "Please, Lord, no," I pleaded. "That can't happen to Seth."

Seth's immediate reaction was to dismiss it as not being that serious. He didn't want to stop running and exercising. In his mind, he would be fine. So he had no intention of stopping anything he was doing. The surgery too, didn't seem to faze him much. After all he had been through, what was one more surgery? That was his initial thought and mentality toward the situation.

Being the worried mother that I am, I begged Seth to please stop running until this was resolved. Though he didn't think it necessary, he agreed to stop running for my sake. He figured he had already put me through enough. He had come through his accident, with a deep gratitude for Chris and me and our whole family and remained very considerate of what we had been through and how we felt.

Chris and I were glad that Seth wasn't taking it too hard, but we knew it was much more serious than what he made it out to be. We called our friend, Matt, who is an anesthesiologist, right away to see what he knew about tracheal resections. He told us that one had never been done here in Grand Rapids, and his opinion was that it was way too serious of a surgery to have done by someone with no experience. We agreed. Even though Dr. Sprik was going to talk to his colleague about possibly doing it, we decided to begin our own research right away. We wanted to find the best and most experienced surgeon for Seth.

My research led me to Cincinnati Children's Hospital. I discovered that doctors there are world renown for their expertise with tracheal surgeries on both children and adults. They have done three times more tracheal surgeries than anywhere else in the world! Chris and I decided we should contact them right away. I emailed them, and they called me the very next day to get information about Seth, so they could begin to look at his case. We were so impressed and grateful that they had contacted us so quickly.

One day later, I received a call from a nurse at Cincinnati Children's hospital. She gathered more very specific information from me about Seth's situation. She told me she would forward all the information to the doctor, and then get back to us to schedule an evaluation. She thought they would most likely have to put Seth to sleep and evaluate him in the operating room (OR), going down into the trachea with a scope in order to get a good look at what was going on in there. We were pleased that they were acting on it rapidly.

Meanwhile Seth was grappling with the question of what he should do with his life. It was a question he constantly wrestled with before his accident, and now that he was recovering, he was right back to worrying about it and trying to figure it out again. Since he was meeting with Fr. Jim on a regular basis, Fr. Jim had some very wise advice, which really struck a chord with Seth. Fr. Jim told Seth that he didn't need to worry about "what" he does, but rather "who" he is. Seth felt that the accident had detoured his life and slowed him down in pursuing "what" he was going to do. That was true, but what he often failed to see was that it advanced him lightyears ahead in "who" he was as a human being and in becoming the man of God he was created to be.

While I was researching hospitals and surgeons, Seth began researching tracheal resections online. He probably shouldn't have. Seeing the pictures and reading about how extensive and serious it was, frightened him. He no longer had a relaxed attitude toward it. On top of that, having to stop running and pushing himself physically toward his goals was very tough on him mentally and emotionally. He had been pushing himself from the moment he had woken up, and now it all came to a screeching halt as he was told to stop and wait. He didn't know what to do with this. It triggered the beginning of a downward spiral of depression.

The emotional rollercoaster continued as we waited to hear back from Cincinnati Children's Hospital. By this time, the fourth of July had come. We were all together at Sandy Pines where we spend most of our summers. Holidays were always exciting because we were all so happy to have Seth there with us. It was so fresh in our minds that he could have died or been severely brain damaged. But again, like Mother's Day, it was actually a discouraging day for Seth.

We played nine square in the air. It is a game that Seth used to be very good at. This time, however, it was a struggle. Seth didn't have his normal coordination back. He felt heavy on his feet and was not comfortable with his body, both how it moved and how it looked. He had lost so much of the muscle he had worked so hard to build before the accident. And now with his breathing issue, he had to stop everything. Feeling like he was moving forward toward a goal had always been a huge part of who Seth was, and now he couldn't. With his whole recovery his whole focus had been to work hard and continually improve. All that was stopped because of his breathing issue. This discouraged him deeply. It made him feel like his recovery was going to take a long time, causing him to miss out on some of the best years of his life.

Seth continued to be painfully aware of how different he was, while the rest of us were just celebrating that he was alive. He felt like everything he was proud of, worked so hard for, and liked most about himself was gone, things like his physical fitness, athletic coordination and abilities, and his singing. They were not anything like what they had been and because of the reduced amount of airflow through his trachea, he could no longer work on improving them.

No one really understood how difficult that was for Seth. He told me that he wished he had lost his personality so that it would be obvious to other people that he wasn't fully himself or fully recovered yet. His friends didn't understand the physical, emotional, and spiritual battle Seth was undergoing. They just expected him to be normal and okay with it all. They constantly joked about how much he slept and his loud breathing. And as far as the possible tracheal surgery, they blew it off telling him he'd be fine, treating it like no big deal.

The breathing issue and possible surgery looming over Seth's head was taking a huge toll on Seth. He looked at his life before the accident as having been so amazing and filled with fun and exciting experiences. He sort of had a glorified view of those memories and felt like his life after the accident would never measure up. He remembered the confidence in the way he talked and carried himself around his peers and how he could command a room as soon as he walked into it. He no longer had that confidence and certainty about himself, neither in who he was nor in what he was capable of. He was no longer comfortable in his own skin or life. Even his friends would make comments saying things like, "Don't take this the wrong way, but I wish I could hang out with the old Seth. He was so dope." Seth would tell them, "I'm still the same Seth," to which they would respond, "Yeah, but you know what I mean."

I tried to have faith that it would all be okay and that God would heal Seth, not just physically, but spiritually and emotionally as well. I knew and believed that God had a plan for Seth even in the unexpected and continued suffering. I really felt like God was recreating Seth and preparing him for whatever the next step in the journey of his life would be. But that didn't mean it was easy. I worried a lot, more than I should have. I worried way too much and trusted way too little. A mother's heart never stops bleeding for her children.

God had shown us so clearly that He was one hundred percent in control of Seth's life and future. I believed that with all my heart, but as a weak human being and mother, I still struggled. Sometimes friends would question me like, "How can you doubt and worry after all that God has done for Seth?" They were right. I shouldn't have worried, but I was weak and fragile after months of watching Seth suffer. I guess I should have put my eyes more on the miracle than the pain. Some days I did, but other days my heart just ached and was tired and wanted it all to be over.

It was difficult for our entire family to accept the continual suffering and struggles Seth had to face. However, even through all the hardships, the man Seth was becoming was amazing. In many ways he was so much more mature, selfless, kind, and thoughtful. He took responsibility for his actions, admitting when he was wrong and apologizing. He was working on building relationships with his younger siblings. I don't think Seth could necessarily see all the changes we saw in him, but they were obvious to the rest of us. It was truly beautiful, and in my heart, I knew God had a purpose in all of this. I just needed to trust and pray. Knowing God was good even in the unexpected, we decided we needed to rally all the prayer warriors again for the grace and strength to get through these new challenges, Seth's next hurdles.

The scheduler from Cincinnati Children's Hospital was trying to set up the necessary tests to evaluate Seth's trachea. Unfortunately, since there were several specialists who would need to see him, they were having trouble finding a week in which they could fit everything in. Chris and I told them we would drive back multiple times for the tests, if they were unable to schedule them all in one week. We realized it was a huge blessing that the hospital with the most expertise and experience with tracheal surgeries in the world, was only a six-hour drive away. We were willing and able to make that trip as many times as needed. But even still, it looked like it could possibly be months before they would be able to even evaluate him, much less correct the problem. We were quite discouraged. And as the waiting carried on, Seth sank deeper into depression.

Toward the end of July, Chris and I were scheduled to take a weekend trip to Appleton, Wisconsin to see my sister, Kathy and her husband, Keith's new house there. We were going to go by boat with Dave and

Sarah, my Dad and his wife, Erma. We had all planned this trip together to celebrate Sarah's fiftieth birthday. As the weekend drew closer, neither Chris or I had peace about leaving Seth.

It was a clear sign to me that we shouldn't go when Chris wasn't comfortable with it either. I tend to worry and sometimes make decisions from a place of worry, whereas Chris is much more levelheaded. I often defer to his judgment for this type of decision. He always helps me stay calm and not overreact to situations. So when Chris mentioned that we maybe shouldn't go, then I was positive that we shouldn't.

Seth had been struggling a lot, and emotionally he was not in a good place. He had been trying so hard to put his life back together but felt everything had been put on hold with the news of the tracheal resection. That completely threw him into a tailspin as he was grieving all he had lost, trying to accept the new challenges in his life, and now suddenly anticipating the unexpected suffering that may lie ahead.

He was pretty emotionally unstable. I hate to even say it, but the fear of suicide did enter both of our minds. I remember one night Seth calling Chris and me at one o'clock in the morning. He was downtown at the building he had fallen through. He was alone in the rain, crying out to me on the phone saying, "This building took everything from me! It messed up my whole life!" I felt helpless as he cried out in emotional agony. Chris and I didn't even know where that building was, so we had no way to get to him. I begged him to please just get in his car and come home. By the grace of God, he did. But incidences like this were why we knew we couldn't go to Wisconsin with my family. Although Seth did not want us to change our plans on account of him, we knew it would not be prudent for us to leave at that time.

About a week later, on July 27th, we received a call from Cincinnati Children's Hospital. They had switched Seth over to a different department, which enabled them to get Seth in quicker. They had scheduled all of Seth's evaluations for Tuesday, Wednesday, and Thursday of the following week, August 1st-3rd. This was an unexpected blessing, and it was nothing short of a miracle! Despite my weakness and worry, God never stopped working out every little detail of Seth's care. Our merciful God continually showed us that He had Seth in the palm of His hand.

Chris and I and Seth drove to Cincinnati, leaving our younger kids in the care of Chris' sister, Mickie and her husband Greg, who spent their summers near us at Sandy Pines, a summer resort in Michigan. We were extremely blessed with the constant support of family. The first day in Cincinnati, Seth was seen by the anesthesiologist, the gastroenterologist and the pulmonologist. In speaking with the doctors, it was very obvious that they knew what they were doing and dealt with conditions like Seth's, and much worse, all the time.

This brought us great peace of mind. We were exceedingly confident that this was the right place for Seth to be. He was without a doubt in excellent hands there.

On the second day in Cincinnati, Seth had triple scope exploratory surgery. They put him to sleep under general anesthesia. Three different specialists went in through his mouth with scopes to evaluate his lungs, trachea, and esophagus. I was nervous about it after having watched Seth unable to breathe in the ENT's office when Dr. Sprik put the scope down into his trachea. But I knew that these doctors were used to doing these procedures and even did them on infants.

Seth handled the exploratory surgery well. Everything looked perfect in their examination, except of course the scar tissue at the sight where his tracheostomy had been. There was no doubt that it would require surgery of some sort. While Seth was in recovery, Dr. Catherine Hart, who was the main physician and surgeon assigned to Seth, talked to Chris and me. She told us that they may be able to do a surgery in which they could go into Seth's trachea through the mouth, make several incisions in the scar tissue and then stretch it to hold it open. She said it can sometimes take a few times to get it opened to the amount desired, but to her it seemed worth taking the chance in the hope of avoiding the very invasive tracheal resection. She explained, however, that if Seth didn't want to waste time trying this, he could opt to just go ahead and have the tracheal resection done. We needed to discuss it with Seth, but the fact that there was the possibility of a less invasive and dangerous option was incredible news to us. Based on what Dr. Sprik had told us, we thought there were no other options.

Seth finished the rest of his testing and evaluations on the third day in Cincinnati. He had five appointments in three days. Then we headed back home. We discussed the options for surgery, and Chris and I and Seth all agreed that it was definitely worth a shot to try the less invasive endoscopic surgery first rather than the resection. Seth wouldn't lose anything except possibly some time, but if he could end up not needing the tracheal resection that would be a total gift and answer to prayer.

About a week later we received the results of all of the labs and biopsies Seth had done in Cincinnati. All the results came out as the doctors had expected, so they scheduled the endoscopic surgery for October 18th. I'll be honest, we were disappointed that Seth would have to wait another couple of months to have the first of what could be a few surgeries and a very long process. However, we were grateful to have a plan and have it scheduled. This is my text to Chris' family on August 13, 2017, explaining everything to them:

"Seth's surgery is scheduled for October 18th. He is also on a cancellation list, so it can hopefully be sooner. They are first going to try a less invasive endoscopic surgery, where they will go

in through the mouth. They will be making incisions in the scar tissue and then trying to dilate it and stretch it open. It could possibly be outpatient or maybe 1 night observation in the hospital. They said he should notice a difference immediately, but that as it heals scar tissue could form again. They will reevaluate him 1-2 months later. If he gets some relief but not full relief, they can repeat the procedure 1-2 more times if there is at least some improvement each time. If that doesn't work then he would need a tracheal resection, which would require a large incision across his neck and actually removing part of his trachea. It would be a 4-5 hour surgery with ICU time, being on a ventilator a couple days, a minimum of a week in the hospital and a minimum of 2 weeks in Cincinnati. So we are grateful for the first option and are asking everyone to please pray hard that he could possibly get in sooner and that it is successful and he won't require multiple ones or the tracheal resection. Thank you! Please also pray as he is now really grieving all the loss he has encountered. He has been extremely blessed, but there is still a lot of work ahead of him and a lot he must grieve and come to terms with. God is really working in his heart and asking him to surrender everything to Him. This summer has been an emotional roller coaster! I believe God has a mission for him and is preparing him! I can't tell you enough how much we appreciate all your prayers and support through all of this!"

As only God can arrange, two days later on the feast of the Assumption of the Blessed Virgin Mary, the

Hospital called with a cancellation. Seth was scheduled to have surgery the next day at 12:30 in the afternoon! Miracles never cease!! I don't know why we were continually so blessed. God was so good to us even in the unexpected.

We immediately packed up and left the next morning at 4am to get there in time. Before we knew it, Seth was in surgery, a surgery that wasn't supposed to happen until October. Wow, how the power of prayer and God's goodness constantly surprised and humbled us.

In surgery, Dr. Hart made several cuts in the scar tissue and dilated it, stretching Seth's trachea open as much as possible. After dilating it, she injected it with steroids to try to keep it open. Dr. Hart was extremely pleased with how well it opened up. It actually worked better than she had expected. She decided not to wait the typical one to two months to evaluate it. She felt she would have more success if she repeated the procedure in two weeks to try to get it opened up even wider. She seemed very hopeful at that point. We were so relieved and thankful.

Seth handled the anesthesia and the surgery very well and immediately, upon waking up, noticed a difference with his talking. Before he had always felt as if he had to talk over something, almost as if he could feel the scar tissue or some blockage as he pushed the words out. After the surgery, he didn't feel that at all anymore. In fact, he said it felt so easy to talk. He was excited and couldn't wait to get home and try running!

Seth was kept one night in the hospital for observation. By the next morning, we were headed home, and Seth had no restrictions at all. God is way too good to us! I often think, "Who are we to be so blessed?" We were continually humbled and overwhelmed by God's mercy and goodness as we rode that rollercoaster of fear and peace, discouragement and hope, doubt and trust, sorrow and joy. There seemed to continually be new challenges with circumstances that changed minute by minute, but God was the one constant, the same yesterday, today, and tomorrow. If only I could learn to surrender and rest in Him, I would always have peace. I am most definitely a work in progress.

For the next week and a half, Seth enjoyed the ease with which he could talk. He also said that in all his normal activities like walking up and down stairs, he no longer noticed his breathing being a problem. However, when he exerted himself, like trying to run, then he realized there was still a limit to what he could do. Overall, he was very happy with the difference the surgery had made and hopeful that the second one would open it up and correct the problem even more.

A couple days before his next scheduled surgery, which was set for August 30th, Seth already felt the same sensation as if he was having to talk over something again. We became concerned that new scar tissue was

322

already forming. Dr. Hart did warn us that could happen and was exactly why she had planned the second surgery just two weeks after the first. It was evident that it was going to be a process. We just continued praying that it would be successful overall, so that Seth wouldn't have to have the tracheal resection.

By this time, it was the end of August and Seth was still struggling quite significantly emotionally. With the second surgery only a couple days away, he worried about his future. He felt like if the surgery was successful, then his recovery would be basically finished. Therefore, in his mind, he needed to know the next step for his life. He felt a lot of pressure to know and be prepared to take that next step, whatever that may be.

Seth felt no particular direction or guidance from God. This made him feel as though nothing had changed in his life. He felt like he was right back to where he had been before the accident, only worse because he had less talents and abilities. He felt like he was no longer energetic, passionate, strong, athletic, or even a good singer. On top of that, the spiritual had faded and the friends he thought were Christian weren't necessarily the support he needed. This is what he had written in his personal notes during that time: *"I thought it was a group of Christian bros building each other up, but it feels more like competition and bragging about things that are truthfully not even Christian. Then I find myself wanting to join in, and I really don't wanna go that direction."* So much had happened to Seth, and so much was still going on inside him as he tried to process and get through all the changes. He wanted to live for God, but he could no longer sense Him and felt no direction. He just really didn't know what he was supposed to do or where to go from there.

We felt like God may have a mission for Seth to share his story and all that God had done for him. Seth thought maybe he did too, and he was completely willing to do that. However, he didn't remember anything that happened. He didn't even remember telling us about it. Even his memory of his time at Mary Free Bed and all the therapy he had done had become a blur to him. I knew Fr. Jim had said he couldn't live in both the spiritual and physical realm at the same time, but I didn't understand why God didn't at least let him remember it. I also didn't understand why God seemed to be hiding Himself from Seth. I wondered and asked God, "Why can't you just show yourself to him? I know he has to live in the physical world, but why can't he experience you, Jesus, in this physical world in the same way we all do and how he used to?" Instead, he felt like he was in total spiritual darkness, like he had actually been closer to God before his accident.

The longer this dark night of the soul went on for Seth, the more anger, aggression, and frustration we saw in him. It was very scary and painful to watch him struggle this way. I felt like he was trying so hard to live for Christ. He was going to daily Mass and weekly confession, seeking God. He seemed to be screaming out to God with no reply. Deep in my heart, I knew and believed God was working in Seth, but I couldn't understand it at all. If I couldn't understand it at age forty-nine, how was Seth, barely twenty-two-years-old, supposed to understand it? Inside, I was scared for Seth, but I kept telling him that he needed to trust God, even though I knew I wasn't doing a good job of trusting God myself. As I would tell Seth to trust God, I knew I needed to also. I constantly felt God saying to me, "Trust Me. I am working in Seth. Be patient and trust." I truly didn't understand what God was doing with Seth spiritually, but in the darkness, I felt God standing over my shoulder once again saying, "Don't worry Chris. I've got this. Trust me."

Seth wrestled with the temptation to think that God did not have a plan for his life. He knew that was a lie, that he had seen God's plan so clearly while in the coma, but at this point he couldn't remember any of it and was desperate to sense even an inkling of God's presence in his life. He felt so alone and abandoned and couldn't understand why. On August 28th, he hit a very low point. Seth told us many times throughout the day that it would have been better if he had died and that he should have died.

It was exceedingly painful for Chris and me to hear Seth say that. Fear gripped our hearts and minds that night. We both laid in bed physically and emotionally exhausted, but afraid to go to sleep and leave Seth alone while he was feeling that way. Seth was so low that even Chris, who as I said, is not a worrier, was extremely scared for Seth. We both continued to fear he may contemplate suicide. Looking back, I don't think Seth was ever at that point, but as parents it is hard not to fear that.

Chris was particularly torn that night because he knew Seth needed support, but at the same time Chris had a long drive for work early the next morning and recently had been fighting to stay awake while driving. Worried about both Chris and Seth, I got up and went downstairs to talk to Seth, so that Chris could sleep with peace knowing Seth wouldn't be alone.

As I headed down the stairs toward Seth's room, I found him listening to Fr. Mike Schmitz on YouTube. This brought me immense peace to know that even in such darkness, pain and doubt, he would still turn to his faith for help. I knew God was strong in Seth, and I believed that through all the suffering, God was molding Seth and working out His plan in him. I needed to trust that God was good even in the suffering and would not test Seth beyond what he could handle. Later, as I finally climbed into bed in the early hours of the morning, I prayed the way I had prayed many times at the side of Seth's lifeless body in the ICU, "Oh Jesus, I surrender myself and Seth to you. Take care of everything. Jesus, I trust in you."

Two days later on Wednesday, August 30th, Seth and I headed back to Cincinnati for his second surgery. This time we decided Chris should stay home to work and be with our other children. Again, we left very early in the morning in order to get there in time. The first part of the trip Seth slept while I drove. Besides the difficulty of it being dark and foggy, the trip was going smoothly, and we were making good time.

At about 6:30am, only an hour and a half into our six-hour road trip, the front passenger-side tire blew out. I was suddenly driving on the rim. Having no sense of direction and blindly following a GPS, I had absolutely no idea where we were. Seth woke up as soon as it happened. I put on my flashers and drove slowly to the next exit. Luckily it was very close, and there was a gas station directly off the exit.

I pulled into the gas station, and as I was calling roadside assistance, before I even had time to panic, a stranger pulled up out of nowhere in a truck and asked if we needed help. Of course, we gratefully said yes, but we were puzzled as to how he even knew we needed help. It was dark and foggy out, and we hadn't even gotten out of our car yet. It just so happened that he had a commercial grade jack in his truck and all the tools he needed. He had our car jacked up and the old tire off before Seth even had the spare tire out of the trunk. It couldn't have been more than ten minutes for him to change that tire from start to finish. Then without hesitation, as quickly as he had pulled up beside us, he got back in his truck and drove away without ever going into the gas station.

Seth and I looked at each other in utter amazement. We agreed that was definitely an angel incident! It all happened so fast that we never had to worry about a thing or try to figure out what to do. Just like that it was done, and we were back on the road again. I was in awe the rest of the day. God continually showed me that He was in control! He was good even in the unexpected challenges.

Seth's surgery was successful again. Just as Seth had suspected, there was already new scar tissue forming, but Dr. Hart was able to get it opened up even further this time. She told us that she wanted to repeat the surgery at least two more times to keep opening it up more as needed and make sure it holds. She felt a couple more surgeries may be needed to get the end results wanted, but she was very positive and seemed quite confident that this route was going to be successful. Seth handled the surgery so well, that they didn't even keep him overnight. He was discharged a few hours after surgery, and we were headed back to Michigan. It was a long day, but a positive and hopeful one.

While Seth may not have been sensing God in prayer, God was still making it very obvious that He was in control and had Seth in His hands. Seth was so grateful and relieved the surgeries had been successful so far. While he would get caught up in his emotions and grief trying to process the recent events of his life, it remained evident that Seth had been changed by God. He continually sought God and thought much about all he had been through. He knew he had been blessed and didn't ever want to take that for granted. This was his journal entry just a couple days after his 2nd surgery: *"I'm feeling retrospective tonight, thinking back on my time at Mary Free Bed. I remember being so thankful for every ability I got back. Now I find myself taking them for granted again. It's so easy. Never take anything for granted. It can all change so fast."*

Seth's third surgery was only eight days after his second one. That time Chris and Seth went together, while I stayed home with the rest of the family. Seth's trachea looked great. It had stayed open and there was no sign of new scar tissue forming. Dr. Hart didn't even have to make any new incisions or dilate it. She simply injected it with more steroids to hopefully prevent new scar tissue from forming.

I took Seth back to Cincinnati two weeks later for his fourth surgery. Once again, it had stayed open, and no new scar tissue had developed. What a gift! Dr. Hart injected it with steroids one final time and told us that unless he had any trouble, Seth would not need to come back for a year! We were elated! After all our worry, Seth never had to have the tracheal resection. We also had worried about the long wait to deal with it. Yet, by September 22nd, Seth was finished with all of it, all the evaluation appointments, exploratory surgery, and four other surgeries. That was truly miraculous when you consider that we had originally been told that Seth probably wouldn't even be able to get in for evaluation until October, much less have any sort of surgery. Our God truly is good. He had shown us countless times that even in new and unexpected challenges, He was in control and that His timing, whether long or short, was always perfect. I was and continue to be constantly humbled by the love, mercy, and greatness of our God. When will I learn to trust even when I don't understand and can't see the plan?

Having anticipated that it may have been our last trip to Cincinnati for a while, Mary and Peter came along with us for the fourth surgery. We rented a nice hotel and made a fun trip out of it. While Seth slept off the anesthesia in the hotel, Mary, Peter and I explored some fun places in Cincinnati. Then the day after surgery the four of us went to the Cincinnati Zoo before heading back home. Having left them behind so many times, it was a blessing to include Mary and Peter and turn some aspect of Seth's journey into a fun memory for them. God is good and brings good out of unexpected hardships.

CHAPTER FIFTEEN
- MINISTRY -
God is Good... in Our Weakness

The next month, in October of 2017, a woman from our parish invited Seth to share his story with her psychology class at West Catholic High School in our hometown of Grand Rapids. As someone who had known Seth growing up and had prayed very hard for him throughout his recovery, she had been very inspired by Seth's miraculous story. She desired for her students' hearts to be opened to Jesus, for she knew that some had already abandoned their faith. Though Seth was not accustomed to doing anything like this, he was willing and ready for God to use him. And God did just that. The class seemed to relate well to Seth. The teacher thought it was beautiful and was very pleased with the response from the class. She began noticing a change in some of her students in the days to follow.

It was crazy to witness how God used Seth, even though he was in a weakened state. First of all, he had very little memory of what had happened to him both physically and spiritually. Yet Seth was always willing to share. Even if he didn't feel like it, he knew he had to. He had to share what God had done for him. And each time he stepped out in faith, God blessed it abundantly and gave him the memories and the words for exactly what he needed to say. It was truly amazing, especially for those of us who knew how much he was struggling, and how much trust it took for him to share. God is always good even in our weakness.

Seth was struggling much more than people realized at this point. He was struggling to make sense out of his life. He didn't know what he was called to do with this second chance God had given him. He was struggling to understand where God was for him after having been so close. He was struggling with extreme fatigue and lack of energy. He was struggling with depression and anxiety. He was grieving the losses in his life. He was struggling with sin and temptation like the rest of us. He was struggling with his friendships, feeling they were pulling him further into temptation. And at the same time, he was having to constantly defend his faith around his friends. Though he had these incredible experiences with God, some of his friends had set out to try to disprove his Catholic faith and tried to fight him on it continuously. He didn't have much support with this besides our family and Tyler, and at this point even Tyler wasn't around since he had gone back to college across the State.

Even though Seth was still recovering and working through so much, my sister, Kathy, wanted him to come spend some time with her in Appleton, Wisconsin. She had been so instrumental throughout all of his hospitalization, rallying prayer warriors around the world. Many of her friends in Appleton had been a huge part of Seth's faithful prayer warriors.

Being in Wisconsin through it all, rather than in Michigan with us, Kathy relied heavily on her community there for support. Her very good friend, Keri, had become her main support and trusted confidant. Kathy shared the details of Seth's accident and recovery with Keri on a daily basis throughout. When Keri saw the news story that WOOD TV8 had done, she was disappointed. Though it was a half hour long and quite comprehensive, Keri knew from Kathy how much more there was to the story, especially all the spiritual experiences Seth had.

Keri had been deeply impacted by walking through Seth's accident and recovery so closely with Kathy. As Seth was recovering and began sharing his spiritual experiences some here in Grand Rapids, Keri started sharing them with various friends of hers in Appleton. She remembers specifically telling them about how thin the veil was and how Seth had stressed that God is right here with us. As she shared, people would just start crying. She knew that Seth's message needed to reach other people, especially the youth.

It became Keri's mission to get Seth in to speak to the students at Xavier High School in Appleton, Wisconsin where her daughter and Kathy's son were both seniors. She thought, "These kids need to he36ar this before they head off to college." Upon talking to both the principal and superintendent, she found out that before Seth could speak there or anywhere in the diocese he would first need to be vetted, meaning approved by the diocese, to make sure he was a practicing Catholic in good standing with the Church. Keri hoped her parish, St. Mary's in Appleton, would be willing to help Seth with that vetting process.

Kathy, too, was convinced that people needed to hear Seth's experiences. While Kathy had updated and informed everyone of Seth's needs and progress on facebook during the time of his injury, she also had spent hours every day responding to all the comments. The sacrifices that friends and strangers alike had made for Seth in the midst of their own pain and suffering were heroic and astonishing. People had prayed and drawn close to God like never before, believing and trusting in His power. Kathy saw firsthand how God had touched and changed lives all over the country through Seth's story.

Kathy and Keri believed that people needed to hear more about Seth's spiritual experiences. While I was still caught up in the day-to-day details and needs of his recovery, they saw the broader picture of what God had done and could continue to do through Seth. They believed it would be powerful if people could see Seth and hear the story directly from him.

The first week of November 2017, eight months after his accident, Seth drove himself to Wisconsin to spend a week with his Aunt Kathy and Uncle Keith and meet Keri and others of their friends who had prayed so hard for him. They also hoped he would be able to meet Fr. Bill, the pastor of St. Mary's, and Theresa who also worked at the parish. They had already talked to Theresa about possibly beginning the vetting process with the Diocese of Green Bay, so she was anxious to meet him.

To be completely honest, it was hard for me to let Seth go that week. Although he was twenty-two years old, he was still going through so much. As he healed, I found myself needing to learn to let go again, but it wasn't easy. For the past eight months, I had been riding an emotional and spiritual rollercoaster over the hills and valleys of every detail of Seth's injury and recovery. I felt like I had traveled from terror to triumph in the first six weeks and was still traveling everywhere in between since Seth had returned home from the hospital. I began to let go when Seth started driving and hanging out with friends again. However, I quickly grabbed back on as he faced the possible tracheal resection and the downward spiral of depression which ensued.

Throughout the past eight months, I had been humbled so many times by my own frailty and inability to let go and trust God. I was continually awed by God's providence, love, and mercy through it all. But even so, I continued to worry and agonize over every aspect of Seth's recovery. My own worry was, quite honestly, what made it even more of a rollercoaster. Time after time, I allowed my emotions to control me rather than trusting completely in God. In hindsight this is easy to see, but at the time, I was pretty blind to it. Worrying had become a way of life for me. I often just accepted the commonly held idea that worry is what we moms do. So the thought of Seth making that six hour drive by himself frightened me. He still didn't have the energy he used to and would often just need to close his eyes and sleep. Many people thought Seth was completely recovered, but I knew he wasn't. Still, I needed to let go. I needed to trust.

Seth met many people that week in Appleton. As each person heard Seth tell of his experiences, they were in awe and knew that his story had to get out. Seth had a humility and raw authenticity that drew people in. Each person was enthralled by his story. And although most of the time Seth only got the memories back when he needed them to share, as Fr. Jim had indicated would happen, nothing he said ever contradicted what he had told us in the hospital or the teachings of the Catholic Church. In fact, after Fr. Bill, the pastor of St. Mary's, had met Seth that week, he was surprised and said that Seth was actually quoting and describing teachings of the Church fathers. Trust me when I say that Seth did not know enough on his own to be quoting doctors of the Church. It was purely God and the fact that Seth had truly experienced these phenomena while in his coma.

St. Mary's parish agreed to sponsor Seth in the vetting process with the diocese. Beyond that, one by one a group of faithful supporters formed throughout the week. Many of them were already extremely involved and committed to other ministries, but they felt God tugging at them to help Seth get his story heard. Anne was one who was already extremely busy. She told the Lord, "I am way too busy. I can't take on another thing." Her plate was full, but she could not deny the prompting of the Holy Spirit. When she heard Seth, she knew she had to get involved. She felt like God was asking them to bring Seth's message of Heaven to as many people as possible. So she joined Kathy and Keri in their effort. Theresa also joined in the mission and immediately began the paperwork to get the vetting process started. And after Seth headed home to Michigan, Kathy, Keri, Anne, and Theresa started meeting and working to set up speaking engagements for Seth at St. Mary's Parish and around the Diocese of Green Bay.

Well into November, Seth was still struggling with significant bouts of depression as well as dealing with anxiety and flashbacks from his time at Mary Free Bed when he was awake but completely helpless. It also became extremely difficult for him to see the pictures or videos of himself in the hospital. We were quite convinced by that time that he was dealing with post-traumatic stress disorder, commonly known as PTSD. Some people didn't understand why he would struggle with PTSD. He remembers his friend's mom asking him how he could have PTSD when he didn't even remember most of it. Regardless of his memories of how it happened, it happened. He would say, "Imagine waking up and not being able to talk or even move most of your body, not knowing where you are or how you got there."

That was his reality, and it was extremely traumatic. Seth was having uncontrollable flashbacks of times in the hospital and throughout his recovery. Whether he could remember specifics or not, deep within him every ounce of his being knew what he had been through and how dramatically it had changed his life. This is one of his personal notes from that time period: *I don't remember a lot of what happened to me, but I live with and notice the differences every day. It's very weird. It's like waking up a whole different person."*

The PTSD got severe enough that Seth felt like he couldn't take it anymore. In many ways it felt like it was robbing him of his life, and he didn't want to live like that. Seth finally called the doctor hoping there may be some medication that could help him through it. He described to the doctor his "episodes" for lack of a better word. He told the doctor that he had very weird feelings of deja vu followed by feelings of overwhelming terror and doom. He said it was a terrifying feeling that he couldn't adequately describe. It seemed like he was having severe panic attacks. Following these weird episodes or panic attacks, he would experience periods of serious depression which stole all of his motivation, energy, and joy. Seth, who had always been extremely active and even through his recovery pushed himself to continually work hard to get better, would just sleep and lay around the house all day every day with no desire or motivation to do anything. Life felt pointless and hopeless to him. It was so not like Seth. It seemed to come and go and would last about a week at a time. And whenever Seth would come out of one of these periods, he would be devastated that he had wasted so much time doing nothing. These are some of his own personal notes trying to describe his life at that point: *"This isn't my life. Feels like a movie, a dark movie. Episodes... Lack of motivation... Seeing no point... Flashbacks... Aggression."*

The doctor prescribed some medication and counseling for Seth. Looking back, it is so awe-inspiring to reflect on what God can do when we simply make ourselves available to Him. The fact that Seth was willing and able to make that trip to Wisconsin while in the throes of PTSD was admirable. Seth even remembers having flashbacks of smells while on that trip. He called us on his way there, kind of freaking out, saying his car smelled exactly like his hospital room. No matter what he did, he couldn't get rid of that smell and sensation. Regardless of Seth's PTSD, God was using Seth. God gave Seth all the grace and strength he needed to get through that week. God always has perfect timing, even when we don't think so. God is good even in our weakness.

Close to a year after Seth's accident, on Christmas of 2017, Seth was feeling quite emotional and retrospective as he looked back over the events of the past year. This is what he wrote late that night:

"This... this was me one year ago... and I think I'm finally ready to make this...

You might ask, what happened? Well... lemme tell you. I wasn't always like this...

In February of 2017, February 13th to be exact...

Something happened that completely changed my life...

Let's go back... this is also me (music videos of himself). Since I was about 16... music was my life... I was going to be one of the biggest names in music... I wanted it more than anything, and I was determined to get it...

I was downtown with some friends location scouting for my next music video... As the sun was setting, me and a friend climbed on a roof to grab a glimpse... Although I don't remember it... I'm sure it was beautiful...

As we climbed back down, I made a jump from one landing down to another when the roof gave out underneath me on impact...

I fell two stories to concrete... I was unconscious immediately... I wasn't breathing...

My friends, freaking out, called 911. The ambulance resuscitated me (put me on a ventilator), and rushed me to the hospital...

I was in a medically induced coma for two and a half weeks...

My parents asked the doctors if I could die from this and they said, "Yes, he could"...

You see I had brain shearing or shredding of the brain... one of the worst brain injuries you can have... The doctors didn't even know if I'd wake up from the coma...

Spoiler alert... I did. But I was different...

I couldn't walk... couldn't even sit up on my own. I couldn't eat... couldn't even swallow...

I couldn't talk...

I was completely dependent on other people... I was a 21-year-old... not even able to go to the bathroom on my own...

All this taught me a lot... things I don't know if I would've learned if this didn't happen...

You see... something happened when I was in a coma... I was with God...

I felt God's love like nothing I had ever experienced before..."

The next day, Seth called me into his room saying he wanted to read something to me that he had written. As I listened to him reading it, my eyes filled with tears. Knowing how little he remembered and how much he had been struggling to process everything that had happened to him, my heart was broken and full, all at the same time. I could not have summarized it better myself. I thought, "Wow, here's a guy who can't remember most of this, yet he had written it so beautifully." There was evidence of healing and understanding in his voice as he read. It seemed he was getting ready to move past the grief and begin to live again, sharing the beauty of what God had done for him. Little did we know then that what he had written that night was truly inspired at just the right time. God had plans for it to be used to touch the lives of many.

The end of the year seemed to bring continued closure for Seth. On December 28, 2017, he had his final appointment at Mary Free Bed. It was for a Neuropsych evaluation to test Seth's neurological function. Seth went through several hours of intensive questioning and testing. When it was finished, the psychologist told Seth that he would be able to do or be whatever he wanted in life. He told Seth he would do fine in college if he wanted. He would just need to use a lot of repetition in his studies to help with his short-term memory. Seth's verbal memory was a little weak, but his visual memory was strong. This had already been typical for Seth throughout his life. He was always a very visual and hands-on type of learner, so this was not surprising to us. Moving forward in choosing a career, the doctor's only suggestion was that Seth not do something that would put him at risk of getting hit in the head! That made sense. "Otherwise," he said excitedly, "The sky's the limit!" After reading Seth's charts and the extent of Seth's injuries, the doctor who conducted this evaluation was absolutely astounded by Seth. It was another very blatant reminder to us of the incredible miracle we had received, and the miracle Seth's life really was!

The new year, 2018, started off on a very positive foot. On January 1st, Seth returned to personal training. It was a blessing for him to begin working again. And after all he had been through in the past year, he had a renewed passion for helping others attain their fitness goals. He started by training a few clients in their homes. Eventually he found a gym downtown where he could train. He loved being a part of the gym and the comradery and environment there. Not only did he help others attain their fitness goals, but he worked out constantly to reach his own as well, regaining the strength and physique he once had.

Along with personal training, Seth was also making music again. He had throughout the past year worked on retraining his voice. All the work he had put into his voice and music before had been stripped from him. He basically had to start all over again. This was very discouraging and even devastating for Seth at times. He had gone through many ups and downs, feeling both hopeful at times and completely hopeless at others. However, he never gave up.

Approval came from the Diocese of Green Bay giving Seth permission to speak anywhere in the diocese. Kathy, Keri, Anne, and Theresa (Seth's faithful supporters in Wisconsin) had wasted no time arranging speaking engagements for Seth. They had several lined up for the beginning of February in 2018. They weren't just trying to have Seth come speak at their parish. They had plans way beyond that. They felt God calling them to help Seth start a ministry, speaking all over. They had even put together some promotional materials for Seth and had set up a meeting for him with a woman who had traveled nationally and internationally speaking at events. She had said she would meet with Seth and mentor him in how to get his ministry started.

This was all a little overwhelming because Seth was not a speaker. He had never been trained in anything like that, and he didn't have any ideas or expectations for how things should go or what he should do. The one thing he did know though, was that he was grateful for all God had done for him and felt strongly that he should share it. The fact that this group of women, from another state, who had just met him in November, felt called and driven to help him do that was incredible. It was another miracle. It was another sign of how God was directly orchestrating every step.

Kathy, Keri, Anne, and Theresa were all part of a moms' group in Appleton. They called it their ROCKS group, which stands for Raising Our Catholic Kids. Their ROCKS meeting was the first place they had Seth scheduled to share his story when he went back to Wisconsin in early February, almost one year after his accident.

The women in that group had prayed so hard for Seth and already knew a lot of his story from Kathy, but they were looking forward to meeting him in person. Through their prayers, they had been part of the miracle that enabled this young man, who they had never even met before, to stand in their presence and share how God had changed his life. Seth was a living miracle that they had been a part of. That in itself was inspiring.

Seth didn't have a prepared talk, so it was pretty informal. Kathy helped prompt him with things to share by asking him questions, and others asked him questions as well. As he shared his spiritual experiences with God, they were in awe. His experience was like nothing they had ever heard firsthand from someone, but Seth was so authentic, real, and relatable. His words were profound, yet raw and genuine. And at the same time, he charmed them with his typical wit. That was Seth, and they loved him. Others of this group felt called that day to get involved with Seth's ministry as well.

Later that same day, Seth was scheduled to speak at Xavier High School after school. This had been thrown together at the last minute, so it was unknown how many kids would actually stay after school to hear it. Nothing had been set up ahead of time, and it wasn't as organized as Kathy would have liked it to be, but she was grateful for the opportunity to have Seth speak there. Quite a few students showed up. It was more than they had anticipated with such short notice.

Since Seth didn't have a formal talk written out, he used what he had written on Christmas night. He began by showing on the projector a picture of himself in the ICU, and he said, "This was me a year ago." Then he showed a clip of himself singing and dancing in one of his music videos and said, "This was me just one week earlier," showing the stark contrast of how your life can change in an instant. He also showed the WOOD TV8 news story to give the students an overview and basic understanding of what had happened to him. Kathy talked too, filling in some of the details and prompting Seth with questions about his spiritual experiences. Then they opened it up for the students to ask questions. When Seth would answer questions about his spiritual experiences, the Holy Spirit would grant him the memories. It was amazing, like watching a miracle every time. Before the talks, he would feel totally unprepared because he couldn't remember most of it, but God never let him down. He would always remember what he needed when he needed it. He was totally inspired during the talks. Then immediately afterward, he wouldn't even remember what he had said. God was good, despite Seth's weak memory. It was crazy.

Many of the students stayed after to talk to Seth individually. Some of the girls who weren't sure if they were going to stay for his talk or not told him that they were so glad they did. They said it was one of the best talks they had ever been to. I know it wasn't because

Seth was an eloquent speaker. It was because the words were God's, and God knew how to reach the youth through this young, willing guy.

Seth was very honest and real with the youth. How can you not stop and listen to a young guy who has stood in the judgment line and is telling you that *the weight of his own sin absolutely leveled him*? He would tell people that *there was no way any human could ever do what Jesus did when He hung on the cross, taking on the weight of everyone's sins. "Only God could bear that load,"* he would say. Seth became adamant telling them, *"If you want to go to Heaven, live like you want to go to Heaven. If you want to go to hell, live like you want to go to hell."* He knew for himself that *he never again wanted to feel the way he had felt when he stood in the judgment line.*

The next morning Seth was scheduled to meet with another group to share his story. Each month all the Youth Ministers and Directors of Religious Education (DRE's) in the diocese of Green Bay met together. It just so happened that their monthly meeting was the week Seth was there. Theresa worked it out so that Kathy and Seth could attend that meeting. They were given thirty minutes on this group's agenda. This was a fantastic opportunity to have representatives from every parish in the diocese hear Seth's story. Since Seth had just started sharing his story, had no formal presentation planned, and struggled with his memory, this was a bit nerve wracking. Kathy wondered how they would fill a half an hour. She remembers trying to put some notes together in her phone while she was getting ready for the meeting that morning. She figured she would give the basic story and then they could ask Seth questions if they wanted.

When they arrived at the meeting with all the diocesan youth ministers and DRE's, they were the first up on the agenda. Seth felt completely unprepared and had been hesitant to even go that morning. Kathy was a huge help for Seth. There were times when someone would ask Seth a question, and he would just get a blank look on his face. Sometimes Kathy was able to rephrase the question in a way that would jog Seth's memory. Other times, even as he was starting to say, "I don't know" or "I don't remember" the memory would suddenly come flooding back, and then he would proceed with the most beautiful and profound answer.

The people present at the meeting that morning were so taken by his story and his answers that it went on for about forty-five minutes or longer. They had a whole lot on their agenda that they needed to discuss that day, but none of them wanted to stop talking with Seth. They were inspired and wanted to hear more. Many commented on how authentic Seth was. The truth of it all was undeniable. It was a phenomenal meeting. So much so that before they left that day, two of the parishes had asked Seth to come speak at their Confirmation retreats that weekend, one on Friday night and the other Saturday morning. As people heard Seth, they knew it was a story that needed to be shared.

The next morning, Seth and Kathy gave a similar presentation at an informal meet and greet at St. Mary's Parish. Seth met and talked to many more people that morning. Each time, he was inspired as were they. Kathy and the group had even made promotional materials for Seth to hand out, so people would know how to contact him to book him for speaking. God is so good, and He was very obviously at work that whole week.

Anne really wanted her friend, Suzi, to hear Seth while he was in Appleton that time. She had hoped Suzi might get involved in the ministry as well. Anne and Suzi had both been very close to the former pastor of St. Mary's, Fr. Mike. However, Fr. Mike had passed away suddenly in recent years, which was devastating for both of them. After his passing, they began an extremely successful nonprofit organization called Catholics in Apostleship (CIA) in Fr. Mike's honor, which they were both heavily involved in. While Anne was excited to have Suzi hear Seth, Suzi was actually quite apprehensive about it. On her way to hear Seth speak that week, Suzi prayed looking for some kind of sign or direction from God. She wasn't sure why she was going and what it was all about. In her prayer, she asked Fr. Mike to let her know somehow that he was there and that this was real and whether it was something she should get involved with or not.

At many of Seth's talks, he would mention how things had been different for him since the accident and how some things that he didn't like before, he liked now and vice versa. Often people would ask him for an example. His examples were often different each time, but typically would be something with some sort of spiritual significance. This particular time when the same question was asked, Seth could only think of one answer, so he blurted out, "Twinkies! I didn't like twinkies before my accident. Now, I love twinkies!" Immediately after he said it, he thought, "That was a stupid answer! Why did I say twinkies?" It was an honest answer. He really didn't care for them before and after he did, but he just felt like it was sort of a dumb answer with no significance. Even Kathy sat in the crowd thinking, "Huh. That was weird."

Suzi, on the other hand, immediately started crying. Unbeknownst to Seth or Kathy, that was the answer Suzi needed. It was her sign. It turned out that twinkies were her beloved friend, Fr. Mike's favorite thing in the world. So much so that he had even acquired the nickname, "Twinkie." That was Suzi's answer. She knew at that moment that Fr. Mike was there with her through the Communion of Saints, and that she should help with Seth's ministry in some capacity. While Seth and Kathy thought it was a strange answer, it was God's answer. It was God working through Seth to speak to Suzi. Perhaps in God's divine providence, that's the whole reason Seth liked twinkies after his accident. It was another miracle! And it seemed that incidences like this happened whenever Seth spoke, relying on the Holy Spirit rather than his own memory. God was powerful and good in Seth's weakness.

After the talk, Suzi asked what she could do to help with Seth's ministry. She ended up using her gifts to edit the news story into a shorter, more straight forward version that Seth then began using in his future talks. What a blessing. God just continually put all the perfect pieces together to develop a ministry to spread His messages.

Seth's Aunt Kathy also went with him to both of the Confirmation retreats, Friday night and Saturday morning, which had been added to his schedule that weekend. They followed the same basic format they had used at Xavier. As always, the Question-and-Answer portion was the most inspiring part. That was always when most of the spiritual experiences would be shared. Kathy never ceased to be amazed by Seth's answers and how God worked in and through him. Though he was nervous to go without knowing what he was going to say, no one else ever knew. No matter how he felt beforehand, Seth always made it look easy. However, Kathy was totally aware that it was completely the strength and grace of the Holy Spirit. She truly was witnessing a miracle every time. The youth loved Seth, and it was evident that hearts were being touched by his message, God's message.

It was a whirlwind of a week with six talks in four days. Kathy, Keri, Anne, and Theresa had also sent out information to diocesan leaders and schools around the area inviting them to some of the events. They hoped to make Seth and his ministry known throughout the diocese. It seemed that each time Seth spoke, more people were tapped by God to help get his ministry going. Terri became involved, and later her husband, Bill, joined too. He had recently retired and was wondering what he should get involved in. He knew when he heard Seth. Andee, too, had recently quit her job and was seeking God's direction in her life. She was extremely talented with marketing and began putting her skills to work in the formation of Seth's ministry. As Kathy told us the stories of how God had called and involved each person, we were in awe of what God was doing.

Though I had been worried about Seth making the trip and how he would do with all the speaking engagements, I discovered very quickly how freeing it was to have it all happening in Wisconsin with Kathy instead of in Grand Rapids with us. As Seth went to speak, I didn't worry. I just prayed for him, and I was able to trust that God would give him what he needed.

Kathy, on the other hand, had taken over my role of worry. You have no idea how difficult it is to relax when you're with Seth before he is supposed to share his story, and he literally doesn't know what he's going to say because he can't remember anything. Kathy found that out rapidly! Seth often needed lots of encouragement at first. He would say things like, "I really shouldn't go. I don't remember, and I have no idea what to say." It was extremely nerve wracking for Kathy not knowing what Seth would remember or say. She would pray so hard with each question he was asked, begging God to give Seth the words. I am extremely grateful for the countless hours she spent helping Seth. It took a lot of sacrifice and trust, but it was absolutely amazing and crazy as she continually watched God at work in and through Seth.

Knowing how much trust it took on our parts, I can't even begin to imagine how much humility and trust it must have taken for Seth. I have often thought that I could never do what he was being asked to do. But that is how God had chosen to work through Seth. God was asking him to live a life of total surrender and dependence on Him. And God did not disappoint! Seth, Kathy, Chris, and I were constantly in awe. Over and over again God had shown us that it was all by His power, not our own. We are called to just simply make ourselves available to Him. That is what Seth continually did no matter where he was in the process of his recovery, whether it was a good day or a bad day, whether he remembered or not. He continually just stepped out in faith. And God never let him down.

Seth often wondered why God had chosen him. In many ways, Seth felt like he shouldn't be the one up there speaking. He didn't feel the spiritual experiences anymore and didn't feel the closeness he had felt with God right after the accident. He knew his own sinfulness. He knew he was far from perfect and never claimed to be. Sometimes, looking at himself, he wondered how God could be changing lives through him. But the truth is, it was not Seth, it was all God - His message, His mercy, His transformative power. Seth was just His instrument. Though sinful and struggling in many ways, Seth still made himself available to be used by God, and God worked miracles. God is good even in our weakness! In 2 Corinthians 12:9 the Lord says, "My grace is sufficient for you, for power is made perfect in weakness." This was an indisputable truth that God continued to show us repeatedly through Seth.

Seth returned home from Wisconsin just in time for the first anniversary of the day of his accident, a day which had shattered his life as he knew it, significantly altering the course of it forever. Seth had been working hard all year to recover and rebuild his shattered life. By the first anniversary, the PTSD seemed to be settling down and he seemed to be handling things better emotionally and spiritually.

Casey Jones from WOOD TV8 called Seth about doing a one-year follow-up interview with him. Casey met Seth downtown Grand Rapids at the building he had fallen through. During the interview, Seth told Casey that over the past year he had returned to that building many times by himself playing the "what if" game and looking for answers. He admitted that he had been dealing with a lot, but said he was feeling better and working through it. While in some ways he still grieved the life he once had, he told Casey, *"I love the person I am now."*

Seth talked to Casey again about his experience with God while in the coma and *how amazing God's love was.* In fact, he even told Casey, *"I've said this to many people, and I'll say it till the day I die: I would do anything to be back in that hospital bed just to feel that love again. If I could go back to that hospital bed to feel that love again, I would do that in a heartbeat."* It astounded me every time Seth said that. I would think, "Wow. God's love must be amazing beyond belief if Seth, a twenty-two-year-old active young guy, would give up everything, to the point of being helpless in a hospital bed, just to experience it again!"

During the interview, Seth told Casey that many people had asked him if he had ever gotten angry at God, asking, "Why me?" Seth said that hadn't been a problem for him because he envisioned it like this: *"God didn't make me get up on that roof. God didn't make the guy who made the roof make it all weak and pathetic."* He said, *"It's all free will. I went up there on my own, and it happened. The roof gave out. **I like to envision God standing over me in the shop, me laying on the ground*** *all bloody and scratched up and God thinking like, 'Oh Seth, what have you done? Well, hold on to me and we'll get through this together.'"* That is how Seth pictured it. He didn't blame God. It was clear to Seth that *God doesn't desire for any of us to hurt.* He said, *"God is always offering his strength to us. We just have to accept it."*

The interview went very well. Seth was obviously coming to terms with his accident and the new realities of his life. No matter how much he struggled at times, his experience was deep within his heart, and he knew that God would always be with him, and he shared this truth every chance he could regardless of how he felt at the time.

In March, a local youth minister invited Seth to speak at his youth group while they were on retreat out at a camp. What Seth had written on Christmas night was still the outline for the talk he would give along with showing the shortened version of the news story about his accident. That was all good, but the best and most inspirational part was always the questions at the end. I had witnessed how God had given Seth the memories back when I went with Seth to talk to the 8th graders at St. Paul in the beginning, but since then, neither Chris or I had heard Seth speak. We had only heard about it from Kathy. Most of Seth's speaking had been in Wisconsin with his Aunt Kathy's help. I was nervous for him to do this. I stayed home and prayed, while Chris went with Seth.

When they got to the Q&A, one of the young girls asked a question that stunned Chris. He wondered how Seth would answer it. She asked him what Heaven looked like. Chris thought, "Wow. How do you describe Heaven?" Without hesitation Seth responded, *"It's not so much what it looked like. More importantly, Heaven was just being in the presence of God."* Chris told me later that Seth answered it so humbly and effortlessly. Chris said all of his answers were like that. They were simple, yet so profound and genuine that there was no denying the truth and reality of his experience.

After the talk, Seth stayed and hung out with the youth for a while. They were so drawn to him. He had such great rapport with them. Many talked to him individually or in groups and several even wanted pictures with him. One of the guys even knew all of Seth's music from before his accident. They all seemed to have a great time. Chris was impressed and amazed by Seth's ease and comfort with the kids and the profound way in which the Holy Spirit had worked through him.

This was not only a great evening for the youth, but for Seth as well. Since Seth had started sharing his story with groups, he had begun to realize that his accident had given him a platform to reach other people. It made him excited for the future. He wanted to inspire others and share with them the love that he knew many

357

were missing out on. He knew in his heart that everything had happened for a reason and while it had been and still was very difficult at times, he was beginning to see how God had been leading him all the way and could bring good through it.

A week later, Seth headed back to Wisconsin. It had become like a second home for him. He was getting to know so many people, and he had his own team of people working their tails off trying to help him build a ministry. They decided their team needed a name. Seth decided to name them #TeamTapped, as each one of them had felt they had been personally tapped by God to become involved in helping Seth develop a ministry.

Seth's trip this time was for four speaking engagements at St. Mary's Parish. He gave one presentation on Sunday morning after Mass during coffee and donuts. Then that evening he talked with the Confirmation students. And the following Wednesday night he did two separate presentations for high school students and their parents at 4:30pm and 6:30pm. After each of the four talks, the members of #teamtapped worked, emailed, and met, when possible, to critique and get feedback on Seth's presentations. They were totally committed to making it the best it could be in an effort to reach as many hearts as possible. One or more members of the team always attended his talks to help support him and ask pointed questions when needed. This is part of

Keri's email to #teamtapped after the Confirmation talk that Sunday night:

"The kids were completely engaged in what he was saying and asked a lot of questions. When Seth talked about how the Holy Spirit was present in the room with us, one girl expressed that that scared her. He told her not to be scared because there is so much love. He told the kids that he is not afraid to die and explained the difference of why he feels that way vs suicide etc. He was VERY relatable to those kids with discussions about who he was before (partying etc) and now wanting to live a life to get to heaven. I guarantee he made all of those kids think about their daily choices and who they are. He also talked about not hanging with the people he hung with as much before the accident because they do not share the same faith values. He mentioned multiple times how lucky we are to be Catholic and how great it is that they are all making a choice to become confirmed in the Catholic church. He mentioned the sacraments and the Eucharist during this time and told the kids to ask questions about Catholicism if they have questions. He assured them that there are good answers to all questions because Catholicism is not made up. Peter (the leader) ended by having the kids form a circle around Seth and pray over him. There was a musician there who played music and repetitive lyrics of 'Come Holy Spirit' that we all sang along… very powerful. In fact, I heard one girl say 'Wow' after we said Amen. They felt it!!
I am looking forward to Wednesday!"

This is Theresa's response:

"Wow - I got goosebumps and tears when I read your comments Keri!!"

Then part of Kathy's response:

"I was there for a lot of the question and answer part of Seth's talk and was also there for Peter's AMAZING prayer (which brought tears). That age group really is where he shines - he's more comfortable with them and has SO much to share.

359

We do DEFINITELY need to find ways to get him away from (his notes on) his phone. He becomes 'alive' and animated when he looks up and engages with the audience as he speaks from the heart.

He was great just talking to the kids...and Keri is right...he was able to address their fears and concerns.

I think he has much to share with adults, too...one lady approached him yesterday morning after the talk, totally in tears! We just need to find a way to put him at ease and get him to the "meat" of his story quicker.

But, as this is God's story that He is asking Seth to share, I have no doubt He will help Seth (and us) develop the skills he needs to keep sharing it.

All for HIS honor and glory!!!"

It was abundantly clear to all of them that God was at work. They continually witnessed it and felt it. They were faith filled and completely committed to doing whatever God was asking in order to help Seth in this mission. Seth was incredibly blessed to have so many amazing people supporting and helping him.

Word of Seth's miraculous healing and experience with God continued to spread. Not only was there the second story on WOOD TV8, but Seth's story was also featured in the Grand Rapids Diocesan Faith Magazine, the Compass newspaper for the Diocese of Green Bay, and on the 700 Club on CBN, the Christian Broadcast Network. Seth spoke at churches, schools, youth groups, conferences, and retreats throughout the Grand Rapids, MI and Green Bay, WI Dioceses.

We witnessed miracle after miracle as Seth shared his story. Seth wasn't a polished speaker by any means, but he had an amazing story and a message that people of all ages could relate to. Seth and I worked to develop his talk, adding more "meat" to it, meaning more of his spiritual experiences. Even though he was more prepared for his talks, still every time, the most incredible part was the questions and answers. This is where you could literally watch the Holy Spirit take over. Seth's answers were directly inspired. They were beautiful and profound. They were exactly what was needed, when it was needed. God never failed to astound us.

Chris remembers another talk he went to with Seth, where another young lady asked Seth a tough question. Well, at least it seemed tough to Chris. She asked, "What did God's voice sound like when He talked to you?" Chris waited with great anticipation, again wondering how Seth would answer her question. With total ease and sincerity Seth said, *"It's not like I heard an audible voice. It was more like I just knew what God was saying."* Seth didn't worry or think about what the correct theological answer would be. He just answered based on what he had experienced. And nothing he ever said contradicted the teachings of the Catholic Church. *He had,* like Fr. Jim said, *experienced what the Saints had seen and reported.* That was undeniable and truly amazing.

In Wisconsin, #teamtapped continued to grow. It had grown to include Kathy, Keri, Anne, Theresa, Terri, Bill, Andee, and Christine. They met several hours at a time, making promotional materials and envisioning how they could grow Seth Alfaro Ministries to reach as many people as possible, particularly high school youth. They worked countless hours planning two big events for the beginning of May. They felt it was important for Chris and me to come and be a part of these events. We were excited to finally meet the members of #teamtapped who had taken Seth under their wings and done so much to support him over the past few months. They had become very special to Seth.

We had heard so much from Kathy and Seth about this group of faithful people and the amazing stories of how each came to be involved with Seth's ministry. After spending only a couple days with them, both Chris and I were blown away by their love and acceptance of our son. It was obvious how much they truly loved him. It was overwhelming and humbling for us to see the love, sacrifice, time, and effort they had put into helping a young guy they had just met. Their enthusiasm and passion for Seth's ministry was electrifying. We could feel it. It was inspiring and contagious.

It had been so easy for us to get caught up in the struggles Seth was still encountering. However, being around them renewed our faith and our joy and gratitude for the incredible miracles we had received in and through Seth. It's hard to explain the feelings we had. We were definitely humbled by their love for Seth even though they barely knew him. We were also humbled by their faith in God and His plan, and their obedience to what God was calling them too. It made me reflect on how I lived my life. I knew I had sacrificed and given a lot for my family, but I questioned if I would do it for someone else, who I didn't even know well, the way they had? These were, without a doubt, incredible people.

Their love for Seth and for Chris and me was overwhelming. Our hearts were full. My heart sort of felt like it was on fire again, burning within me as it had been at Mary Free Bed when Seth was first sharing his experiences with us. Chris and I left there renewed and excited about what God was doing through #teamtapped and the possibilities of all that He could do in and through Seth's life.

Music had also become a way for Seth to share God's message. One of the first songs and music videos he made after his accident was "Check in the Bank." The first half he wrote before his accident, and the second half after. The video tells Seth's story, much like that of the prodigal son. At the end it depicts his dad running after him and embracing him. Seth has shared it with many youth, and the message is clear. God is merciful and relentless in pursuit of us. Seth tells them, *"Just like my dad came running to me, God is always running after us. We are the ones who turn away from Him. He is always offering His love and His strength to us. We just have to accept it."*

As Seth shared his story, God continued to reveal more and more to him. It wasn't until two and a half years after Seth's accident, that he had the realization that he might actually have been the injured player he saw on the ballfield. Seth recalled seeing Jesus' face looking at him, as if he were the one injured on the ground. Seth said to me, ***"I think I'm the injured player. I think we all are. And God is right next to us crying."*** As Fr. Jim had said, Seth will probably be unpacking these experiences throughout his lifetime. I have no doubt I will be too. It is amazing how even several years later, I am still discovering new and deeper meaning in the messages God gave us through Seth. It is my hope that by relaying these messages to you in the same manner that we received them, that the Holy Spirit will enlighten you with their meaning as needed throughout your lives as well.

It was no surprise that as Seth continued to speak, we noticed more and more spiritual warfare. Of course, the enemy does not want God's messages to be shared. It was interesting to watch how Seth got extremely sick right before many of his talks. Seth had to rely completely on the Lord's strength. He was determined not to let anything deter this message from being spread. Sick or not he was still going to go. Even if the talk was in Wisconsin, he still made his way there one way or another.

One example was when he was supposed to speak for a Parish Mission in Wisconsin. He was so sick that he hadn't been out of bed for a few days. He was way too sick to make a six-hour drive. So instead, he drove himself to the ferry and took it across Lake Michigan. When he arrived at his Aunt Kathy's house, he looked horrible. She kept looking at him questioning, "How on earth is he ever going to get up in front of a crowd to give a talk?" Regardless of how he felt, Seth continually made himself available to God and completely reliant on Him. And as he did that, God never let him down and the miracles never stopped! It's amazing what God can and will do if we just show up.

Only one hour before the talk, Seth could barely stand. He was so weak and miserable. But then, by the grace of God, he got up in front of the people, and no one could even tell he was sick. It was crazy. It was truly miraculous! There was never any doubt that Seth was doing God's work, and that God was in total control, no matter what obstacles tried to get in the way. Our God is amazing!

Another time when he was supposed to speak out of state, he got pneumonia. I changed my work schedule at the last minute and drove him to Wisconsin. It was incredible to watch how the Lord gave him the strength he needed when it was time to give his talk. That particular time, teens and adults from several parishes and different towns had come together for the talk. Some of them drove in buses from parishes over an hour away to bring their teens to hear Seth. At the end, one man stood up and asked everyone to extend their hands in prayer for Seth. He was profoundly impacted and convinced that Seth needed to continue to speak and reach as many people, especially youth, as possible. He led the two hundred plus people in a beautiful prayer asking God to bless Seth and enable him to continue his ministry. It was extremely powerful and touching. Seth did not let his health or how he felt deter him from speaking, and God blessed it abundantly. God is definitely good in our weakness.

CHAPTER SIXTEEN
- THE AFTERMATH -
God is Good... in Sacrificial Love

Hearing Seth share his story and witnessing all the miracles that continually surrounded his ministry, always gave Chris and me renewed joy and peace about all that had happened. We were healing and, in many ways, felt ready to move forward. However, in May of 2018, fifteen long months after Seth's accident, it quickly became apparent that not every member of our family was at that point. After the ride we had been on for well over a year since February 13, 2017, I guess I should have been prepared for the rollercoaster to drop, but I wasn't. Sadly, I never even thought of the aftermath and devastation that had been left by the trauma of it all. The roller coaster speedily spiraled downward as my eyes were suddenly opened to the brokenness and healing which still needed to take place in our other six children. Here are a couple of my journal entries from that May as I tried to process everything.

May 7, 2018

To the world, it appears that everything is done, but it is not. We still watch Seth struggle with his short-term memory, and odd things happening as the brain heals. About every four to five weeks Seth has weird episodes, and everything seems really weird afterwards for about a week. It steals his motivation and is quite scary for him. He also doesn't have the passion he used to have, and he is still working on his coordination for running and his singing voice. Right now, he is feeling numb and emotionless, which is so not like him. These are all constant reminders that his brain is still healing.

Chris and I just had dinner with Michael and Meg. They have both been struggling. They feel stuck in the "grief" stage of this whole thing. They know Seth is okay and are thankful, but can't seem to get past the hospital, and they aren't sure why. It's like it was so difficult emotionally that they just shut it off and now can't seem to turn it back on. They are both struggling emotionally and spiritually. Michael is stuck on a day at Mary Free Bed (March 8, 2017) when he was with Seth. There were two nurses in the room trying to clean Seth and his bed after an accident. Apparently, they left Seth sitting naked in a chair while they cleaned his bed. Seth sat there dazed, and Michael felt they treated Seth as though he wasn't even there. Watching his twenty-one-year-old brother go through this, just broke Michael's heart. It was so painful that Michael pretty much just shut off his emotions from there on out. Then Seth started to get better and so Michael never really dealt with the emotions. It was supposedly over and all better, like he was just supposed to let it go, forget and move on. But unfortunately, it doesn't really work that way. Michael was broken inside... and so he continues to be.

On February 13, 2017, Seth fell through a roof, and Michael was faced with the unimaginable, losing his twenty-one-year-old brother. How could this be? Michael dropped everything and went straight to the hospital, meeting us there just in time to hear the doctor tell us that Seth had a serious brain injury, was on a ventilator, in a coma and could die. He stood at his brother's bedside with uncontrollable tears streaming down his face thinking, "Seth, what have you done?" But then when Andrea and Ethan came, Michael just naturally stepped into his role of big brother and stopped his tears in order to be strong for them. Michael stayed all night, getting very little sleep in the ICU waiting room chair. He prayed at his brother's side for God to spare his life. For the next two and a half weeks while Seth was at Spectrum, Michael basically lived at the hospital with us and Seth. He sacrificed his work, his wife, and his two sons. When he did have to leave, it was to go to work, and then would head right straight back to the hospital, not knowing if Seth would live or ever wake up or what he would be like if he woke up. He grieved the loss of his brother as he stared at his lifeless body in the bed. Day and night he sat there in silence and darkness praying right beside us. He spent countless hours at Seth's side holding his hand. The place where Michael could best express his emotion was when he was alone in his car. Michael drove in his car just yelling "No! No! No!" as he punched the ceiling of his car over and over again.

Michael did have some moments early on when he felt hope, sometimes when we were at our lowest. But having studied physical therapy. [Michael knew how devastating left side neglect could be, so] the left side neglect made him very nervous. Then that day at Mary Free Bed... It's like something snapped. Knowing they needed to change and clean up Seth, I had stepped out of the room to give him his privacy. I remember Michael coming out to me in the hallway so upset. He said he couldn't take it anymore and just wanted to run away from it all. He kept saying, "that's my brother in there, naked and dazed and unable to care for himself at all!" It is a day stuck in Michael's head and heart. This picture in his mind of his brother awake but unaware, dazed, naked, and unable to use his left side, seemingly disregarded by the hospital staff helping him at that moment, has left Michael unable to move. He is stuck there, in that room, with that pain, and he doesn't know how to get out and move forward past it.

Emotionally, I think Michael did run away that day, and now he is struggling to find his way back. Michael feels like it is selfish for him to have these feelings. After all, this isn't about him. "Seth is better, so he should be too", Michael tells himself. But inside he knows he is not okay. He is broken and doesn't know how to fix it.

People all over the world have prayed for Seth, and God heard and answered all of our prayers. People's lives have been touched and changed through Seth's story. The thing is, it's not just Seth's story. This is also Michael's story. Plenty of people have asked Michael how we are and how Seth is, but no one asks Michael how he is. He tells himself it doesn't matter, that it

370

is actually Seth's story and our story. But it is actually our whole family's story.

Meg too is broken and stuck in a place of grief and struggling to experience Christ's peace. She gave up everything the day Seth fell. She loves Seth like a brother, but she put her own desire to be at the hospital with her husband and all of us aside in order to help us. She put our needs above her own. The minute she heard about the accident, she drove straight to our house to be with our other children. Even when Andrea got the call from us after we first talked to the doctor, she and Ethan went upstairs to talk, but Meg stayed downstairs. She didn't want to leave Caleb, Mary, and Peter alone, even though she would have liked to go upstairs with Andrea and Ethan to find out how Seth was. Throughout the whole thing, she constantly died to herself out of love for us. She and [her two sons] Christopher and David moved into our house to take care of Caleb, Mary, and Peter. This was difficult on the boys, not seeing their Dad and messing up their routines and sleep schedules. It had an impact on their sleep and behavior, being only three years old and about eight months old. Meg, through her sacrifice and help, made it possible for us and Michael, Andrea, and Ethan to all be together at the hospital with Seth. She literally took care of everything, the children, all the calls and offers of food and help, the house, everything, so that we would not have to think or worry about anything other than Seth. I am so grateful for her help during this time, and so proud to call her my daughter. She displayed the selfless love of

371

a mother, throughout those six and a half weeks, which was felt by all of us. I know it was a total comfort for me to know that she was with Caleb, Mary, and Peter. And they too, have since commented that having Meg with them was a great source of comfort and security. But it didn't come without great sacrifice and pain on her part. Because of her selfless love, she didn't get to be there at the hospital with us to go through it together and process it. She felt very alone going through it all. Then when she would get to come to the hospital, she didn't allow herself to cry because she wanted to be strong for us. She locked up her emotions right from the start and is still having a hard time unlocking them now.

Andrea is the closest in age to Seth. She was twenty-three when Seth had his accident. She was in the middle of a class for a certification for her job. She dropped everything and left class as soon as she got the call, and never returned to complete it. She will have to take it another time. She couldn't focus on it. Her mind and heart were with Seth. I think her every thought and whole life became about Seth. She and Seth had been quite close growing up. I'll never forget how sad Seth was when Andrea started Kindergarten. He used to sit and stare out the window and cry for her every day after we dropped her off at school. Andrea too, like Michael, missed work as much as she possibly could. She and Michael really became Chris' and my main support both emotionally and physically throughout it all. Day after day she sat with us at Seth's side, praying and holding his hand for countless hours. I remember one night in particular when she laid across three hard straight-back chairs, and that was how she slept. She didn't ever want to have to leave the hospital. Those were long and difficult days in the ICU.

During that time, Andrea had a boyfriend who was supporting her. I was thankful she had someone looking after her needs. Then ten days after Seth's accident, he broke up with her unexpectedly. My heart broke for her, but sadly I'm afraid I was not much comfort because I was so consumed with what was going on with Seth. She was too, actually. She said that in comparison, the breakup was the least of her concerns, but it was difficult because it kind of left her alone to deal with things. I remember her saying that she had no one to talk to, because Seth would have been the person she would have talked to about the breakup, and her boyfriend was the one she talked to about Seth. But at that point in time, she didn't have either of them. Those were heavy crosses for Andrea to have to carry, but she did not complain. She was just there, faithfully with Seth and us day after day no matter what. She is one strong woman. Then when we got to Mary Free Bed, Andrea stayed with Seth every weekend, so Chris and I could be home some. She fed Seth. She took him to the bathroom. She did whatever was needed to help him. I think this experience has impacted her in many positive ways, yet I also know it was extremely painful for her, and she still has deep pain that she is still trying to process.

Ethan, Caleb, Mary, and Peter all sacrificed much during this time as well. They were basically left without their parents for six and a half weeks. We were pretty much at the hospital as much as possible. We would go home to shower and eat sometimes and occasionally sleep a night at home. Caleb, Mary, and Peter all slept in our room when we weren't home. It was a source of comfort for them. Each one of them was our support through this. In so many ways they kept their own needs to themselves out of love for us. They continually died to themselves so that we could focus our time and attention on Seth. Looking back, it is amazing to think about, and Chris and I couldn't be more proud of each of them.

Ethan was in the middle of his senior year of high school at Grand Rapids Catholic Central. He missed school most of that first week. He was at Spectrum with us as much as he possibly could be. Then once Seth got to MFB, he would walk there after school many days. Then he would go home and later bring us dinner and also bring Caleb, Mary and Peter there almost every night. He took on a lot of responsibility for the younger kids once Michael and Meg went back to their own home.

Ethan lived a nightmare for many weeks. The day before Seth's accident, he and Seth had a big fight. The words said in the fight were the last words they had spoken to each other. Then suddenly Seth is in a coma, fighting for his life. Ethan stood at Seth's side sorrowful, crying, praying, and thinking that it can't end this way. He needed to tell Seth he was sorry and didn't mean what he had said, but he didn't know if he would ever get that chance. Ethan carried an extremely heavy cross that few will ever understand. Ethan is a very kind, sensitive, and compassionate young man. This was a lot of weight for him to carry, but he did it with grace and love.

However, as time went on, he became numb to the pain and just went through the motions. He sort of buried his pain and then became stuck in it. Ethan felt very alone, like many of his friends didn't understand. He carried his pain long after Seth was home and better. Surprisingly, it ended up being someone Ethan hadn't really cared for that reached out to him. It meant a lot to Ethan to have someone who had been through something similar, reach out to him. It made him realize he wasn't alone. It also made Ethan think about whether he had actually cared or even thought about others when they were going through difficult times. It challenged Ethan to grow as an individual and look more outside himself.

Caleb, Mary, and Peter in many ways felt left out. They said that they sort of felt like outsiders rather than part of the family. This breaks my heart. It was definitely not our intention. Because they were younger, we didn't want to scare them. We weren't home to tell them anything, and we didn't communicate to our older children what we wanted them told. Truthfully, I don't think any of us knew what to tell them or how, and so they weren't really told anything. We also didn't bring them to the hospital to see Seth for a while because we thought it would scare them. Seeing him that way was extremely frightening. I didn't want the kids to be home, scared, and having nightmares when I couldn't even be there to help them. They also didn't have cell phones, so when I sent our kids updates on Seth's condition, they didn't get those either. Sometimes they got their information from facebook or misinformation from classmates at school. That should never have happened. When I would go home to shower or sleep, I sort of assumed they knew, but to be honest, I didn't know what they knew and didn't take the time to find out. In hindsight, I wish I had. I should have, but at the time, I was exhausted and wrapped up in my own emotions. For that, I am so sorry. I never wanted to hurt them, and I didn't mean to discard their feelings.

Caleb was fourteen and in eighth grade at St. Thomas. Because of his age, he didn't know how serious Seth's injury was. He had some really great friends, whose families kind of took him in and had him over quite a bit. In some ways, he was having a great time. We were glad that he was distracted. It helped us to know that Caleb was happy and well taken care of. It wasn't until we talked to the kids about the MRI results that Caleb realized how bad it was and that Seth could have died. When he found out, he was kind of mad that he hadn't been included in all of that. He also felt really guilty that he had been having fun with friends and hadn't been more worried.

Caleb also found comfort and security in Meg being at our house with them. When Woodtv8 interviewed him, he told them that Meg, being a mother, was a great comfort because there is nothing like the comfort of a mother. He was a fourteen-year-old navigating through this family tragedy and other typical struggles of a teenage boy pretty much on his own. I feel bad. Looking back, I wish I would have recognized his struggles and spent more time talking to him about how he was.

Mary-Kate was in seventh grade and had just turned thirteen only two weeks before Seth's accident. She and I had just spent a weekend away together for her thirteenth birthday. I am so thankful we had that time together before all of this happened. She was having a tough year in school with her classmates. We had been in the principal's office many times trying to work things out. Mary had been dealing with bullying in her class and felt very alone. She had not found a single friend who she felt had her back and would support her or stand up for her when she tried to stand up for what was right. She was up past midnight many nights, unable to go to sleep or crying herself to sleep because she was worried about going to school the next day. When we were preparing for our trip to California, we were worried about leaving her for just one week, but instead we essentially ended up leaving her for six and a half weeks. And during that time, being at school got harder for her, yet she never said a word to me about it. She knew we needed to be with Seth and focus on him. She even sent me a text late the night of Seth's accident telling me that they were okay and not to worry about them at all. She has since told me that she was crying as she wrote and sent that text because she was scared and definitely not alright, but she didn't want me to worry. What an amazing example of true selfless love. Throughout Seth's hospitalization, when I would ask how things were, she told me many times, "I'm alright. Seth needs you right now." That was extremely selfless and very mature at only thirteen years of age. Her love was heroic and sacrificial like Christ's. She seemed happy and okay when she was at the hospital with us, but she told me later that she was breaking inside because she felt so alone.

It is heartbreaking to know now that she was not alright and hurting so much. In fact, things had gotten much worse for her at school. Classmates teased her about Seth's accident and used it against her. Because of it, she had a lot of trouble sleeping. She would be up until three or four in the morning crying, sometimes even having panic attacks. Then she would cry almost every morning, begging Meg not to make her go to school. Mary has deep hurts from those times at school. Hurts and insecurities that she still carries now and is trying to overcome. I am so proud of the way she supported me through this time by her sacrificial love. I wish I had done a better job supporting her. I wish I would have questioned her more, listened more and been emotionally more present to her during that time.

Peter was nine years old and in third grade, the youngest of the family. We didn't talk to him too much about any of it. He still has such a beautiful innocence. He is our happy little boy, who seemed to adapt and roll through it all pretty gracefully. We probably should have talked with him more about what was happening. In many ways, he must have felt alone during that time. He is still upset about not being home the day Seth came home from Mary Free Bed. He wanted to be there, but I thought it would be better for him to go on his field trip with his class.

It is something he says he will always regret. There are undoubtedly many things I would do differently had I known what I know now. I think Peter understood more than we gave him credit for. Our little Peter never ceases to amaze us with his depth of thinking and character, like the day he hugged me and comforted me saying, "It's okay Mom because life is really about getting to Heaven." The wisdom, beauty, and purity of a child...

May 8, 2018

As a mother it is extremely painful to see how each of my children have suffered through this. And it is painful to see how I was not present to them and able to care for them. I wish I had taken better care of them and tried to help them through it more, but I was so wrapped up in my own pain and Seth's recovery. I neglected their needs at the time. I can't help feeling that I have let them all down. For that I am truly sorry. Chris and I are so proud of each and every one of our children, and the sacrifices they each made out of love for their family. They were our main support, and we couldn't have done it without them.

Sometimes when I talk about this and how Seth's siblings were all there for him through it all, he feels very bad. He feels like we all gave so much to him, and that he gave nothing to us. It makes him feel helpless again. Yet Seth gave too...He told us over and over that it would have been easier for him to just die. He told us how incredible it was to be in God's presence and how amazing God's love is. Yet he begged and pleaded for his life. Why? For us. He told us that he saw us, felt our love and could not leave us. So day after day of therapy, every painful step of it, every humiliating step of it, he gave for us. And all those hours in the hospital, all the sacrifices we made... they were all because we just wanted Seth back. None of us want him to feel bad for anything we did. All we wanted was Seth back because we couldn't imagine life without him. Our family just isn't complete without him. So Seth asks what he did for us? Well, he fought every day to come back to us and went through the pain for us and appreciated us and allowed us to love him every step along the way. That is no small task. It required a lot of hard work and a lot of humility.

I see all the suffering in my family, the brokenness, the pain, the insecurities... It has not been easy for any one of us. I feel their pain, and I worry about my family. Then this morning I opened my Magnificat and was reminded that this pain is God's grace drawing us each closer to Himself. It is walking through the crosses that make us into the men and women He desires us to be. When Seth fell, God had a specific plan for each of us through it all. He had all of us in mind and knew exactly how it would affect and change each one of our lives. It is not just Seth's story; it is all of our story. God continues to hold us now, as He always has. We are indeed his masterpiece, but we are most definitely still a work in progress.

Sadly, it wasn't until this time, May of 2018, fifteen months after Seth's accident, that I realized that my other children, too, still needed to heal right alongside Seth. I suddenly became acutely aware that our journey was not over, and it may not be for quite some time. Until this time I had been pretty oblivious to how deeply they were still hurting and the fact that many of them had never processed the pain and trauma they experienced.

No one really knew the extent of their pain and what they had been through. Their lives had also been shattered on February 13, 2017, but in many ways their feelings were overlooked. Even in the news story, the other kids were such a small part of it, that it hurt as they watched it. Caleb wasn't even in the picture of the siblings. As much as they told themselves that these things didn't matter, they did.

None of this is written to complain or to make light of the amazing miracles God gave our family. There is no doubt we were blessed beyond our wildest dreams. Rather it is to show our humanity in it all, and to bring hope to other families that may be suffering in similar ways. Such traumas are difficult to process, and even when everything turns out good, they can still leave wounds that need healing.

It was exceedingly painful for me as a mother to see how alone and destroyed my children felt inside. I was ashamed to realize that I had been so wrapped up with Seth's needs and my own emotions that I hadn't been emotionally present to my other children. It is my biggest regret in all of this. If only I had looked more at them and their needs, rather than my own, maybe things could have been different for them.

I am constantly humbled by the Lord's mercy and His patience with me. He has shown me so many times throughout my life that He is in control, yet I still struggle to surrender and trust Him completely. Thankfully, holiness is not in our perfection, but rather in our constant striving.

Life is a journey, and God uses everything along the way to mold each one of us into the man or woman He created us to be. I have had to continually surrender all of my children to Christ, and trust that, in all that He allows, He is working in their lives, loving them, and leading them where He desires them to be.

Chris and I have seen God's grace and beauty so abundantly in each of them, in their total sacrificial love for us and each other. John 15:13 says, "Greater love has no one than this, that one lay down his life for his friends." This is exactly what we had witnessed in each of our children throughout all of this time. We could not possibly be more grateful and proud of them and the tremendous sacrifices they each made out of love for God and their family. I know that God is holding each one of them in the palm of His hand. Their sacrifices have not gone unnoticed. In fact, God's goodness has been clearly seen in their sacrificial love.

CHAPTER SEVENTEEN
- THE EPISODES -
God is Good... in the Ordeal

Seth continued to deal with his strange "episodes" of anxiety and subsequent periods of depression, not knowing what they were, for over a year. They continued to happen cyclically about every four to five weeks. When Seth realized the anti-anxiety medication and counseling hadn't resolved the issue, which we had thought was PTSD, he eventually stopped both and just tried to live with and manage the episodes on his own.

As time went on, Seth began researching his symptoms online, and diagnosed himself with complex partial seizures. I didn't want to think that could be true. I feared Seth may lose his ability to drive and much of his independence as a result. Though Seth had tried at different times to describe the episodes to his doctor, the doctor never mentioned seizures. Seth eventually brought his research and suspicion to his doctor's attention.

Finally, several months later in November of 2018, Seth was referred to a Neurologist and was officially diagnosed with complex partial seizures, just as he had suspected. Fortunately, complex partial seizures are very different from what most of us think of as seizures. Seth never lost consciousness with them, therefore his ability to drive was never revoked. He was started on anti-seizure medications right away, which at first significantly reduced the occurrence and severity of his seizures.

As Seth's seizures spaced out and got less severe, we would start to relax and think he would be able to manage them okay as long as they were mild and not very often. However, after a while, his body seemed to adjust to the medication and the seizures began to come more frequently again. When this happened, Seth's doctor increased his medication dosage, which again reduced the rate and severity of the seizures. However, a pattern developed as this happened repeatedly over the next couple of years. After about 2 years of unsuccessful attempts to eliminate Seth's seizures with medication, the neurologist scheduled Seth for seizure monitoring.

In September of 2020, Seth was admitted to the hospital in the Epilepsy Monitoring Unit (EMU) for an unspecified number of days for seizure monitoring. Upon arrival, Seth was hooked to an Electroencephalogram, commonly known as an EEG. He had several small sensors attached to his head in order to pick up the electrical signals produced by his brain. He was confined to the bed, except for using the bathroom, for the duration of his hospital stay, which we were told could last a week or so. The EEG monitored his brain continuously, and the hope was that it would record his brain activity during a seizure. Obtaining information about how and where the seizures were taking place could help the neurologists to determine the best course of action for treating Seth's seizures. We didn't know much about this monitoring going into it, but throughout Seth's stay we learned that the main purpose of it was to determine if Seth would be a good candidate for brain surgery as an option for eliminating his seizures. This for me was a very scary prospect, which I didn't want to think about.

While being monitored with the EEG, Seth was weaned off his anti-seizure medications and was sleep deprived in order to try to trigger a seizure faster. This, combined with being confined to a hospital bed for days, was tough on Seth. He is one who, since his brain injury, really needs sleep, and at the same time, he is also one who does not like to sit still. Not surprisingly, he was going a little stir crazy. Because of Covid, only the same two people were ever allowed in his room. So throughout his stay, Chris and I took turns sitting with him trying to keep him occupied and awake. It was a very strange feeling just waiting for and wanting him to have a seizure.

It was not only strange waiting for a seizure but also quite stressful, because the timing had to be right in order to get the optimal testing desired. For starters, there was a button that Seth had to push when he was having a seizure, which would mark the start of the seizure on the EEG. This was a little difficult for Seth, since his seizures were sometimes mild and hard to detect at first.

The good thing though was that Seth's seizures usually came in clusters, meaning he would have several over the course of a day or day and a half. So if Seth missed the first one, he would most likely have more relatively soon after. But the hard part was that during specific times, the button was also connected to a device that when pushed would inject a small amount of low-dose radioactive material into Seth's IV. This is called a SPECT test.

In a SPECT test, the injected radioactive material creates a detailed, 3D map of the blood flow activity in the brain during a seizure, which is what the doctors really wanted. However, the SPECT test was only set up at specific times, and if the button got pushed and the radioactive material was injected mistakenly when Seth was not having a seizure, they would have to wait another day or two to try again. And when you're stuck in the hospital, confined to a bed, and periodically being sleep deprived, waiting for another day is not desirable. So we prayed and waited, hoping Seth would have a seizure at the perfect time to produce the results needed.

Within four days Seth had a seizure and it was while the SPECT test was hooked up. Having gotten the information the doctors needed, Seth was then able to go home. In retrospect, four days doesn't seem that long, but going through it with Seth, it sure felt long. Needless to say, we were happy it was over.

Seth's neurologist told us that it would most likely be months before we got any results from it. He explained that Seth's EEG during his seizure would be compared to his baseline EEG and very specialized and detailed mapping would be done to study the activity in his brain during his seizure. In the meantime, life went on as usual for Seth, continuing to deal with the weird episodes, known to be seizures, each month or so as he waited for the results.

In 2021, Seth was hired by a heating and cooling company. We thought this could be a great career opportunity for him. Being such an active, physical person, and visual, hands-on learner, Chris and I had thought Seth might end up working some sort of trade, and HVAC was one he had thought about on and off. Seth liked the work, but to his surprise, he was having a tough time remembering from day to day what he had done the previous day. Usually doing something himself would lock it into his memory. But this time something was extremely different.

To help, Seth started taking pictures of things as well as taking notes on what he needed to do. He would go over the steps and procedures at night for the next day and then again in the morning on his way to work, yet when he got to the job site and looked at the unit to be installed, it felt almost as if he had never seen it before. This was exceedingly frustrating and confusing for Seth. He even contacted a friend of his who worked with HVAC and had him go over it with him several nights, but still Seth struggled. He had no idea what was happening to him.

This brought back very disconcerting feelings, like ones Seth had after his brain injury. Once again, he suddenly felt like he didn't know who he was anymore. The way he had remembered and learned things his whole life was not working. It was like a part of him was gone. He would tell me, "I don't even know who I am." At the time, I didn't realize the gravity of how difficult the job was for him, and I kept wondering why he was reverting back several years, grappling with who he was again. It didn't make sense to me. I just kept encouraging him to stick with the job. I was sure it would click for him at some point. After all, this was Seth. This was exactly the type of thing he was always good at.

Right around the same time in midwinter of 2021, Seth's neurologist called saying he had the results of his seizure monitoring, but that before he went over them with Seth, he wanted Seth to have another neuropsych evaluation like he had back in December 2017, about ten months after his accident.

Seth's second neuropsych evaluation was devastating. It showed that Seth's visual memory, which was strong over three years earlier in December of 2017, was no longer strong. In fact, it was pretty much nonexistent, which explained everything Seth had been experiencing at his new job. As horrible as this news was, it gave Seth a little relief to finally have an explanation for what was happening, instead of him just feeling like he was going crazy.

Not only did the neuropsych evaluation confirm all Seth was feeling, it also confirmed the findings of his seizure monitoring. The monitoring showed that Seth's seizures were taking place in his visual memory center. And based on Seth's recent evaluation, it had become clear that his seizures, over the past few years, had literally been killing his brain cells in that area. This news crushed me. Actually, it made me really angry. I felt like he'd already had enough loss and deficits to deal with. Why did the seizures have to attack one of his strengths? I struggled to accept this.

There was no longer any doubt that the seizures absolutely had to be stopped. Seth's neurologist told us that based on their findings so far, Seth may be a candidate for surgery. As I said before, this was a very frightening prospect. I had at first thought it sounded extreme and had hoped that maybe Seth could just live with the seizures. Afterall, he had learned how to cope with them quite well. But after the discovery that the seizures were doing damage in his brain, and the fact that the anti-seizure medications had not worked for him, surgery was beginning to look like his only option. However, we were told he would need further testing before they could be sure.

Before this time, we had not realized that the seizure monitoring he had in the EMU back in

September, was only phase one of the testing. Phase two, we learned, was much more invasive and difficult. In fact, we found out that he was going to have to have brain surgery in order to even do the testing! Phase two would involve more monitoring, only this time it would be done using electrodes that went directly into his brain.

Seth's brain surgery and epilepsy monitoring was scheduled for July 26, 2021, and this time we were informed that the monitoring could take anywhere from one to four weeks. Since the last time he was monitored took only four days for him to have a seizure, we felt somewhat confident that this time would likely be pretty quick as well. The scary part this time was the brain surgery to begin with.

Remember the bolt that Seth had in his head while in the ICU to measure his intracranial pressures? Well, this surgery was to place not just one, but ten of those in Seth's head. The surgeons were going to have to drill ten small holes in Seth's skull and insert wires into them and very carefully feed those wires into very specific and precise places in Seth's brain. This would all be done so that when Seth had a seizure, they would hopefully be able to pinpoint the exact location of his seizures. The thought of them placing all these wires directly into Seth's brain was extremely scary.

The week before Seth's scheduled surgery and monitoring, Seth began having the typical feelings he gets just before he has his monthly cluster of seizures.

This was very worrisome since Seth typically only had seizures every four to six weeks. Based on Seth's history, if he had seizures before entering the hospital, it would be unlikely for him to have more seizures for at least another month or longer.

We began praying and asking others to pray that Seth would not have seizures before his hospital stay. This put a lot of stress on Seth. He was trying not to have seizures, when in fact, that was not something he could control. Sadly, Seth did end up having his normal cluster of seizures just days before his admittance to the hospital. He was scheduled for surgery to place the leads in his brain on Monday morning, and the seizures took place on the Saturday before. So with it being a weekend, he wasn't even able to talk to his neurologist about it first.

I had been an emotional mess inside that whole week prior, worrying about the surgery, worrying about him having seizures beforehand, and just plain worrying. The day before the scheduled surgery, was our son, Caleb's nineteenth birthday. We had the whole family together that day to celebrate. It was nice, but difficult all at the same time. Tension was high that day, with the next day on everyone's mind.

I was trying hard to focus on Caleb, but it was difficult. Seth was very obviously and understandably uptight, and as a result, things were getting blown out of proportion and sort of blowing up among the brothers.

Let's just say that it was a tough day for all. However, by the grace of God, we all pulled it together and ended the day with praise and worship and praying over Seth in preparation for his surgery and all that may lie ahead.

During the praise and worship, all the worry and emotion I had bottled inside that week finally came pouring out in healing tears as we prayed for Seth and reaffirmed our trust in God. As we prayed, one particular Scripture passage kept coming to mind. It was not one that I wanted to hear or accept at that time. Nonetheless, I felt the Lord saying to me, "My child, if you aspire to serve the Lord, prepare yourself for an ordeal." (Sirach 2:1) I didn't want to admit it, but after receiving this message, I had a sinking feeling that things were not going to go as smoothly this time around.

Surgery began between 7:30-8am the next morning and was expected to last around four hours. Family and friends had signed up to take shifts praying for Seth during his surgery, making sure he was covered in prayer the whole time. As I sat in the surgery waiting room, I struggled to surrender my will for Seth's life. I was anxious and fighting God's will. I just plain did not want to be there and be in that situation. I worried for Seth's life and the possible risks and dangers associated with brain surgery. In the depth of my heart, I really did believe that God's will for Seth was best, but I also knew that God's will is not always easy. So humanly, I was very scared.

Seth came out of surgery in extreme pain. Between the anesthetics and the pain, he also woke up from surgery very nauseous. Just trying to get him from recovery to his room, he began vomiting which caused tremendous pressure in his head and bleeding on the side of his head where some of the leads had been put in. That was very nerve wracking.

Seth had a bit of a rocky start, but as the nurses got his nausea under control, things settled down. Seth was awake, coherent, and able to move everything! What a relief it was to see that he was okay. I could finally breathe freely. My prayers had been answered, and my fears regarding the surgery had been dispelled.

Seth's CT scan after surgery showed that the leads were all placed correctly, exactly where the neurosurgeon wanted them. It also confirmed that there was no bleeding in his brain from the procedure. Though it was difficult to see Seth in so much pain, we were incredibly grateful that he was through the surgery and that it had been successful. We were told the rest of that day would be focused on pain management, and then the following day, they would begin slowly weaning him off his anti-seizure medications.

The last time Seth did epilepsy monitoring we had no idea what to expect. Therefore, we weren't prepared at all. Being veterans this time around, we came prepared with lots of Seth's favorite comfort foods and drinks to help pass the time and keep him awake during periods of sleep deprivation. However, we were not veterans to phase two and the surgery part. In fact, in our ignorance, we completely overlooked a major part of this experience... pain! Four of the leads going into Seth's head were in his right temple and went directly through his jaw muscle. This was one of the most painful areas for Seth and actually made it exceedingly painful for him to use his jaw to even talk, much less eat.

By the second day, Seth's nausea and the pain in his head were both being satisfactorily controlled with medication. However, the pain in his jaw was still intense, continuing to make it very difficult for him to talk or eat. On top of that, the sleep deprivation had already begun. He was not allowed to sleep at all that day, even though he was still completely worn out from the surgery and pain.

Seth was also put in arm restraints twenty-four/seven and was told he had to be restrained for his entire stay in the hospital. This was new from last time too. I thought being stuck in bed was bad enough before, but this time he was literally tied to the bed. With the electrodes going directly into his brain, they couldn't risk him having a seizure and accidentally pulling them out. That would be extremely dangerous.

There were ten wires going into Seth's head with over one hundred contact points in his brain. His head was wrapped tightly to hold the wires in place. The wires then all came together like a ponytail cascading down the side of his head. They were then connected to a machine near the side of Seth's bed, which in turn was plugged into an electrical outlet. So in essence, his head, with ten holes and wires in it, was tightly wrapped and hooked to machines, while his arms were tied to the bed; he was in pain, couldn't eat, and was forced to stay awake hours on end. This seemed like torture. And on top of it all, we were told that it could go on for one to four weeks.

Last time had only been four days, so we held onto hope that it would be relatively short again. However, we had doubts, especially since Seth had just had his typical cyclical seizures just two days before. We also found out from the doctors that the surgery often delays seizures. I had thought maybe the surgery would irritate the brain and cause seizures, but I was wrong. We learned that the surgery actually does the opposite. So the odds were stacking up against this being quick, and I have to admit that in the back of my mind, I was sort of plagued by the words from Sirach that the Lord had spoken to me, "My child, if you aspire to serve the Lord, prepare yourself for an ordeal." To me, Seth having to do this for a whole week or even two seemed virtually unthinkable and unbearable, but all we could do is take it one day at a time, supporting and encouraging him through it.

We typically received daily reports from the epileptologists, the neurologists who specialized in epilepsy. Each day they would come into Seth's room and tell us what they had seen on Seth's EEG over the past twenty-four hours. Right away the day of the surgery, the EEG recorded some unusual activity in Seth's brain. It wasn't exactly seizure activity but was somehow related. The doctors told us that they sort of expected to see this type of activity since Seth had just had seizures two days before coming into the hospital.

On day three when the neurologists gave their report, we were told that the EEG recorded Seth having constant tiny seizures for ten hours straight from 4pm on day two until 2am of day three. They reported that sometimes they were coming as quickly as every fifteen to twenty seconds. The crazy part is that Seth never felt them at all. He felt a little weird or off at times, but that didn't seem unusual given his sleep deprivation and the heavy pain medication he was on. The fact is, while the EEG recorded seizures in his brain, he didn't feel any of his normal seizure symptoms. It made me very sad to realize that so much was going on in Seth's brain that we weren't even aware of. It's no wonder his thinking got foggy at times and his memory was being affected.

This was disheartening news, but what made it even worse was that these seizures were in a different area than the activity they recorded the first day, which now meant that there may be two different parts of the brain involved. Based on these findings, it was already looking like things may not be as clear cut for Seth as the epileptologists had hoped. All of this was going on, and they hadn't even recorded the actual seizures he typically

396

felt yet. The doctors would still need a lot more information to get a clear picture of what was going on, but I was already feeling very discouraged about this. The words the Lord had spoken to me were starting to feel very real. Things were seemingly shaping up to be quite an ordeal. We were back on the rollercoaster of ups and downs as we had to once again just wait and trust.

Typically, after a night of sleep deprivation, Seth was allowed to sleep the next night. But even if he didn't sleep well that night, he would still have to do sleep deprivation the next. Within the first few days, after a very restless night when Seth didn't sleep well due to a lot of pain and discomfort, he was sleep deprived again. He had to stay awake until 4am. Then he was allowed to sleep only four hours until 8am at which time he was awakened and required to stay awake all day until 8pm. Other nights he was kept up until 5am and then only allowed to sleep for three hours before they woke him up again. This sort of pattern continued as the days turned into weeks, waiting for Seth to have a seizure. It was brutal. By the 11th day, Seth felt like he couldn't do it any longer. With his sleep schedule so messed up and the continual sleep deprivation, Seth was literally exhausted and at the end of his rope. We didn't know how he could possibly continue on much longer. Everyone was praying so hard for him to have a seizure and put an end to this misery.

Doctors also tried to induce seizures using methods such as light stimulation, making him hyperventilate, as well as giving him alcohol when he was exhausted, right before he was allowed to fall asleep after being sleep deprived. All these things can often be triggers for seizures, but for Seth it was all to no avail. And as the days and weeks went on, it got more and more difficult for Seth to stay awake, and it was getting nearly impossible to wake him up in the mornings after only having a few hours of sleep.

By this time, nearly four and a half years after Seth's accident, our family had grown in number as well as age. We had welcomed two new grandsons and a new daughter-in-law. Michael and Meg now had four sons, Christopher, David, Brandon, and Damian. And on July tenth, just a couple weeks before Seth's surgery and hospital stay, Ethan had married his high school sweetheart, Elle, whom he had newly been dating at the time of Seth's accident. Also, Seth's youngest three siblings, Caleb, Mary, and Peter, who had felt very left out during the time of Seth's accident, were now ages nineteen, seventeen, and thirteen. They had grown much closer to Seth after his accident and provided tremendous support for him throughout this time.

In fact, Caleb, who had just turned nineteen, became the MVP this time around. He decided that summer that he would keep his schedule free in order to help Seth in whatever way was needed. Throughout

Seth's hospital stay, Caleb took the night shifts with Seth. He would stay with Seth and help keep him awake each time Seth was being sleep deprived. It was a huge help to Seth and to all of us, to be honest. It was an incredible blessing for Chris and me to be able to go home to sleep every night and know that Seth was in good hands. In fact, Seth looked forward to Caleb coming every night. I think staying awake through the nights with Caleb was actually easier for Seth than the daytime. They had their stash of Monster energy drinks, coffee, and other caffeinated pops to help, and although it was under very difficult circumstances, it was a very special time of bonding for Caleb and Seth as brothers. Seth was no longer the big brother caught up in his own life with little interest in his younger siblings. He had, since his accident, invested time and energy into knowing and caring for them. Caleb was no longer just the little brother who had been left out. He had become the person Seth counted on and Seth's main support during this time. Not only had they grown as brothers, they had also become very close friends.

Daytimes were often a bit more difficult for Seth. I would usually show up at the hospital at 8am and have the job of waking Seth up after only a few hours of sleep. I typically stopped at a coffee shop on my way to help entice him to wake up with his favorite coffee and breakfast sandwich. Besides Chris and me, Michael, Meg, Andrea, Ethan, Elle, Mary, Peter, Aunt Sarah,

Uncle Dave, Grandpa and Aunt Kathy also helped out with this morning duty as well as at other times during the days when Seth had to stay awake. Having different people to visit with definitely helped motivate him to wake up and stay awake.

Even without the added discomfort of sleep deprivation, most people would struggle being confined to a bed day after day. However, many would still at least be able to find some fun ways to pass the time, like playing video games, binge watching season after season of a favorite show, reading, or even playing cards or board games. But none of these activities were fun to Seth. He's never been a big reader or TV watcher and the games he likes to play are active ones. He's never liked sitting still at all. He likes to be on the move and doesn't like wasting time. So unfortunately, this continuous time of doing nothing was particularly challenging for Seth.

Day after day he passed the time on social media, basically watching other people out living their lives while he could not. As the days passed, this whole ordeal moved far beyond physical discomfort, feeling much like mental and emotional torture for him as well. Imagine going from working full days for a construction company to being confined to a hospital bed when you feel perfectly fine. Seth wasn't even allowed to go to the bathroom on his own. He couldn't even get up and walk around his hospital room without assistance from the nursing staff. And not only was he physically confined, it also became a sort of prison in his head, because all he could do was think about and talk about what he wished he could be doing. It became a huge mind game, and it was getting increasingly more difficult for him to stay positive and hopeful as the days passed.

By Seth's 3rd week of monitoring, the epileptologists began to do some cortical mapping. Given that Seth had intracranial electrodes with over one hundred contact points deep inside his brain, the epileptologists could systematically stimulate each of those areas in an effort to trigger a seizure. It was quite crazy to watch, and even more crazy for Seth to experience. With a simple click of a button on their laptop, the doctors would stimulate an area of Seth's brain and then wait to see if it caused any response on Seth's EEG as well as any physical or emotional responses in Seth. There were areas that produced no reaction at all, and other areas that caused Seth to have immediate emotions or feelings. At one point, the EEG did show seizure activity and Seth had the exact symptoms and feelings he typically had during his seizures. This gave them a good indication of where his seizures may be taking place. It was one more piece of information the neurologists could add to the whole picture of what was happening in Seth's brain.

Seth was super hopeful that since they were able to record a seizure on the EEG, that would be enough, and they would let him go home. Although it was good information, when Seth's neurosurgeon did her rounds the next day, she told him that it absolutely was not enough information for her to feel confident doing brain surgery with. To pinpoint exactly where his seizures were and get the full picture of what was happening in his brain, they really wanted Seth to have his typical seizures on his own. Hearing that was super disappointing for Seth. He felt desperate to go home by this point. However, the neurosurgeon's thoughts were definitely understandable. If part of Seth's brain was going to have to be removed, none of us wanted them to be guessing about which part to remove.

It could have been easy for Seth to give in and lose hope, but he worked hard to stay positive. Most of the time he enjoyed talking to his nurses and nurse techs. He joked around with them trying to brighten their days and spread joy and laughter as much as possible, but as the weeks passed it got harder and harder for him to maintain that positive attitude. By the end of three weeks in the hospital, Seth was losing the battle and had become quite depressed. It was hard to see him so down, but none of us could blame him. Waking up each new day became almost unbearable as it held nothing except for more waiting for something that may never actually happen.

The thought of Seth going through all this and never having one of his typical seizures was unimaginable, but as the weeks passed, it was becoming a real possibility. Typically, they didn't like to leave the electrodes in the brain more than four weeks due to the risk of infection. And no one had ever been in the EMU longer than five weeks. Going longer than that was too risky. So as the weeks progressed Seth was sort of "on the clock," which definitely added more pressure. I couldn't even bear the thought of him going through all of this potentially for nothing.

Along with scattered bouts of pain, there was also a lot of itching from the tightly wound head wrap. By the beginning of the fourth week, the itching was so intense that it was causing him immense physical pain. He said it felt like there were a thousand needles stuck into his head. He felt like he couldn't take it any longer. He was in so much agony that he wanted to just rip everything out and go home. At times, he was literally losing it, and I was getting scared that he was going to accidentally pull the leads out with all his frantic scratching.

Through it all, Seth clung to a quote that Caleb had given him by Pope Benedict XVI. It really spoke to his heart and inspired him. Writhing in pain and discomfort, he repeated Pope Benedict's words over and over again, "The world offers you comfort, but you were not made for comfort. You were made for greatness."

Seth definitely had moments when he lost his composure, and he also struggled through some very depressive days, but they were few and short considering the length of time he spent strapped to a hospital bed. The neurologists and medical staff were actually amazed at how well Seth was handling all of it. His neurosurgeon told him he was one of the best and most cooperative patients they had ever had in the EMU. They said many people lose it after so much time! Without the prayers of many, he probably would have lost it too. Hope seemed very dim at times. But during one of his most agonizing days, with tears in his eyes, he still was able to say with full resolve, "I can do this. I am a son of God." It was obvious that many people were praying for Seth. As Fr. Jim once told him, prayer is not just words. It is active energy that goes from the one praying to God and then to the one in need. It was evident that much grace was being showered on Seth by all the prayers of the body of Christ.

By Seth's fourth week, a couple of his friends started coming in daily to hang out with him, sometimes even staying most of the night even though they had to work the next day. That was a tremendous blessing, which truly helped to pull Seth out of the depression he had been experiencing. We also started trying to get creative and come up with different things to help pass the time. We brought dumbbells in so that Seth could lift some weights while sitting in the bed. It had been extraordinarily hard for him to not be able to work out all those weeks. Working out is one of his greatest passions!

We also brought in ping pong paddles and balls. We began counting how many times we could hit the ping pong ball back and forth in the air! I think the record was somewhere around one hundred and forty! It was toughest for Seth because not only was he confined to the bed, but his arms were also in restraints, so he had limited range of motion. However, Seth always enjoys a good challenge! Activities like this definitely lightened the mood and allowed Seth to have a little fun.

The nurses also started having a little mercy on him too. They couldn't take the restraints off, but they would sometimes give them quite a bit of slack so that Seth could move his arms more. There were times they were so tight that he couldn't even itch his own nose, and then there were times when they were so loose that he could rest his hands behind his head as he sat in the bed. One of the nurses even allowed Seth to get out of the bed and do some pushups while she was in the room. Of course, they had the permission of the doctor. The nurses were understaffed due to Covid, and therefore were extra busy. But when they had time, they would stay in the room and let Seth get out of bed and walk around the room and stretch for a few minutes. These little things were very helpful for Seth.

It got really difficult staring at the same four walls for four straight weeks. So since the nurses station was right outside Seth's room, they started letting him walk out into the hall, as far as the wires from the EEG would allow, so that he could attend their staff change meetings at 7pm. By this point, they all knew him, and he knew them quite well too. The nursing staff was great the entire time Seth was in the EMU.

As Seth's stay lengthened, it became more and more difficult, not only for Seth but for the family as well. Caleb ended up completely on a third shift schedule, awake at night and sleeping during the days. So we didn't see a lot of him, except for when he came to the hospital at night as we were leaving. Mary was still working her job at Sandy Pines, a camping resort about a half hour away, where we typically spend our summers. So she was back and forth, which left Peter home alone a lot. I was also still running a daycare out of our home two days a week. Mary specifically asked for those two days off work each week, so that she and Peter could help watch the kids when I needed to be at the hospital. Or they would go to the hospital when I needed to be home. Then when Mary needed to work at Sandy Pines, Meg and Ethan and Elle took different days and stayed out there with Mary and Peter so that Mary didn't have to be alone and so that Peter could still enjoy the end of his summer out there before the new school year began.

I felt extremely torn throughout the weeks. I knew Seth needed me, but my younger children needed me too. There was also my job and Mary's to juggle as well. In the midst of it all, I didn't want to neglect the needs of my other children, as I had when Seth first had his accident.

Seth's twenty-sixth birthday was quickly approaching on August 23rd, the school year was about to start for Mary and Peter on August 25th, and Chris had a flight to California on August 26th to surprise his Dad for his eightieth birthday. Never did we imagine Seth would still be in the hospital waiting for a seizure at this time. This would have been completely unthinkable and unbearable if we had known this at the start. As the first couple weeks passed, the goal for Seth became to at least be out before his birthday, but by the fourth week, Seth had become pretty much resigned to the fact that he was going to spend his birthday in the hospital. Seth's birthday was the first day of his fifth week in the hospital. Family and friends came throughout the day and we celebrated with cake that night. It was obviously not the birthday Seth wanted, but it was still a celebration of the gift of his life and the gift he is to all of us.

Throughout Seth's entire stay in the hospital, my sister Kathy posted on Facebook, rallying all the prayer warriors, seeking prayers for Seth's specific needs. She is such a beautiful writer and has such a deep faith. Her post from Seth's birthday shows the kind of love, faith and prayer we were continually being supported by.

August 23, 2021
Today is Seth's 26th birthday. It's also the beginning of his fifth week in the hospital.
None of us expected Seth to be spending his birthday with over one hundred leads still attached to his head and inside his brain. This wasn't a part of our "plans." It wasn't a part of Seth's plan. It wasn't even a part

of the medical team's plan.[OBJ] But, somehow, we trust that it is a part of God's plan. Only He can see the bigger picture...the top of the tapestry...while all we see are the threads and knots underneath.

On one hand, I am so sad and discouraged that Seth is spending his birthday still in the hospital and without the information his team needs. On the other hand, I can't help but be grateful that Seth is spending his birthday here on earth with us, with his faith strengthened and sense of humor and personality intact, when he could've so easily died or spent his life as an invalid as a result of his fall.

And so, today on the 26th anniversary of his birth, I am choosing to be grateful... I am grateful for his life, grateful for his miraculous recovery...grateful for his tremendous faith and for how much my faith and the faith of so many others has grown through his witness. I am grateful for the advances in medicine that allow his team to pinpoint where his seizures are occurring and then give them the possibility of removing those parts of his brain in order to eliminate them...[OBJ][OBJ][OBJ] I am grateful for my sister and brother-in-law and their whole family, whose strength and faith and unconditional love continually amaze me. I am grateful for family, friends, and even strangers who have prayed unceasingly for Seth for so long. And, most of all, I am grateful for our amazing God and Father who loves us more than we can possibly know or understand, and for His Son, our Lord and Savior who cares for us every day, who stretches us, who leads us, who nurtures us, and who calls us to take up our cross and follow Him, and then gives us the grace and strength to do so.

Jesus, we trust in you! In our weakness, You are made strong!

Seth, may God bless you with strength throughout this difficult trial and may He gift you with many more birthdays to celebrate His love with those you love, and with those who love you. We are all praying for you more than you know! #birthdayblessings #sethstrong #allforhishonorandglory #miraclesdohappen #prayersdomatter

On Seth's birthday, the surgeon told us that she would most likely do surgery to remove the leads from his brain on Friday, August 27th, regardless of whether or not he had a seizure. She explained that it was too dangerous to leave the electrodes in any longer. Seth's EEG had been showing interictal activity in his brain for over a week. Interictal activity basically means the brain is irritated and wanting/getting ready to seize. So we thought for sure he would have a seizure, but it just wasn't happening. We tried to pray for God's will, but humanly we wanted Seth to have his normal seizures in order for the neurologists to have the most accurate information possible for Seth's treatment. However, as each new day passed that 5th week, it had become increasingly clear that after all this time, he would likely go home without having a seizure.

There were varying opinions among the neurologists about whether or not they had enough information to proceed with any kind of plan for surgery to eliminate Seth's seizures altogether. They told us they would all have to meet for a long consultation to discuss all the information they had gathered and make a decision about how to proceed if Seth, in fact, didn't have a seizure before he left.

After nearly five weeks in the hospital, doctors began preparing Seth for surgery by starting him on IV anti-seizure medications. They needed to make sure the medication was fully in Seth's system before surgery the next day. The last thing they would want is for him to have a seizure while they were removing the leads from inside his brain. That same day, the day before surgery,

Chris flew out to California as planned. It was hard for him to leave Seth, but we knew at that point that Seth was almost finished with this ordeal, and we felt that it was important for Chris to go be with his dad. It would be a nice break for Chris too.

I think the three of us had all experienced the gamut of emotions throughout those five weeks. And as I rode that roller coaster of emotions, I continually thought about the Lord's words from Sirach, "My child, if you aspire to serve the Lord, prepare yourself for an ordeal." In His mercy, He tried to warn me, but even in my wildest thoughts I never imagined it would go on this long, certainly not without Seth ever having a seizure. To be honest, deep down I feared that it could happen but didn't truly believe it would. I wrestled with the fear and fought it for about the first four weeks, before I could finally let go and surrender it all to Christ. Here is my text to a friend the day of Seth's surgery to remove the leads: "Seth has not had a seizure, but he will be having surgery today around 1pm to remove the electrodes. It's crazy and kind of unbelievable that after five weeks of this Seth will be leaving without having a seizure. I can't really think too much about it. I just have to trust. If God wanted Seth to have a seizure and the doctors to get that information, He would have made it happen. So I am trying not to worry about it. It took me four weeks to accept it, but I do have peace now. I have come to believe that all this has been about so much more than just Seth's medical needs!" I finally was able to let go and trust that God could and would use all suffering for good.

Seth continually offered his suffering each day. It was obvious to see that Seth was continually receiving great grace from all the prayers being said for him. We all were. Once again, his prayer warriors had held him and our family up in prayer throughout the whole ordeal. God is good even in the ordeal!

Seth's surgery to remove the leads went very well. So well in fact, that they actually discharged him from the hospital that same day! You would think I would have been excited, but honestly it was a bit disconcerting. It was frightening for me as they gave the discharge instructions on what to watch for in case of bleeding in his brain. That was terrifying for me, especially with Chris across the country in California. Seth didn't worry about it though. He was a free man and extremely happy to be!

Even though the anesthetics from the surgery should have been knocking him out, Seth had so much pent-up energy that he wasn't tired at all. At 1am the first night home he still wanted to go out and do something. After five weeks of laying around, he was determined to live life to the full! All the things he had thought about doing, he was going to do! Strangely, it seemed like he had a chip on his shoulder, like he had something to prove. He said he felt that way too, but neither of us knew why.

There were other factors that also made it a tough transition for Seth coming home. He said he felt super weird again, like he had when he first came home from Mary Free Bed after his accident. Nothing felt normal to him. That was a feeling he had hated before, and sadly it was back again. It took some time for things to feel normal again for Seth.

Within a couple days of being home, Seth also began to have severe side effects from the new anti-seizure medication his neurologist had started him on. The doctor had warned us that this particular drug, Keppra, was known to cause what was referred to as, "Keppra rage" in some people. Unfortunately, it turned out that Seth was one of those people, and we saw Keppra rage firsthand. Let's just say, it wasn't pretty. It was frightening in fact. It's been eye opening and nerve wracking to see how many strange and unpredictable things can happen when you start messing around with the brain. Seth stopped taking the Keppra immediately and was started on a different medication instead. Thankfully Seth was feeling much more like himself again within a day.

Despite the Keppra rage, medication changes, and the weird feelings he had, Seth was determined not to let anything stop him. Only one week after leaving the hospital, Seth, Caleb, and some friends traveled out of state for a weekend music festival. After returning home, Seth and his music producer, Julian, cranked out several new songs. After five weeks of being stuck in bed, Seth was taking life by storm. One of the songs he wrote and recorded was called, "Say Less." It's about doing more instead of just talking about it. All he could do in the hospital was talk about what he wanted to do. Now he was ready to stop talking and start doing. He was motivated by the desire to make sure he didn't make a liar out of the Seth in the hospital who talked big about all he was going to accomplish when he got out. Being confined to the hospital from July 26th to August 27th definitely made Seth appreciate the freedom and joy that is open to us every single day, which we sadly, so often take for granted.

Seth's neurosurgeon and all the epileptologists who had worked with Seth during his hospital stay met together and agreed that the best course of action for Seth would be a right anterior temporal lobectomy, which is a surgery to remove part of the temporal lobe of his brain. This was a very scary proposition, but the hope was that if they could safely remove the area of the brain where the seizures were occurring, they could successfully stop his seizures. However, before proceeding, they needed to do one more test on Seth to make sure that he would not experience any significant cognitive or motor function deficits with the removal of that particular section of his brain.

The test was called an Intracarotid Methohexital Procedure, which they refer to as the Wada test. The test was done on September 30, 2021. While Seth was hooked to an EEG, the doctor injected medication into the right internal carotid artery in the groin area, which basically put the right temporal lobe of Seth's brain to sleep. While this area was not functioning, they evaluated Seth's motor skills and also put him through a series of cognitive tests specifically involving language and memory. All of his function was appropriate with the right temporal lobe shut down, meaning his left temporal lobe was functioning well, as they had expected. This was the result they were hoping to see, showing that Seth's language and memory would still function adequately if part of his right temporal lobe was removed.

Once the right side was awakened, they then put the left temporal lobe to sleep. And repeated the testing on his right side. With the left side asleep, Seth's memory was significantly affected. This was also what the neurologists had anticipated. Much of his memory function on his right side had been destroyed by his seizures. The test confirmed that the left side of Seth's brain was already compensating for this loss, and that removing this portion of his right temporal lobe would not cause significant increased loss or side effects. This was very good news. It was exactly what all the neurologists had suspected and hoped for.

The positive test results along with the danger of future seizures that, if not eliminated, could do significant damage in other areas of Seth's brain, it seemed there was no other choice but to proceed with the surgery. The neurologist who ran the Wada test said that everything lined up perfectly for surgery, and that if it were his son, he would have him do it. While his words brought some sense of comfort and confidence, they were unfortunately not able to distill all of our fears. Yes, they were able to test cognitive and motor functions, but at the same time we were told that there was no way for them to test or predict how complex things like personality would be impacted by the surgery. For Seth, as well as the rest of our family, this was terrifying.

This weighed very heavily on our hearts and minds. And as the date of the surgery got closer and closer, it became increasingly obvious how worrisome it was for Seth. With each passing day, the frightening question got stronger and stronger, "Is this it for me as I am? Will I ever be the same?" Many "what ifs" plagued Seth's mind, and no one could answer these questions for him. Once again, he, and all of us could only wait and trust. None of it was in our control.

We arrived at the hospital at 5:30am the morning of November 5, 2021, with surgery scheduled for 7:30am. It was heartbreaking for me to watch Seth in pre-op as he made a video on his phone saying, "This is my last video as a normal person." He was not just being dramatic. It was an actual, legitimate fear for which there was no relief.

As they wheeled Seth away to the operating room, Chris and I returned to the waiting room, where all we could do was helplessly wait and pray. Seth was in the surgeon's hands and most importantly in God's hands. It was several hours of waiting, once again not knowing how our son would wake up. Even once Seth was in recovery, we were not allowed to see him. We arrived at the hospital at 5:30 that morning and at 5:30 that evening we were still waiting to see Seth. By that point he had been in recovery for about three and a half hours. We had never had to wait so long to see him after a surgery. Apparently, the hospital was so full that they were having a hard time getting a room for him. And as the time went on, I got more and more uptight, not knowing if Seth had woken up or how he was doing.

Around 8pm they finally had a room available for Seth, and at that point we were sent to his room, where we would finally get to see him after twelve hours of waiting. When we arrived at his room, Seth was not there yet. So we quickly went to the cafeteria to grab some food. We would have had time to get food earlier, but we didn't want to leave the surgical waiting room and miss an update on Seth while he was in surgery. Nerves were high. And once Seth was in recovery, we still didn't dare leave, hoping we may get to see him at any time.

After quickly eating a little something, we returned to Seth's room only to receive the devastating news that he had just had a grand mal seizure. He had never had one of those before... When we saw him, he was completely out of it and seemingly unaware of anything going on around him. Doctors and nurses were doing constant neuro checks asking him to move different parts of his body. I stood there in horror as he barely moved his left side, if at all. It brought me right back to the days in the ICU when he was just coming out of his coma. I thought, "Oh my gosh! What have we done? He was perfectly fine when we brought him in this morning." I was terrified. I couldn't help but think that maybe the surgery had been a mistake.

After twelve worrisome hours of waiting, this was certainly not how we expected or wanted to see Seth. He was so "not there." We had been told that the first twenty-four to forty-eight hours after the surgery would be the most critical because of the risk for serious complications like brain bleeds or stroke. Knowing these risks and now seeing Seth looking so similar to how he was after his brain injury, was enormously terrifying.

Only one of us was allowed to stay the night at the hospital with Seth. We decided it should be Chris since he would be able to help the nurses stand Seth up to go to the bathroom if he was able to get up. So after a very long day, I left the hospital at around 10:30pm without ever getting to see Seth awake or know if he was okay.

The fact that Seth was barely able to move his left side and had not woken up or become aware at all before I had to leave, was awful and exceedingly painful and unsettling for me.

I had a lot of heavy and frightening emotions running through me. While I didn't want to leave, I also didn't feel like I had the strength within me to stay. I was exhausted and afraid of what might lie ahead for Seth, and by this point my nerves were shot. Basically, I was a complete mess. I could no longer maintain my composure. I tried so hard to hold back my tears until I got out of the hospital, but I failed. I could not contain them. They just rolled down my cheeks uncontrollably. I finally got into my car and utterly fell apart. I had expected Seth to be a little out of it. Afterall, it was a major brain surgery. But I was not at all prepared for him to have a grand mal seizure and be in the condition he was in. I feared that something had gone terribly wrong with the surgery.

As I drove, I sobbed and yelled, pleading with God to please let Seth be okay. I arrived at my son, Michael and his wife, Meg's house, where most of our other children were together. I was going to pick up my youngest, Peter, who was fourteen at the time. When I got there, I tried to collect myself before going into their house, but when I saw my other children, I lost my composure once again, falling apart in their arms. I am exceedingly grateful for the loving family I have. They all stopped what they were doing and were so kind and compassionate toward me. As a mother, it was an extraordinary gift to have the children, whom I always tried to take care of and comfort, turn and take care of and comfort me instead.

As I was crawling into bed that night shortly after midnight, I received a text from Chris informing me that Seth had woken up. He told me that Seth had his eyes wide open, was eating a cracker on his own, and was talking and had asked how the surgery went. He was able to move his left side and even walked to the bathroom mostly on his own! This news was the answer to my prayers. I was deeply encouraged and relieved beyond words. I went to sleep filled with gratitude.

Early the next morning, I went back to the hospital to relieve Chris, who had only managed to get a couple hours of sleep during the night. When the team of neurosurgeons came into Seth's room later that morning, they explained that the decreased motor function on his left side, immediately following surgery, was something they had completely expected. That was definitely good news, but I sure wished that I had been aware of that the night before. They also said that they believed the grand mal seizure was just an immediate effect of the trauma to his brain from surgery but not a lasting effect. It wasn't anything they expected to ever happen again. Many of my fears were dispelled upon hearing this.

That first morning after surgery, Seth was still pretty disoriented as to time and day, but that was totally understandable considering the heavy pain medications he was on and the fact that he basically lost a whole day being in surgery. Seth was also in considerable pain. He said he had a headache like no other headache he had ever had before! That means something coming from a guy who had ten holes drilled into his head with wires going directly into his brain for nearly five weeks.

Thankfully, the pain did not keep Seth from being able to sleep. He actually slept a lot that day, which was very good. And every time Seth woke up, he was alert and aware of what was going on. Throughout the day, Seth steadily became more and more "with it," and by evening was pretty much talking nonstop. That was extremely encouraging. Seth would have a lot of pain to deal with in the coming weeks and a long recovery ahead, but it seemed as though our Seth was back, personality intact, and all things considered was doing very well. Less than twenty-four hours after Seth got to his room, the doctors were able to remove the drain from his head and were confidently sending him home. Unbelievable!

We were grateful beyond words and once again overwhelmed by the number of people praying for Seth and us. Their prayers were answered, and God's grace through them was abundant. We can never adequately thank our community and all of Seth's faithful prayer warriors for this. We will be forever grateful for them and for my sister, Kathy, and her beautiful writing, which constantly "rallied the troops" and gave all glory to God. The following is her facebook post the day after Seth's surgery.

Nov 6, 2021
We have WONDERFUL news! Seth is being discharged in a little while and is going home!!!
I am actually blown away by the goodness of God and how well Seth is doing! He has been doing GREAT today!!! His mom says that as the day has gone on he has been more and more "with it" and is now "talking up a storm!" Her description literally made me cry—tears of joy, relief, and thanksgiving!
Thank you, Lord!!!!
He has a long recovery ahead of him, and lots of pain to deal with, but the difference between last night and today is tremendous!!!
Thank you! Thank you! Thank you!!! Thank you for storming the heavens for Seth. Thank you to our many prayer warriors, some of whom I actually ran into—yesterday in Wisconsin and today in Michigan—all asking me about Seth and telling me how much they are praying for him and his family! Thank you to our Facebook warriors, the many prayer groups, parishes, and other numerous friends and family members who have spent days doing novenas and hours in front of the Blessed Sacrament on his behalf. We can't tell you how much this kind of love and prayer support means to Seth and to each of us. We are so very grateful.
Each time we have reached out to you for prayers, you have answered. The number of people who love Seth and have prayed for his recovery, is unreal! And now you each have a part in his story…a story that he will continue to share with so many…a story that will hopefully continue to lead others to know and love the Lord. Words of gratitude are simply not enough. May God thank you in ways only He can!
I will continue to keep you informed on Seth's healing and progress. In addition to prayers for his continued recovery, please offer up prayers

of thanksgiving. Our Lord has once again performed a mighty work, and we are truly grateful. #allforhishonorandglory #sethstrong #prayersreallymatter #miraclesdohappen

Although Seth had constant, intense pain in the days to follow, he handled it very well. God's grace was evident in him, and he had an incredibly positive attitude in the midst of it all. That grace was a true blessing as his pain began to increase about four days after surgery. The side of his head and face began to swell as he had been warned about by his surgeon. While this was normal and expected after surgery, it caused a lot of extra pressure and pain for him. On top of that, Seth also ended up contracting a bad head cold and cough. Along with the already bad pain and swelling from surgery, his cough was so hard that it caused even more intense pain to his head each time he coughed, while his severe congestion caused increased pressure in his head. He was in bad shape for quite a while. He had to stay on a strict schedule of pain medications around the clock for several weeks following surgery.

Before the surgery, doctors had told Seth that they couldn't predict how his personality might be affected by the lobectomy. We were relieved when we got to see that Seth was still Seth. However, unbeknownst to us at the time, when Seth woke up from surgery, he knew immediately that a part of him was gone. He felt very different. Seth always had a certain intensity to his personality, almost like an energy that he couldn't contain. It was noticeable in him even as a baby, and as a little boy it often came out as aggression or extreme excitement. As he grew, it turned more into drive, passion, and self-confidence. Then after his accident, it showed itself more as a sort of pride or chip on his shoulder that drove him, almost like he had something to prove. However, when he woke up from the temporal lobectomy, he instantly felt as if all of this were gone. It felt so strange and empty to him. He had lived his whole life with this energetic, driving force inside of him, and now it was suddenly gone. He felt like something was seriously wrong with him. This was something that he grew more concerned about with each passing day. It was something he wanted to talk to the doctor about at his follow up appointment.

Despite this and the tough recovery being sick and all, Seth was excited for what the future could hold. He felt like he was finally going to be done with all these medical issues and would be able to move on with his life. This surgery marked, for him, the final step in his recovery since the night of February 13, 2017, nearly five years earlier. The last several months especially had been so focused on all the testing and steps needed to get the surgery done, that he felt like he had been in constant recovery mode. It seemed he was always recovering from something, which had made it nearly impossible for him to get excited about and focus on anything beyond the surgery. It was beautiful after the surgery to see his excitement return and grow as he began to look toward the future.

Physically, Seth was told he shouldn't workout for about four weeks, and that he would probably need to be off work for about six weeks. This led us to believe that his recovery would take about six weeks total. When Seth went to his six-week follow-up appointment, he was told that the incision was healing well and that it would be fine for him to go back to work and start slowly working out again. This was all good and what we had expected to hear. However, as Seth began to talk to the neurologist about the differences in how he felt, the doctor said something we were not prepared for. While he couldn't explain the changes Seth felt, the doctor told Seth that he needed to look at his surgery like another brain injury, meaning that it would take a long time, possibly as long as one to two years for Seth's brain to be completely healed. This was a huge blow and super discouraging for Seth who had been waiting to be done with all these changes and begin to fully live and move forward with his life.

There were definitely changes in Seth after the surgery. He seemed to mellow out a lot. He even went totally silent on all of his social media platforms. They no longer held the same importance in his life that they once had. The amazing part of it all was that he finally felt like he was able to move past the age of twenty-one. Whereas before the surgery, it often seemed like he was still in pursuit of what he thought he had missed out on and lost when he had his accident at twenty-one years old. Finally at peace as a twenty-six-year-old, Seth put his head down and began to focus on what was right in front of him. He stopped living for his twenty-one-year-old dreams and began to focus on the here and now.

To us, his family, it seemed almost as if Seth had matured overnight. For the first time since before his accident, he was finally happy and content with the age he was. He was ready to move forward with no more looking back, desiring what he once was or thought he wanted. He was growing and maturing at a rapid pace and beginning to live life to the full as a twenty-six-year-old man. Even Michael, Meg, and Andrea finally felt like they had Seth completely back for the first time since that fateful, life shattering night of February 13, 2017.

Ten months after Seth's brain surgery, in September of 2022, Seth had a post-surgical neuropsychological evaluation. This evaluation went very well. It showed no evidence of any continual decline of his visual memory, since he was no longer having seizures. And even some of the functions that were tested showed as having been mildly improved, indicating that the left temporal lobe was functioning well and compensating some for the loss of the right anterior temporal lobe. The test results were consistent with what his doctors had expected and hoped the surgery would accomplish for Seth. This was great news and a huge answer to prayer.

Though the evaluation was good and Seth was finally content with his age and life, he still missed the intensity he always used to feel inside. Without it, he had become a much more patient and humble person. He was grateful for that change but wanted both. He prayed continually for God to give that intensity back to him, promising he could handle it and still stay patient and humble.

The morning of November 6, 2022, the day after the one-year anniversary since Seth's temporal lobectomy, Seth woke up and knew instantly that his intensity was back! These overnight changes have been extremely "trippy" for Seth to adjust to. But this one Seth had wanted and had been praying for. So thank you Jesus.

There is no doubt that dealing with Seth's seizures was an ordeal. After each surgery Seth has had to rebuild. Actually, for nearly six years now, Seth has been rebuilding, or rather, God has been rebuilding him. God tells us, "If you aspire to serve me, prepare yourself for an ordeal." Sometimes, we must be shattered in order to be made whole. All of us need to be willing to be broken, so that God can mold us into the men and women He has created us to be and needs us to be in order to fulfill His purpose. And no matter the ordeal we are faced with, He will be right beside us all the way. For God is good in the midst of the ordeal.

CHAPTER EIGHTEEN
- TRUE SURRENDER -
God is Good... in All Circumstances

Throughout the writing of this book, Seth and some of my other children have asked me how and where I would end this story? To which, I repeatedly answered, "I honestly don't know. God is going to have to show me." Now, with Seth's temporal lobectomy having been over a year ago, it seems that from a medical standpoint, this is a good place to end. Seth has now moved forward and finally put all of this behind him. But the reality is that it is not something that will ever be over and done with because it is an experience far beyond just a medical one. It is an experience that will continue to impact all of us in many ways for a very long time, and it will most definitely affect Seth, in particular, the rest of his life. Fr. Jim had told Seth that the out-of-body, spiritual experience he had was a gift that will take a lifetime to unpack. I didn't necessarily understand that statement when Father said it, but I certainly do now. Those words ring true more and more with each passing day.

God gave Seth an extraordinary gift through what once appeared to be a life shattering tragedy. It wasn't a gift just for Seth or our family. It is a gift that is meant to be far reaching and touch each one of us. Seth is continually searching for how exactly God is asking him to share his story. He has given talks, concerts, shared with many over coffee or a meal, and even shared with strangers on the streets when the opportunity presented itself, but he is still searching for that plan that God had revealed to him in his coma.

I have often wondered why God didn't allow Seth to remember that plan, but I have come to the conclusion that God does not want Seth, or any of us for that matter, to seek a plan. Rather, He wants us to seek Him. In fact, He is continually waiting for us to seek Him and come to Him, as He so clearly expressed to Seth when He said, ***"Look how they all pray because you are injured, but I am here always."***

Whether we see or understand what it is or not, God's plan is happening in the various circumstances we encounter each and every day, and God is good in all of them. According to St. Faustina, true surrender is lived by praising and thanking God in all circumstances. I know I have a long way to go to live that kind of total surrender.

Caleb once asked me if, after knowing about the spiritual experiences Seth had and how it had changed him, I would go back to the night of Seth's accident and make it never happen if I could. Looking back at it, I realize that, in essence, he was asking if I would take Seth being physically okay over spiritually okay. It was clear that the accident had truly changed Seth spiritually, yet we still had no idea how much he would recover physically.

Sadly, at that moment, I couldn't answer Caleb's question. However, as I have contemplated it since, I have realized that it is a question that each of us answers simply by how we live our lives every single day. Let me put it to you this way: What is your priority? Are you pursuing your physical talents, abilities, and earthly success? Or are you pursuing the heart of Jesus? Both are important, but which one comes first in your life? How about for your children and grandchildren? Which one are you pushing them most toward?

It's humbling for me to admit that in many ways I had still been putting Seth's physical abilities over his spiritual well-being. It took me a while to realize that while I had still been worrying about what Seth's life on earth would be like, God had actually answered the greatest prayer of my heart for Seth: that he would know God, be in relationship with Him, and give his life completely to God. This is the greatest prayer and deepest desire of my heart for all of my children and loved ones. The greatest miracle in this story was, is, and will always be JESUS, right in the middle of the suffering.

The truth is, when Seth fell that day, February 13, 2017, his life and every member of our family's lives were shattered. But our Lord picked up the pieces and began that day a new and very blessed spiritual journey not only for Seth but for all of us, hopefully for each one of you now as well. It is a journey that should not end until we reach our final destination in Heaven.

Throughout the writing of this book, it has dawned on me that none of our stories will be finished until the day we die. However, as I look back over my life so far, I see how every piece ties together to make a beautiful whole. In fact, the times when my life felt the most shattered, are precisely the times when God was making me whole. I started to see this more clearly when I was asked to speak about Seth's story at our parish's Advent by Candlelight women's night. Let me explain...

Speaking was something I had never done before. It was not me. I was always scared to even ask a question or make a comment in small groups, much less try to speak to a crowd of about two hundred people. It was way out of my comfort zone, but I knew that after everything God had done for Seth and our family, I couldn't keep it to myself. No matter how scared I was, I had to share it. I had to give glory to God for this miracle in any way I could, and I had to thank the incredible people of St. Thomas parish for the way they had supported us through it.

As I began preparing for the talk, I knew I couldn't just tell Seth's story. I had to include the journey God had taken me on through the births and deaths of four of our babies. It was that journey that taught me what true surrender and joy really were. I didn't get the miracles of healing that I had prayed for, but when I finally learned to surrender my will to God's, I was given a joy and peace that I had never known before. And the crazy part was that it was right in the middle of my deepest pain and grief. Jesus brought me complete healing. I realized that Jesus, himself, was the true miracle, and He came right in the middle of my suffering. Fifteen years after that experience, I finally wrote a book about it called, "The Delight of My Heart." I had actually just finished the first draft of it right before Seth's accident.

Through the writing of that story, God brought back to the forefront of my mind and heart all that he had taught me fifteen years earlier about trusting Him and surrendering to Him. It wasn't until I was preparing my talk for the women's Advent by Candlelight, that I realized how God had used the writing of that book to prepare me for the journey that, unbeknownst to me, I was about to take with Seth.

As I continued to prepare and pondered my experience with Seth, I realized that through Seth, God had shown me the same exact thing; that He was the miracle. When Seth woke up from the coma, he had a peace, joy, and love like never before. And it wasn't because he was healed. It was at a point when he was unable to walk or talk or care for himself at all. Seth's greatest joy was right in the middle of his greatest suffering, simply because he had encountered Christ.

Once again, Jesus was the miracle… and once again, it was right in the middle of the suffering.

It is often not until we step back and look over the events of our lives that we recognize how God's hand was in all of it, directing every step. He is a merciful God who walks with us, right beside us through it all. I look back to those excruciating days in the ICU with Seth, not knowing if he would live or die, and now after everything Seth has told us, I picture Jesus standing right over my shoulder, crying with me, whispering in my ear, "Don't worry. I've got this! I've got Seth, and I've got you."

I have often mentioned the rollercoaster ride this experience was. The truth is, life is a rollercoaster ride full of peaks and valleys. This is where surrender comes in. If our joy comes from our circumstances, it will go up and down with the peaks and valleys of our lives. However, when we surrender every moment of our lives, trusting that our God is good in all circumstances, our joy will be steady and complete.

Sadly, I did, many times, allow the circumstances of Seth's journey to steal my joy. John 10:10 says, "A thief comes only to steal and slaughter and destroy; I came so that they might have life and have it more abundantly." Abundant life comes in that surrender, when we trust God with every detail of our lives no matter how grim the situation may look. It requires us to trust that God's hands are always good.

433

In April of 2017, I had the privilege of meeting a beautiful nun, Mother Mary Catherine, who, as a young novice, worked very closely with Saint Mother Teresa of Calcutta. During a talk she was giving, someone asked her what the biggest obstacle to surrendering was. Her answer was simple, "A lack of trust that my Father's hands are good."

Our Blessed Mother is a great example for us in this. She surrendered completely when she told the angel, "Behold, I am the handmaid of the Lord. May it be done to me according to your word." (Luke 1:38) I have often reflected on the joyful mysteries of the Rosary and thought that for me, as a mother, they do not seem like joyful times. I mean, just think about giving birth in a barn and laying your baby in hay. That would be a terrible situation, which I'm sure I would complain about for a long time. Then at the presentation of Jesus in the temple, Simeon tells Mary that her heart will be pierced with a sword. That would be frightening, not joyful. And I don't know about you, but for me, losing my twelve-year-old for three days would be a nightmare. Yet, somehow, for the Blessed Mother, these are described as the joyful mysteries. Her joy obviously was not dictated by her circumstances. I have wondered why these were named joyful mysteries, but then I realized, they are just that... mysteries! Life is a mystery. But if we live a life of surrender as our Blessed Mother did, we will live in joy no matter what our circumstances are.

I often think, "Who am I to grasp the mysteries of God?" In Isaiah 55:8-9 it says, "For my thoughts are not your thoughts, nor are your ways my ways, says the Lord. As high as the heavens are above the earth, so high are my ways above your ways and my thoughts above your thoughts." I will never fully understand the ways of God, but I believe that if I surrender my will to His, He will continually reveal more. I have no doubt Fr. Jim was right. It will take a lifetime to unpack this gift. I also believe that the messages God gave us through Seth can touch and impact each individual differently according to their need and God's will. I sincerely hope and pray that it will be a gift that we, you included, are all unpacking throughout the rest of our lives.

The ways of God are a mystery and will remain so until the day we die. Yet through Seth, we were blessed to have a small glimpse of that mystery, a glimpse of God's amazing love for us. And as Seth has told us ***God is standing right next to us no matter what we are going through. He is always offering His strength to us. We just have to accept it.*** He is our joy and our peace right in the middle of the suffering and the unknown, if we let Him be.

It was not a coincidence that Seth's first message to us upon waking from the coma was, "My God is good." It was also no coincidence that he said it while he was completely helpless, instead of later when he was healed. Our joy will be complete, and we will live life abundantly when we can proclaim *"My God is Good!"* regardless of the situation we are facing.

No, Seth's story isn't finished yet. It's ending remains a mystery, as does mine and yours. Not one of us knows what lies ahead, but one thing is for sure: We have a God who loves us personally and walks with us every step of the way. As Seth adamantly repeated, *"He is right here."* Proverbs 3:5-6 tells us, "Trust in the Lord with all your heart and lean not on your own understanding; in all your ways submit to Him, and He will make your paths straight."

One warm, summer day in 2023, six years after Seth's accident, he and Megan walked hand in hand excitedly. The air was warm, and the sun shone brightly on their backs as they walked, hands swinging, conversing joyfully about all their hopes and dreams for their future together. As they approached the door of the parish rectory, the nerves began to well up from the pits of their stomachs. Yet at the same time, there was a peace that filled and surrounded them. This place had become like home for them. Upon entering, they were kindly ushered into Fr. Jim's office and asked to take a seat. Waiting in silence, Seth's mind was flooded with memories of the many times and ways Fr. Jim had been a part of his spiritual growth throughout his entire life. There was so much to be thankful for as Seth sat there with this beautiful young woman by his side. A beautiful young woman who had just been baptized and confirmed into the Catholic Church by Fr. Jim a few months earlier at the Easter Vigil Mass. Fr. Jim had become a spiritual father for both of them. They felt blessed as they waited to have their first meeting with him to prepare for marriage. As they were reminiscing, Fr. Jim walked in joyfully and greeted each of them. At the end of the meeting, Fr. Jim looked intently across the desk at Seth, smiled, then glanced over at Megan, whose hand was locked with Seth's, and said, "Now we know why God sent you back!"

Indeed, God brings good and beauty in all things. Even when we feel completely shattered and see no way out, God does and will make us whole again. Let us rest confidently in that and seek Him in everything. For as a helpless, yet enlightened, young man in a wheelchair once wrote, *"My God is good."*

EPILOGUE

God is Good... Yesterday, Today, and Always

It has been seven years since Seth fell through that roof and life as we knew it had been shattered. Seven years later and all the pieces finally feel as though they've been put back together, although maybe not perfectly in places. Before publishing this book, our family gathered once a week for several months to read through it and process what we had been through together...

Chris and I felt as though we had processed much of it as we went through it. However, as the years passed, we both became more and more convinced that God desires us to spread His messages through this story. So in 2022, we sold our home of twenty-two years and moved in order to make it possible for me to quit my job and start a fulltime speaking ministry sharing our story, the goodness of God, and the true joy in surrender to God's will. Through it, the lessons to be learned from within Seth's story continue to be unpacked and revealed. It has been an amazing journey for us to witness how God is continually touching hearts and lives through it. To learn more, you can check out my website: www.surrendering-all.com

Our youngest three children, Caleb (22), Mary (20), and Peter (17) live at home with us while working

438

and going to school, seeking direction for their lives and the purpose and plan God has for them. We joke that Caleb and Mary have taken over Seth's role of wondering and worrying about where their lives are headed.

Through the reading of this book, deep hurts and wounds were exposed in Caleb, Mary and Peter that some of them didn't even realize were there. We discovered that because they had not been told of the seriousness of Seth's accident at first and were not included in that, they carried deep insecurities within them, feeling like they were insignificant members of our family. Reading the book together gave them an opportunity to recognize and express their feelings openly with the family. It also gave Chris and me an opportunity to explain our actions as well as take responsibility for and ask forgiveness for any hurts we had caused them by the way we handled things. They were able to forgive us, and we prayed over each of them for healing, renouncing in Jesus' name the lies they had come to believe about themselves and replacing those lies with God's truth of their worth and importance in our family. It was freeing and healing for them, and they can now think about that part of the story with a different outlook and feeling toward it and themselves.

They've found healing in other parts of the story as well. For instance, Peter says he no longer regrets not being home the day Seth got home from Mary Free Bed.

At seventeen years old, he understands it now and has a new confidence in himself as a valuable member of our family. It's been beautiful over the past seven years to watch Caleb, Mary, and Peter grow from children into young adults. Their maturity and depth of faith is noticeable and admirable. It is typical in families for the older siblings to help the younger ones. But over the past year, it has been particularly special to see the many ways that the younger siblings now help the older ones as well.

Ethan had just started dating Elle a few months before Seth had his accident. So she journeyed through this story quietly in the background supporting Ethan. She has since become a beloved and important member of our family. Her support and love for Ethan has been a tremendous help for his healing and a true blessing in his life. Ethan and Elle have been married for three years now and have one son, Patrick Jacob, who was born on January 6, 2023, and are expecting their second baby in January 2025. Sitting in the hospital with Seth day after day throughout his injury and recovery led Ethan to his current profession as a nurse. This is another very practical example of how God uses all things to direct and lead us where He wants us.

While Ethan and Seth still have very different personalities, their relationship was forever changed for the better through Seth's accident. They both learned firsthand the importance of repentance and forgiveness.

It is something I imagine they will never forget. As Ethan stood in the ICU beside Seth's lifeless body, he begged God for another chance to have a close relationship with Seth, and God granted his request. Through their second chance, they set aside all their past hurts and resentment and forgave each other. They have since developed a bond of mutual respect and love for one another, recognizing and appreciating their similarities as well as their differences.

Reading through this book together was interesting for Seth, as he doesn't remember much of it until the end. Most of Seth's memories from his accident are based on pictures and what we have told him. But as for the spiritual experience, the Lord continues to give it back to him whenever he needs it! And as Caleb pointed out, "Seth may not remember all the spiritual, but he lives it every day!" While he is still very human like the rest of us, it's easy to see that the messages God gave him truly are written on his heart. He has become a true evangelist, willing to share God with anyone, anytime, anywhere, which is what led him to Megan.

Megan was not raised with faith, but when she met Seth, she was searching for it. Finding faith for her was not about a set of rules to follow, but rather about discovering a God who loves and desires her and learning how to embrace and accept that love and love Him back. Her wide-open heart to Christ and pure faith

441

have been an incredible blessing and gift to watch unfold.

Seth and Megan were married on June 15, 2024. Caleb was Seth's best man and every single one of Seth's siblings and their spouses were in his and Megan's wedding! He continues to hold faith and family as his greatest blessings.

Andrea has endured much of her own suffering over the past seven years. With the support of family, she has continued to push through the suffering. In fact, knowing firsthand how much it would have hurt our family to lose Seth has strengthened her own self-worth, knowing beyond all doubt that she has a family who loves her and will always be here for her, a family who desperately needs and wants her. Despite more than her share of sick days, she has continued to be successful in her job and has been promoted many times.

Andrea is engaged to be married in September 2024 to Boris. He is a young man who knows suffering all too well himself, losing his dad way too early in his life. Boris is a faithful, kind, and compassionate man. The way he loves and cares for his mom is admirable, and I am confident he is the perfect man that God had planned for Andrea.

Michael has found great healing and freedom in recent years. He had felt stuck for a long time. However, through the help of counseling with a priest, he realized that he had been crippled by fear. Fear of what more God may ask of him, fear of losing those he loved, particularly his wife, Meg, and their children. Father prayed with Michael to renounce that fear in Jesus' name. Michael was set free that day and has never looked back since. He has shared his story of how he had been gripped by fear, which controlled his life, and then how God healed and set him free with all of us. Through it, he has continued to be an amazing role model and example for his siblings.

Meg too, no longer feels stuck in the pain and broken from it all. Reading through this book as a family really helped her to process the experience. She feels whole and at peace moving forward. It has actually been incredible and inspiring for Chris and me to watch Michael and Meg raising their four boys with deep faith and trustful surrender to the will of God in their lives. They are expecting their fifth baby in March 2025.

Tragedies have a tendency to either make you or break you. By the grace of God and through the prayers of thousands, we received a miracle that, in the end, helped to make us the close family that we are today. I imagine there are parts about this whole experience that we may continue to process and unpack for many many years to come, but thankfully none of us feel stuck in it any longer. We have all moved forward from it with joy and hope in our lives.

Over the past seven years, there has been both heartache and joy, but through it all, it has been beautiful to see the growth in our family. As our children have grown into young men and women, we have witnessed their steadfast commitment to their Catholic faith, even in difficult times when they don't necessarily feel God near to them; their continual striving to trust and surrender when they can't see the path ahead and no good human solution even seems possible; their recognition of God's providence and praise of Him when He works things out better than they can imagine; their acceptance of their crosses and willingness to offer their suffering up for others; their willingness to wrestle with the Lord and stick with Him even when they don't understand; their commitment to family, dying to themselves to support Chris and me and one another in all circumstances; and their respect for each other even when they don't see eye to eye.

We are not perfect by any means. We each have our own issues and struggles to deal with as we face the various challenges of our lives. Sometimes we deal with them well and sometimes not so well. However, Fr. Jim has always said that our holiness is not in our perfection. Rather, it is in our constant striving. Seth's accident and miraculous recovery has aided us in our striving. I do wholeheartedly believe that it has strengthened our faith. It has in one way or another helped to solidify each one of our commitment and resolve to live out our Catholic faith. And it has also strengthened us as a family. Our children, almost all adults now, have become the closest of friends. And each member of our family knows with complete certainty that if we ever needed anything, we have a family who would drop everything in an instant for us.

We just celebrated Mother's Day 2024. As I sat with my family gathered around me, I told them that they are my dream come true! My faith, my husband, my children, and my grandchildren are more beautiful than anything I could have imagined for my life. It's everything I ever wanted and more. Though trials may come and go, I have everything I could ever need or desire. I am blessed beyond words, and my heart is overflowing with gratitude to our God, who truly is good!

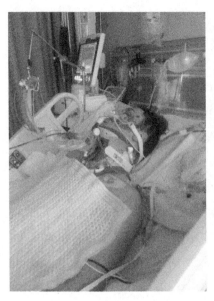
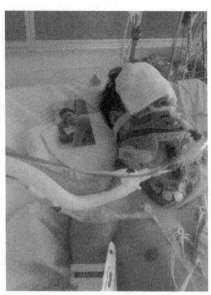
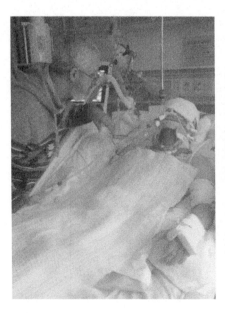
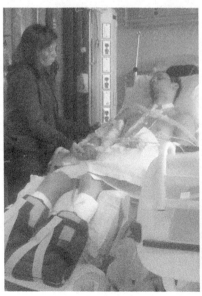

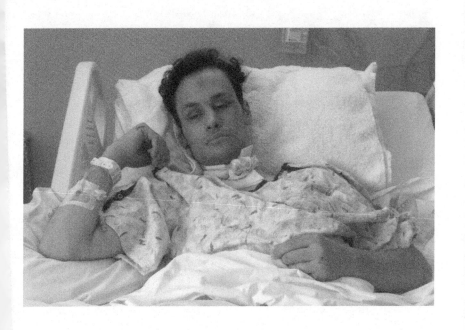

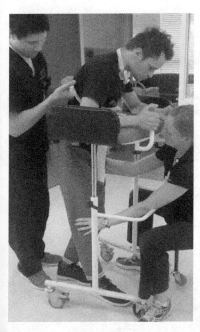
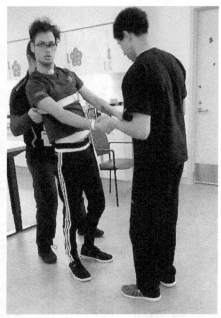

About the Author

Christine Alfaro was born and raised in Rockford, Michigan. At nineteen years old, she met her husband, Christopher, while attending Franciscan University of Steubenville in Ohio. They got married on December 17th, 1988 and have been married for thirty-five years. They have eleven children ranging in age from seventeen to thirty-four, and eight grandchildren. Christine and her family currently reside in Grand Rapids, Michigan.

Christine published her first book, *The Delight of My Heart - A Mother's Journey Through Grief,* in 2019. It is a story of surrender, which is largely taken from her personal prayer journals as she grappled with the births and deaths of four of her babies. She was just about finished with the rough draft when Seth had his accident in 2017.

After Seth's tragic accident and miraculous recovery, Christine was invited to speak and share her story at her home parish. Since then, she has spoken at numerous other events in multiple states. She is currently working full time on growing her speaking ministry. It is her and her husband, Chris' strong conviction that these experiences are not just for them but are meant to be shared with others. Christine hopes that sharing her story will help lead others to the freedom and peace that comes through total surrender to God's will, no matter what life's circumstances may be.

To learn more about Christine's ministry visit her
website <u>www.surrendering-all.com</u>

To contact or book Christine, reach out via her website or
email her directly at christinealfaro1028@gmail.com

Made in the USA
Monee, IL
30 August 2024

64897298R00252